Win It or Wear It

ALL-TIME GREAT SPRINT CAR TALES

by Joyce Standridge

To Bill Reynold —
Best wishes,
Joyce Standridge
[signature] Allen Horcher
[signature] Kevin Horcher

COASTAL 181
PUBLISHER

CREDITS

Book Design and composition *Town and Country Reprographics*
Cover Design *Joyce Cosentino Wells*
Front Cover Photos *Allen Horcher, Mike Campbell*
Back Cover Photos *Allen Horcher, Doug Johnson*

Every reasonable effort was made to locate and credit the original copyright holders and photographers of the photos included in this book. If your photo appears in this book and you are not properly credited, please contact the publisher.

ISBN 10: 0-9789261-5-3

ISBN 13: 978-0-9789261-5-1

For additional information or copies of this book, contact:

Coastal 181
29 Water Street
Newburyport, MA 01950
(877) 907-8181, (978) 462-2436
info@coastal181.com
www.coastal181.com

First printing November 2008

Printed in the United States of America

Table of Contents

Acknowledgements

Joyce Standridge

We started out with a simple premise: The book had to be about sprint car racing, and it had to be entertaining.

It was a concept that sounded like something we would want to read, too, so my publishers at Coastal 181 and I thought we were on to something. But it didn't turn out to be all that easy. "Entertaining" is a pretty broad term, after all. And then we remembered how much fun we've had over the years "bench racing." Throw the checkered flag, break out the refreshments, and we have always been off and running. Lots of laughs, a few tears, fantastic memories. Best of all, we knew there was no shortage of people who were just like us.

The style of the book was another issue to wrestle with. There have been some terrific general racing books done, at least one of which was about sprint cars. Joe Scalzo's *Stand on the Gas*, long out of print, was an inspiration. And we knew sprint fans would probably like to read about some of the more famous folks to ever strap in, but here it was a little more problematic. There have been several sprint car autobiographies and biographies written or that are in some stage of planning—usually associated in some fashion with Indiana-based Dave Argabright. (I strongly encourage you to make the effort to find and read these books, especially *Lone Wolf*, co-authored with Doug Wolfgang.) But with books done or planned about Steve Kinser, Sammy Swindell, Tony Stewart, Doug Wolfgang, Jan Opperman, Brad Doty and Jack Hewitt, to mention a few, we really didn't want to re-hash a lot of the same stories.

Then we stopped to think about the fact that there were—and are—so very many other racers who have fantastic stories to tell. I think every one of the people you are going to read about in some detail here also had a complete book in their life stories, but by combining their memories into a single tome we had something really extraordinary to work with. That's my justification, anyway, for taking the liberty (and having the tremendous fun) of talking to so many stars.

Deciding whom to interview was pretty easy. I started with a list of just a few of the drivers I admire. I was not in the least disappointed. So, the first laurels go to the people who gave so freely of their time and patiently answered so many questions.

Particular kudos to Shane Carson, Rick Ferkel, Hooker Hood, Lynn Paxton and Jimmy Sills, who gave extended interviews and provided some of the best material I've ever come across in more than 30 years of writing about auto racing in all its forms.

Other drivers who provided exceptional material for us to use include:

Bobby Allen, Richard Griffin, Johnny Herrera, Skip Jackson, Bubby Jones, Lenard McCarl, Lealand McSpadden, Curt Michael, Daryn Pittman, Danny Smith, Mares Stellfox, and Gary Wright. I was a fan of these drivers before I started. Afterwards, I was simply in awe of them.

The only frustrating part of this experience is that even after adding considerably more research about other racers, we realized that we had barely scratched the surface. As I wrote these chapters, other fantastic drivers' names would pop into my head along with interesting experiences that I simply couldn't figure out how to work into an already lengthy book. Ah, well—perhaps there's a Volume Two in all this.

I want to also note that our staff tried very diligently to verify the stories shared here to make sure they were accurate. We tried to find dates, locations and concrete confirmation, but quite often these stories were being told in print for the first time. For that reason, if there are errors herein, please feel free to contact the publishers. It's possible there will be future editions, at which time we will try to make corrections. However, bear in mind that what has been shared here was done so with good humor and great affection for all. No one with whom I spoke had anything deliberately hostile or aggressive to say about another racer. A little gentle needling was the most I heard, and that is worth remembering as you read the pages.

We also did something a little different in that we jogged the memories of diehard fans, family and photographer/fans. That was some of the most fun (and laughter) I had through the entire experience. I wouldn't take a millions bucks and the Knoxville Nationals trophy for it. So, to Allen, Kevin, Wanda, Randy, Rita, Ronnie, Mary Lee, Janet, Jeff, Jerry, Dan, Ed, Ray, Dennis, Tracy, and George, thanks for some hilarious and also some thought-provoking stories.

Many thanks to my daughter-in-law Dawn for setting up the interview appointments and my sister Kathy for serving as informal editor during the writing process. Both also helped me tremendously by assisting with the transcription of many, many hours of tapes. (I think they had almost as much fun with that as I did.)

As always, the staff at Coastal 181 provided inspiration and encouragement along the way. I can't imagine working with a better group, and even if it sounds unprofessionally personal I have to say that through three books together I have come to love them all. Particular appreciation must be paid to publisher Lew Boyd (who went well above and beyond a publisher's task in helping gather information), my copy editor and the book's production manager Cary Stratton, and the world's best cover designer Joyce Wells.

Dick Berggren has been friend and colleague for 30 years and gave us enthusiastic encouragement and support for this project. We will never be able to adequately express our gratitude. And then, when we hadn't asked enough already, we also coaxed him into writing the Foreword!

Thanks also to Tom Schmeh, Curator, and Craig Agan, Marketing

Director, at the National Sprint Car Hall of Fame for assisting us in locating many of the people to whom we wanted to talk and for helping us find some rare photographs. I have also appreciated for many years the honor in serving on the Hall of Fame's Selection Committee, which has provided insight into truly great sprint car drivers who otherwise would likely have escaped my attention.

It's hard to believe that at the beginning of the project we actually were a little worried about whether we would be able to find photos to illustrate the stories. By the time you get to the end of the book and realize what extraordinary photos we gathered—and we barely scratched the surface—you'll also realize how ludicrous that concern turned out to be. How can I begin to thank our photographers? Coastal 181 has established a reputation for exceptional attention to photography in all their books, but this was a huge challenge, as we were all over the place with geography, eras and types of racing. You stepped up to the plate for us, and I'm convinced the readers of this book will be forever grateful for the time and effort you put in to helping us find the best possible illustrations. Every photo that appears here has meaning and added value, but I would be remiss if I did not add special kudos to Allen and Kevin Horcher, who became involved with the informal bench racing, too. Mike Campbell, Steve Hardin, and Gene Marderness were the best surprise our team could have come across in our research. Photographers like Bill Taylor and Keith Wendel dug back through their archives, scanned negatives and scrambled to provide priceless shots as we headed towards our deadline. Special thanks also to Al Consoli, Max Dolder, Todd Gould, Doug Johnson, Steve Lafond, Windy McDonald, Tom Parker and Keenan Wright for providing multiple images. Many others gave us permission to use their photos, and the gracious sharing of their images will benefit the readers enormously.

We also thank the drivers who shared photos from their personal collections, along with Jeff Moe, Mary Standridge and Brian Eaves, who allowed me to peruse and select photos from their collections, too.

Love and appreciation, as always, goes to family and friends, who somehow manage to put up with me through the arduous and lengthy process of creating a book. It takes a long time and a lot of attention, which takes away from them. So, thanks for bearing with me through yet another book.

Most of all, enduring love for my all-time favorite driver (now retired from sprints), my husband Rick. Not only does he have to put up with the most headaches during these projects, but this time we also talked him into directly helping us by reading for content and searching his brain for stories, too.

It was a challenge to figure out how best to tell these tales. Good stories have a voice, or a cohesive sound that comes into your mind as you read, and in my previous efforts that was fairly easy because the stories emanated from a single individual. But now we were going to try to be a conduit for literally dozens of people.

A much bigger challenge.

By the time our team had pulled together all the many elements that comprise *Win It or Wear It*, we realized that we had bench raced our way through some of the greatest, funniest, most heartwarming stories ever associated with sprint car racing. Among the things you are likely to remember long after you close the back cover are:

- The race car built from a children's swing set.
- The driver hanging over a billboard yelling at a competitor that's he's a "dumb ass."
- A jack-knifing motorhome that slung a driver out of the bathroom.
- The wreck that ended with a nitro-loaded car under the grandstand and everybody running for their lives.
- A driver who promised he would quit racing if he won a certain race—and he won it—and he walked away.
- The greatest driver you've never heard of who had to beat the Ku Klux Klan, too.

Okay, enough with the teasing. It's time to send you on to read these—and dozens more—memorable tales.

Enjoy!

JOYCE STANDRIDGE
COLLINSVILLE, ILLINOIS

Foreword

If you have ever watched JJ Yeley drive his sprint car down the entire backstretch at the dirt track at Lowe's Motor Speedway with both front wheels high in the air, or were fortunate enough to have seen Doug Wolfgang march through the alphabet of qualifying races at the Knoxville Nationals or Jan Opperman race against Kenny Weld, you have witnessed the best of what racing can offer. Sprint car drivers do things with cars that are simply incomprehensible until you see them.

As *Win It or Wear It* accurately explains and whose extraordinary photos so convincingly prove, this is a very dangerous activity. The center of mass of a sprint car is high in the air to encourage weight transfer to the right rear tire when cornering. But that high center of mass also encourages tip-overs that can brutalize drivers and their cars. In today's world where NASCAR stock cars have become so safe that drivers walk away from 200-mph wrecks without a bruise or scrape, sprint car racing is still dangerous enough to send some of its participants to their graves.

Sprint car engines burn methanol, which produces an exhaust so toxic that a few breaths bring tears that run down your face. As they sit idling, sprint cars literally shake. There's no clutch or transmission, only high gear. The driveshaft is right between the driver's legs. His knees are an inch behind the engine. Not many people wear fireproof underwear to work, but sprint car drivers do.

America's highways have at most a double guardrail to contain crashing cars and trucks. At Knoxville, Iowa's iconic sprint car track, the guardrail is eight rows high because when these cars turn over, they fly like airplanes, right out of the place if the wall's not got some altitude. Especially challenging are sprint cars without wings. Their grip on the track is marginal and when they begin to flip, they keep flipping on and on and on. (Just read about Perry Tripp who flew so high at Godfrey Speedway he discovered that a backstretch restroom had no roof!)

But whether it's the danger, or the camaraderie among racers built through nights of eating dirt together, or the quantities beer consumed telling tall tales afterwards, sprint car racing is life itself for drivers like Steve Kinser and Doug Wolfgang. So it is for Richard "Gas Man" Griffin, Bubby Jones, Hooker Hood, Curt Michael, Lealand McSpadden, and so many others profiled in *Win It or Wear It*. Once people start, try though they will, there is no miracle antidote to help a driver quit racing sprint cars. Rick

Ferkel will tell you he was hooked after his very first lap behind the wheel.

Nothing can replace the thrill of this sport. For those who travel from track to track there's the lifestyle, the opportunity to live with like-thinking people who thoroughly enjoy mud on their shoes and hot dogs as a basic food group. As children riding a carousel reach out for the brass ring, sprint car drivers reach deep within themselves to win the next race. And every one of them knows that the more they race, the greater the chance of winning—and winning is what they live for.

I have spent the past 40 years covering all forms of American motorsports, from street stocks to Indy, from NASCAR's big league to sprint cars. Along the way, I've driven stock cars, supermodifieds and sprint cars, losing more often than I won. With all that as background, I'm here to tell you that the most colorful and interesting people in all of racing drive and maintain sprint cars.

The racers described in *Win It or Wear It* are not "normal" people. This is a wacky crowd. They are more vibrant, more fervent than the rest. And their pursuit of a good time always somehow revolves around the next race.

In this book Joyce Standridge has captured the unique spirit of sprint car racing–the drama, the danger, the tremendous fun, and the deep love these racers have for their sport. In the pages that follow you will read stories–some shared in print for the first time–that preserve forever the soul of America's most outrageous road warriors.

DICK BERGGREN
IPSWICH, MASSACHUSETTS

Introduction

We took what might loosely be called a victory lap around the track.
It was Friday night, April 27, 1973, and the racing season would begin two nights later—but when Sunday came the track lights would be on, there would be a couple thousand people in the grandstand and more than a hundred race cars instead of just my '72 Cougar flying around in the dark at a speed that would have made the engineers at Mercury cringe.

Rick and I had gotten married in church, but there convention ended as our reception was held in the Springfield Speedway's "penthouse," a slightly down-at-the-heels, discount-house-decorated room atop a storage

*Springfield Speedway's entrance in March 1973.
(Allen Horcher Photo)*

*Front stretch grandstand at Springfield Speedway in 1975.
That's the "penthouse" to left; the roof in the center is
the clubhouse, and the double wide trailer at right is
where Joe Shaheen lived. (Photo by Marvin Scattergood,
Collection owned by Terry Young)*

shed on the property. It took only a moment's look at the unpainted grandstand and the derelict vehicles on nearly every corner of the property to realize that the room was penthouse by comparison only. And this was during the track's heyday.

As we got ready to leave the reception we found the car parked down on the track at the start-finish line. Rick took that to mean that our friends and family expected us to take a lap or two. Later, the track owner Joe Shaheen asked if there had been cars on the track, and we, of course, had to deny our all-time favorite memory for many years. But Joe's gone now, so is the track, and confession is good for the soul, right?

Not a lot of people choose a race track as the site of a wedding reception, but a lot of people don't spend their courtship rebuilding a sprint car either. Rick's dad had gotten a brand new Trostle frame and gave his old CAE to Rick so he could move up to the sprint class. We spent that winter in an old two-car garage that listed slightly to one side. It had a cracked, concrete floor colder than Simon Cowell's heart because the stove put out only two or three BTUs of heat, and then only about the time we quit for the night. At least a thousand old race car parts were hung or rested on the rafters, and how nobody ever got beamed by falling junk is a testament to God's good humor.

It's impossible to see through the mud to tell who this is—but there were many nights that the sprinters looked like this after hot laps at Springfield Speedway. (Courtesy Jeff Moe Collection)

Two nights after our wedding ceremony, Rick put that old CAE on the track and I was absolutely riveted. It's one thing to go to sprint car races and root for someone. It's altogether different when it's your car, your husband, and, sooner or later, your hard work flipping higher than the wood retaining wall. The track got so many sprint cars—35 to 40 a night was common—that youngsters usually got to run only a heat race and a semi at *Little Springfield*, so named in deference to the imposing one-mile dirt track across town at the Illinois State Fairgrounds. On an exceptional night, the kids transferred into the feature. As a result, our car made the main event no more than a dozen times all season.

It didn't matter. You had to earn your way into the feature—there was no buying speed at that time. Rich daddies today say that they don't want the kids learning bad habits in junk, but I love what my long-time pal (and one hell of a good sprint car driver once upon a time) Ken Schrader contends: "Anybody can drive a good car, but if you can make a shitbox competitive, you're a real driver."

In time, Rick earned his way into rides owned by guys who weren't raising two kids and working a couple of jobs just to keep the garage roof over the race car. A sprint car track championship came at another track years later, but it was always Springfield that was our measuring stick. If you could win races there—something Rick's three brothers also accomplished many times over—you could call yourself a sprint car driver and nobody could argue the fact—even the fans who thought there were too damned many Standridges around the place.

In researching this book, I spoke to dozens of accomplished race drivers from all over the country and Australia, and I found that anybody old enough to have driven at Springfield recalls it as a premier destination to test their mettle. Oddly enough, the track was developed and thrived thanks to stock cars; the owner loved and owned some really good midget cars; but it was *sprint cars* that cemented the track's reputation and made it far more famous than it otherwise would ever have been.

The great sprint star Bubby Jones cut his racing teeth at Springfield, winning so many championships that everybody else racing there was beyond delighted when he took to the road. It was also Bubby who convinced the wonderful Ohio gypsy Rick Ferkel to come try the track, and it took just one visit for Ferkel to find out why Little Springfield had

That #0 climbing the fence is Rick Ferkel in his only visit at Little Springfield. Considering it took months to recover from his injuries, there's little wonder. (Kevin Horcher Photo)

such a tenacious reputation.

"Car owner Bob Hampshire told me that if I'd seen my crash, I'd never race again, it was that scary," says Ferkel. "It's probably good when you don't get to see them."

Several days in the hospital were followed by a fairly lengthy recuperation at home for a head injury that also severely impacted his eyesight for some time. Ferkel now laughs, "Bubby Jones kept telling me, '*You gotta come to Springfield, you gotta come to Springfield*,' but for some reason we never had. Well, I think that was the only time I was ever at Springfield. I never went back."

Nearly every great sprint car star of the 1970s and 1980s raced Little

Jan Opperman at the 1975 Illinois State Fairgrounds Super Weekend race. (Courtesy Kathy Stewart Collection)

Springfield at some point, usually for Super Weekend, a two- or three-day event that combined racing on the little quarter-miler with an afternoon on the ferocious one-mile track at the State Fairgrounds. Talk about extremes and testing your courage.

A couple of drivers were killed at the Fairgrounds during this period, including one fatal wreck that happened right in front of me. For several years my mother-in-law and I had worked as track timers and scorers—that was until I figured out that writing about racing meant marginally fewer instances of being yelled at. As it happened, I was scoring the event on the stage across from the main grandstand when local champ Jerry Camfield blew his engine right in the middle of the long front stretch. Two more cars came upon him too quickly to avoid his car. Larry Kirkpatrick had the worse-looking flip, but as seems to happen with racing wrecks, he got out and walked away. When the rescue squad started to remove Cliff Johns' helmet, however, they immediately slipped it back in place so the thousands of people in the grandstand wouldn't see the amount of blood. There was no need to rush to the hospital because he was gone before the car finished going over, and who knows if today's personal safety equipment would have made any difference. It was The Mile, spoken of in hushed tones. The danger aspect made driver's palms sweaty just thinking about it. Wives lost sleep, trying to figure out how to talk their guys out of running it.

What really contributed to the legends of Super Weekend, as much as the shrinking *cojones*, however, was a heart-stopping and unbelievable race between Bubby Jones and the legendary Jan Opperman, in which they were doing slide jobs to each other—crisscrossing back and forth, lap after lap, *at 130 mph*!

And then they got out of their cars in Victory Lane and hugged each

Mike Allgaier congratulates Bubby Jones following the Shaheen Super Weekend race at the Illinois State Fairgrounds in 1975. Mike is the long-time owner of Hoosier Tire Midwest and father of ARCA driver Justin Allgaier. (Courtesy Mary Standridge Collection)

other because, Bubby says, they'd had so much fun!

"We weren't as close friends as a lot of people thought we were," Bubby said many years later, "but we had a great time on the track and we had respect and trust—and on the track you can't ask for more. It was a lot of fun."

Racing—and wrecking—were a lot less stressful at the short track. For a while, Falstaff Beer sponsored a huge, painted bulls-eye high on the fence between turns three and four—and at least one driver hit it. Beyond that, a lot of drivers nervously joked about flipping high enough to get over the catch fence and into the Kmart parking lot just outside turns three and four. Some now make the claim, but in reality the only driver I'm positive made it all the way over the fence was my youngest brother-in-law, Rob.

Rick and other brothers Randy and Ron and sister Carol beat the rescue squad over the track fence, the catch fence and into the parking

(Starting upper left) Terry Shepherd has just taken a shot at the fourth-turn light pole at Little Springfield. A few minutes later, Rob Standridge hits the same pole and clears the fence, going into the Kmart parking lot next door. Apparently, a lot of people followed him over. In the final photo, that's sister Janet—back on crutches—standing behind the car. (First three photos Allen Horcher; final photo Joyce Standridge)

lot. That turned out to be a bad thing because the brothers were ready to fight off the rescuers who arrived to get Rob out. Everybody—including the squad—knew that common sense didn't necessarily run alongside this goofy bunch. The most amazing sibling, however, was sister Janet, who managed to climb that six-foot tall wooden fence with a sprained ankle and then swing her crutches at anybody who got in her way. The only sane, calm person on the scene, in fact, was 18-year-old Rob. (Teenagers know they're not going to get hurt, don't you know.) He was pretty proud of that altitude record, even if it did cost him a race car.

It was a Herschel Jenkins wreck that maybe best epitomizes not only Springfield Speedway but short track racing everywhere during the golden age in which any working guy could afford a car if he had a garage, a single-axle open trailer, friends or neighbors who could be conned into helping, and a wife who could do magical things with the checkbook. Herschel was Everyman Racer. He ran a neat little muffler shop in a nearby town, had raced every type of car that ever ran at Springfield, and he knew how to win without spending more money than a Rockefeller. He was lucky, too, until the night he flipped violently going into turn one and cleared the fence at that end. He landed in the beer garden, narrowly missing a passel of people, some of whom had never before sacrificed a beer to run and climb that fast.

It wasn't the flip that hurt Herschel—it was the landing. He spent a lot of sheet time, but recuperated and returned to racing. Herschel was too tough to listen to anybody else even as his intensity began to fade in those latter years, just like Joe's, the track's promoter.

Joe Shaheen, mid-1980s. (Terry Young Photo, Jeff Moe Collection)

Joe Shaheen was a character beyond character. Son of a Lebanese immigrant, Joe had a distinctive, gravelly voice, was rough around *all* the edges, and possessed an ego bigger than all the drivers combined who'd ever walked through his gate. That included A. J. Foyt. Joe had a love-hate relationship with the racers that resulted in several *strikes*. "We'd all mill around in the parking lot, grousing and complaining about how tight Joe was and how rich he was getting off us," recalls Bubby. "And then we'd all cave in and go race—and somehow he never paid us an additional dime."

There were rumors that Joe had been involved with some pretty shady types during Prohibition, including a guy who crossed the Mob and disappeared under questionable circumstances. Regardless of the truth of that matter, what was unquestionable was Joe's ability to prepare a track. He was so good, in fact, that he was flown down to prepare the track when the Houston Astrodome ran indoor midget races in the 1960s. Throughout the years, other track operators all over the country used to call and ask for advice.

And that was the reason behind the desire of so many drivers to make the trek to a mini-Mecca of speed, where the track record was in the 10-second bracket at a time when other quarter-mile tracks were lucky to get down to the 12-second range. The side-by-side duels among drivers were so good that bragging fans called all around the country in the age when there were no calling packages and it cost 40 or 50 cents a minute to talk.

Most touring groups came into Little Springfield, including the All-Stars, early World of Outlaws (WoO), and quite frequently, the United States Auto Club (USAC). I don't think USAC—in spite of meticulous record-keeping—asterisked the race at Springfield that was red-flagged to remove the German Shepherd dog chasing race cars and biting the tires.

(Honesty compels me to admit that the dog also was a Standridge. He belonged to my brother-in-law, who lived just a few blocks from the track. It wasn't the first time Thor had broken his leash and shown up at the track, but it was the only time he tried to eat the race cars.)

It had to be the track that built the legend. It certainly wasn't the ambience.

In the front corner of the parking area was Joe's used car lot, and a sorrier collection of vehicles would be hard to find in the entire state of Illinois, then or now. But Monday through Saturday, buying and selling junkers, then squeezing the last dime out of people who barely had a dime, seemed to be Joe's reason to live.

Adjacent to the car lot—so much so that it was almost indistinguishable, was the double wide trailer in which he lived. He could have afforded to live in one of the mansions overlooking toney MacArthur Park, but that would have meant giving up the first dollar he made. And everybody knew that wasn't going to happen.

Behind the track was one of the all-time, awesome junkyards ever created. Little kids loved to scare the crap out of each other by making up tales about what was really buried out there among all those decrepit, rusting hulks. (There were adults who believed the truth might be scarier than any kiddy fairy tale, in fact.) Climb to the top of the backstretch grandstand, and you could see into the junkyard. But you'd have to ask yourself why you would want to.

The grandstands combined might have held a couple thousand people, but they had to be hearty souls because they could count on being absolutely pelted with mud clods most of the night. Several times people were carted out of the track in an ambulance after being knocked out cold by a clod—seriously. However, a bruise that didn't require a trip to the emergency room was a badge of honor—though even that wouldn't get you a free beer. Joe's sister Mae ran the concessions, and free *anything* was an oxymoron.

Mae was nearly as notorious as Joe for being tight-fisted—and tough on the help. It was always 110 degrees in the under-grandstand concession stand, even when it was 40 degrees everywhere else, but every poor gal who ever worked there was expected to hustle it up in case a would-be customer lost patience, and Mae lost a sale.

She had a huge horse trough in which all the soda and beer was iced down—and it was so deliciously cold that everybody nearly forgave her and Joe for the inflated prices. Mae could also go around a 30-foot, L-shaped railing, take two dozen orders at a time, hand *exactly* the right refreshment back no matter how large the orders had been, and make correct change almost without looking at the bills. We knew she could recognize denominations by touch, but remembering all those orders was pretty impressive.

Another fixture in an incredible pack of characters at the track was Pencils Jim Warner. A developmentally challenged individual, Pencils lived in various corners of the facility's buildings with his Tower-of-Pisa stacks of newspapers, one change of clothes that got washed annually whether they needed it or not, and several hundred pencils—as many as possible stuck in his shirt pocket. A lot of people thought it was very charitable of Joe to take Pencils in as otherwise he would probably have been institutionalized, but Pencils did most of the grunt work around the property—and it truly was grunt work because Pencils grunted and grumbled about it at every opportunity.

Everybody who raced regularly at Little Springfield came to love him, though. Pencils' childlike heart allowed him to embrace racing with his entire being and he couldn't wait for Sunday night so he could share the latest gossip. When he and Joe both got to talking, it was like ground-up glass—in stereo—and that alone was worth the price of admission.

One of Pencils' plethora of jobs was shooing everybody out when the bar ran out of beer three or four hours after the races. The bar was the one truly fabulous structure on the property, with steps made of cylinder heads and interior decoration consisting of walls covered in priceless racing photos. For a while there was even a mini-Indy car in among the tables and chairs for kids to climb all over when Joe wasn't looking.

Track veterans say that some of the biggest laughs (and crushing truck dents) came when it rained during the races at Little Springfield. With sprint cars pitted in the infield, the extraordinarily high banks were a challenge-beyond-challenge to climb when the track surface got slimy.

That fact was used by a prankster driver who used to sneak up on other racers with a water-filled extinguisher, hide behind a truck and squirt in the air just to watch nervous teams start loading up so they could get out of the infield before the expected downpour. Hearty fans would sit in the grandstand, in the rain, and bet on how long it would take for some of the haulers to get out.

Springfield Speedway opened in 1947 and closed in 1987. It should be like rival facility Macon Speedway, which is alive and thriving in the hands of Tony Stewart, Ken Schrader, Kenny Wallace and Bob Sargent. Joe and Macon's original builder Wayne Webb were contemporaries who co-promoted any area racing event that they couldn't steal away from each other and back-stab in the process. But when Wayne got old, he passed along the track to others to run, and eventually sell. Joe honestly didn't believe anyone could ever run the track as well as he did, even in

Before Springfield Speedway was bulldozed for a shopping area, the track was shuttered for a couple of years. This forlorn sight is what greeted fans before the track disappeared forever. (Joyce Standridge Photo)

his eighties when the storied surface got dusty and rutted. And so, when Joe died, the heirs sold it. They knew it had considerably higher value as development property than as a race track—and they nursed what seemed to be considerable distaste for many of the people who frequented the place anyway. Today, a number of businesses reside at Clear Lake Avenue and Dirksen Parkway, including a Starbucks, McDonald's and Walgreens. Heaven knows, the world didn't have enough of those franchises.

But Springfield Speedway isn't quite dead yet. Those of us who were privileged to spend a portion of our lives there won't let it rest in the grave. Happily, the lights of scores of similar tracks around this country still flicker with special memories of glory days.

I've told you a little about Springfield because that's the first place I ever heard the phrase, "*win it or wear it.*" It was reserved for drivers like Ron Milton. Although he ventured around the country occasionally, most

It's easy to be impressed with the big, famous tracks and marvel at how well they present their facilities. But if you have your own lesser-known Saturday Night track and it's a neat and clean little place like Spoon River Speedway in Canton, Illinois, life is good. (Steve Hardin Photo)

of his career was spent at Little Springfield and nearby tracks, so you have to be a real sprint car fan to have heard of him. Because he came from my hometown, all the way back to my teen years I was paying attention to him. Let me tell you, every lap, it was the wreck that didn't happen.

Except when it did.

When you get two or more racers or fans together, from any era or geographical region, the conversation—guaranteed—will turn to the great wins and the incredible wrecks they've seen. Longtime fans appreciate—even love—*win it or wear it* drivers. It has always meant fans could count on those drivers to do absolutely every possible thing on this side of fairness to win (and there were a few who didn't mind stepping over that line). If he wasn't going to get the trophy girl's kiss, it was only because the driver had *worn it*—wrecked so badly that what remained was a steaming heap. It was the most testosterone-driven compliment ever conceived, and for many, it remains the highest praise possible.

Win it or wear it racers have never been bad guys—try to find a murderer or child-molester among them. It doesn't happen. But orneriness, contrariness, and a slightly off-kilter view of the world have driven most of these people from lap one of sprint car history. Heaven forbid these people should have a brush with *ordinary*. Maybe this will help further explain: Some years ago, a famous race driver was asked to describe another one, and he said, "You couldn't castrate him with a chainsaw."

That pretty much sums up people who race sprint cars—and perhaps their fans as well. They are not left-brained or right-brained. Observations to the contrary from outsiders who just don't get it, neither are they bird-brained. Sprint car folks are not stupid, nor careless—just hopelessly obsessed. They choose to selectively ignore what could happen, even if it has happened to them or others, and then they focus with such total, single-minded intent on what-is-gonna-be. And that is limited solely to the adrenalin rush at the checkered flag—a feeling that most freely admit rivals the best sex ever.

Whether it's Outlaws or outlaws-with-a-small-o, this book is their own anecdotal meander through racing history. No crowd races harder, laughs more frequently, nor cries more when the painful losses inevitably happen. In this smaller-than-used-to-be era, these are larger-than-life individuals who have embraced what they accomplish, with an abandon we can only envy.

It's not just Springfield Speedway where wonderful memories were created one lap at a time. There are drivers, participants and fans all over the world with tales worth preserving and sharing.

Let's savor a few of those memories.

1

Wrecks

If we sprint car people were right in the head, bench racing would center on fantastic wins or tales of great courage and racers overcoming tremendous obstacles. The focus would be on supportive families and the changing face (and wallet) of sprint car racing. But what everybody jaws about—absolutely guaranteed and sometimes to the exclusion of all the other deserving topics—are the wrecks.

Psychiatrists would find some kind of label for this, possibly the Socially Acceptable Wreck Observers Syndrome, if only we could finally be considered socially acceptable people. No matter how much fans and racers deny that they are at the track to see the wrecks, it's a niggling little bug in the back of almost every brain. You know you will see somebody win, hopefully in spectacular and satisfying fashion. You know you will be entertained. What you *don't* know is whether somebody is going to *wear it*—and, best-case scenario, walk away from the wreck with nothing but the wallet injured.

Considering how often wrecks occur and how exceptional many sprint car crashes are, it would be a lie to say that it's not part of the appeal. Sprint car participants and fans never want to see a serious injury or fatality—although most have done so if they've been around the sport for any time. But if there weren't at least a subconscious desire to see equipment torn up and brave people walking (or limping) away from the scene of the accident, we wouldn't go to the races. Don't try to deny it.

For the drivers, there is something inescapably thrilling about being tougher than something that ought to beat them silly. The bad stuff always happens to The Other Guy, because if drivers didn't convince themselves of that so-called fact, they would all park the cars and take up golf. But there is a certain kind of individual who can never experience life without testing the limits. Thank goodness, because otherwise we wouldn't have cops, firefighters, military personnel—or sprint car drivers.

Racers can't always pull it back out when the limit is found, and that's why there's a graveyard of bent-up aluminum wings behind most sprint car garages. It happens.

For fans, it's maybe even more complex. They're smart enough to avoid getting in the cars and testing the limits, even if it's finances more than intelligence that keeps them from stuffing their knees into that claustrophobic cockpit. But, gosh, who doesn't live to be the first to tell other sprint car friends about being at the track when somebody who needs arm restraint straps flew higher than the American flag, and then climbed out of the steaming mess to shake his fist at the clown he thinks started the wreck and *got away with it?*

Although the car is lettered to reflect Rich Vogler as the driver, he had just quit the ride and Cliff Cockrum was hired to drive it. He goes for a ride at Paragon Speedway on April 17, 1983. (Kevin Horcher Photo)

Nothing, but nothing, can make a driver sorry he's racing in Florida rather than back home shoveling snow in February—unless he's crashed and he thinks he's got an alligator chasing him.

For decades, racers have listened to the Speed Weeks siren, luring them to spend a few days getting a nose-peeling sunburn—and wadding up a sprint car now and then on an unfamiliar track. Sometimes there could be more to the wreck than just worrying about fixing the race car, however. Drivers will say that if a wreck goes on long enough, you have time to think about how much it's going to hurt when the car makes contact with the track, or how much it's going to cost to fix it. Any number of things. But what was going through Cliff Cockrum's head as he cleared the wall at a mid-Florida track was that all week long people had been telling him there were alligators in the pond just outside the track.

Even before the rescue people could react, Cockrum came running out of the dark and vaulted back over the wall onto the track—without his race car. He had set a world record for unbuckling his harness, and he had absolutely no intention whatsoever of finding out whether there were gator tails—or just gator tales beyond the wall.

Exaggerations are often part of crash stories, but there are a few tracks where embellishment is rarely necessary to make a point. Knoxville, Eldora, Williams Grove, Winchester, Salem, and all the mile tracks have been sites for great races and fabled wrecks that have added much to racing lore. But very few tracks can exceed Manzanita Speedway on the gritty southwest side of Phoenix for memorable mishaps. Part of the reason is that over the years so many cars have exited the track's racing surface and cleared the fence. Some land out by 35th Avenue, which means more than one innocent street driver was fiddling with the radio dial one second and trying to dodge disintegrating sprint car parts the next.

Manzanita Speedway at the corner of 35th and Broadway in Phoenix. The photo showing the proximity of 35th Avenue to the track shows why tales of passersby dodging flipping sprint cars is no exaggeration. The junkyard off the third and fourth turns, however, is no more. Gone with it are some great stories of dazed drivers being chased by guard dogs. (Steve Hardin Photos)

Even more storied are the junkyard crashes. Off the third and fourth turns at Manzy for many years there were disgruntled scrap proprietors who didn't appreciate uninvited vehicles, especially those that arrived airborne. In recent years, the track owners have bought the junkyard, closed it down and cleared it out, but there was a time when it was like a racer's badge of honor to have Doberman bite marks on a Nomex suit. You wanted to be conscious when the race car came to rest on a stack of smashed cars so the dogs couldn't get you.

One particularly vicious wreck there involved Midwestern driver Ron Milton, out west on a vacation-racing tour. He took such a bad ride that he ruined a brand new helmet. And it made him mad enough that he called the manufacturer to complain.

"It's totaled," he complained. "I can't ever use it again."

And the company rep asked, "Well, what happened?"

"I flipped at Manzanita," he barked, "out into the junkyard."

"And where are you calling me from?"

"Home," Milton responded.

"Well, then—*it worked.*"

Ron had survived the wreck, towed the battered remains of his car 1,500 miles and been lucid enough to call Bell Helmets, so you can't argue the validity of the company rep's observation.

At least Milton's helmet stayed on. There was no such luck for Johnny Herrera during a rookie-year mistake. Late in the season he traveled from Albuquerque to Erie, Colorado, with a car owned by his dad. In the ensuing crash, the strap broke and the helmet came off—before the car came to a rest.

"I was knocked out."

Knocked out? Herrera was lucky he wasn't knocked off, the usual outcome of the separation of helmet and head mid-wreck. With a serious concussion that also affected his equilibrium for a while, Herrera could have been forgiven if he'd chosen to walk away from what he still considers the worst wreck of his long career. But, perhaps that's why so many sprint car drivers are young—if they don't think they're bullet-proof, they probably won't come back from that kind of wreck. Especially when they see what's left of the car afterwards.

"We had killed the race car," he confirms. "Dad gave me a little time and then he wanted to know if racing was still what I wanted to do."

Herrera had the good sense to pause and think about it. But within a month, "Hollywood," as he's known to fans, was back behind the wheel. And continues to race more than 20 years later.

Safety equipment is intended to protect drivers through bad wrecks, but even if it gets tested in its maiden voyage like Milton's helmet, it's done its job. However, safety equipment is good *only* if a driver actually uses it.

The vast majority of drivers have—at least once in their careers—

Everybody stayed buckled in and then walked away from this heat race crash at the 2008 Knoxville Nationals. (Doug Johnson Photo)

caught the release lever on a seat-belt system and popped it loose during the running of a race. The appropriate response, and it's the one that 99.99999 percent have chosen—is to immediately slow down and exit the track to someplace where the driver and the other twenty-some people are not running at over 100 miles per hour.

That .000001 percent? Supposedly, it's Gary Bettenhausen.

Onlookers insist that he ran nearly an entire feature with his seat belt undone.

At Eldora.

The baddest, meanest, most *chew-em-up* and *spit-em-out* half-mile dirt in the country, if reputations are to be confirmed. You wouldn't even want to ride in a push truck around the track without a seat belt hooked. And the legend is that Bettenhausen wouldn't pull in *because he was leading.*

Priorities, drivers say.

Not everybody walks away. Beyond Rick Ferkel's devastating Little Springfield wreck that left him with a serious concussion and out of commission for a lengthy period of time, there have been some bad outcomes, and it's not particularly surprising that some involve spinal injuries. The back is especially vulnerable in those accidents that result in a rapid and violent stop. Ferkel is among the drivers to have suffered a broken back. And while his occurred in Webster City, Iowa, hundreds of miles from his native northern Ohio, another broken back proved that it's not necessary to leave home to get really messed up in a crash. Not yet 40 years old, Curt Michael has already accumulated five United Racing Club (URC) championships, but he has also suffered a broken C6 vertebra in a collision with a lapped car at his home track, Delaware International Speedway in Delmar.

"I jumped the right rear with my left front and it started going," he says. "As soon as I hit the track, I knew something was wrong because I couldn't breathe."

Thanks to careful extrication and good, immediate medical care, not only did he recover but he avoided the specter of paralysis. "It hurts every day," he says, "and I imagine it'll really hurt 20 years from now. But it could have been a whole lot worse."

Knoxville can be tough, as a couple of guys found out during the 2007 Nationals. Brandon Wimmer (#8) tried a slide job on Chad Kemenah that didn't work. Mark "Dynamite" Dobmeier from Grand Forks, North Dakota, took a major tumble when a right rear wheel broke in half. They were both okay. The cars were not. (Mike Campbell Photos)

Although it took 11 weeks to recuperate, Michael's pain was compounded when he returned to the track and an official admitted that the lapped car Curt rode over in the crash was in the wrong position on the restart and should have been *behind* Michael instead of *ahead*. But rather than slow the show by putting the lapped car where he belonged, they let it go. The rest was history, as Michael's aching back will attest.

Really serious wrecks are rare and becoming more so over time. When drivers recover they can look back at the wrecks with a wince and a chuckle. But it's harder for some other drivers, especially those whose wrecks changed—or ended—their careers, such as Bob Christian's moment at Riverside International Speedway in West Memphis, Arkansas.

Bob Christian at Haubstadt in 1981. (Allen Horcher Photo)

Bob had struggled to get his car ready for the feature that night. At the last second as cars were lining up for the race he told the first alternate, "Sorry, young'n, but I'm gonna make it."

He shouldn't have. In one of those "if only" moments racing has spawned too often, the exhilaration of getting through a thrash and then joining the field on the track yielded to disaster. Within a few laps, Bob's life changed forever when he lost his arm in a wreck.

Another driver, who asked not to be identified because "I don't want to be remembered for my wrecks," nonetheless recalled a couple of nasty ones that got him some pretty serious sheet time. The first was during the brief period in the mid-to-late 1970s that Champaign Motor Speedway in east central Illinois was open. He remembers, "They had gotten the water truck stuck down in the second turn and it kept dumping water on the track. When I went out to qualify, I hit that water and got really sideways. The car turned over and over and went way up over the light poles and came down on the nose of the car. Blood came through my skin. I ruptured my kidneys, and collapsed my lungs. Pretty much busted everything."

Later, "At Granite City, Illinois, I got in the fence upside down and backwards. It broke the cage off and the car landed on me four or five times. When I got stopped, it was on top of me and part of the roll cage was stuck in my shoulder. The wreck broke my cheekbone, some ribs, my back, and my arms and legs. That one should have killed me. I think I survived because I was small. If I'd been a bigger man, it probably *would* have killed me."

Most of the time, though, crashes result in less-sobering results.

Like bell-ringers.

You won't find a definition in Webster's, but here's the explanation: Racer wrecks. Rescue personnel ask pertinent questions—what's your name, what day of the week is it, who's president—and the racer answers correctly unless he hasn't voted in a while. Racer walks back to the pit area, but later can't remember any of this.

On May 17, 1991, at Eldora, it turned out to be a good thing that Jack Hewitt and Lealand McSpadden were already good friends. A slide job that didn't work resulted in Lealand going for a ride. And Jack, who had his bell rung, too, apologized more than once. (Allen Horcher Photos)

For example, Tempe, Arizona's Lealand McSpadden, one of the best to ever come out of the Southwest, and Jack Hewitt, a legendary Ohio star who lived near Eldora and has probably accumulated more racing stories—happy and horrific—from that track than anybody, were battling for the lead on the high banks and crashed. Both flipped hard and after the race, according to an observer, Hewitt went down to McSpadden's car to apologize for a slide job that didn't work.

And then, a little while later, Hewitt walked down to McSpadden's car to apologize—because he didn't remember he had been there earlier.

That's the definition of a bell-ringer.

Richard "The Gas Man" Griffin was the good-luck recipient of inheriting the Eldora win when McSpadden and Hewitt crashed, but the Southwest ace knows what it's like to get a bell-ringer, too. His most memorable one occurred in 1984 at Ascot Park in Gardena, California. "It really knocked me out on the first flip and I don't even remember waking up until I was at the hospital," he recalls. "Didn't have anything wrong with me except a concussion. But, my car—they actually had to bring an end loader out to get it off the fence while I was still in it and knocked out."

Bobby Allen, a Pennsylvania transplant from Florida and one of the most-admired drivers of his time, also knows what it's like to have some teeth-rattling experiences. "I was running down the straightaway at Williams Grove, getting ready to pass Dub May, when he blows a tire and that pulls him over to the right. I climb his wheel and it flips," he says. "I remember being in the ambulance, and I thought it was really great that I woke up."

So did everyone else.

Proving that drivers don't always have the best judgment, especially after a bell-ringer, Allen got back in a race car a couple of days later, against doctor's orders. Bobby was able to keep his mind together long enough to set fast time, but one lap isn't the same as a 25-lap feature. "I just rode around," he admits. "I just knew not to get hurt again."

As if there was a choice.

Any driver who stays at it long enough and races as hard as Bobby Allen probably is going to have more than one *uh-oh* moment. Allen's other especially painful encounter with immovable objects was at East Alabama Motor Speedway in Phenix City, Alabama. The right rear wheel broke going into the corner and Allen shot up the embankment.

Not a problem.

And then it came back down on the tail.

Problem.

Allen painfully broke his shoulder blade. As he recuperated Bobby also learned another of the axioms of racing: If somebody films you crashing big time, you can expect to see it, and relive it, in racing commercials until the cows come home or somebody takes more air crashing.

What a shame no one was filming the very colorful and talented driver Clarence "Hooker" Hood on a particular evening back in the sixties at his hometown track, the ever-challenging *Ditch*, a.k.a., Riverside Speedway in West Memphis, Arkansas. Hooker was driving a car powered by a ridiculously fast flathead Ford engine during a match race. The two drivers came out of the fourth turn toward the checkered flag, got tangled up and Hooker went for a ride. Up, up, *up*, over the fence, and just as he thought he was going to hit the concession stand (and the girl working there), the car nosed down and just barely missed her.

Ah, but the tale does not end there. When Hooker landed on all four wheels, the throttle stuck and the car blasted on at least 35 or 40 feet beneath the grandstand. Finally at a stop, Hooker bolted from the car, hollering at the officials, "My car's 'bout half full of nitro! You better get out of here because that grandstand's gonna *blow up*!"

They stopped running toward Hooker, did an about face and started back through the scrambling fans running for their lives—or so they thought. Happily for sprint car fans who've been going to West Memphis for decades since, the car must have decided it was starved of fuel, shut itself off and the grandstand didn't explode into a shower of splinters.

Hooker says he avoided nitro after that.

On another occasion, Hooker didn't drive under the grandstand at West Memphis. He took an airborne route off the track instead. "I came down the main straightaway and something broke in the steering," he

The "No Whining, Just Race" sign at West Memphis is world famous. (Joyce Standridge Photo)

Like a lot of sprint car drivers, Rick Ferkel loved a track with a lot of bite and challenge to it (and a big ole wing to take advantage). What he didn't add is how this type of track can grab a wheel if you slide too hard—and snap you on over. This is Ferkel at Riverside International Speedway, West Memphis, Arkansas, on Nov. 24, 1976. (Courtesy Rick Ferkel Collection)

explains. "I hit the fence and it made me into Evel Knievel."

At the end of the turns was a walkway that allowed fans to get from one side of the track to the other. Fortunately, Hooker's flyover came at a time when most people were in the grandstand watching the race rather than wandering around. But not everybody.

"There was a lady and her husband who were walking around the end there," Hooker explains. "I hit the wire fence on the inside and the force pushed the mesh up on her, trapping her. And she was pregnant."

Needless to say there was a bit of hysteria accompanying the realization of what had happened. Quickly, Hooker was out of the car and consoling the woman when his father worked his way through the mass who'd gathered round.

"Boy, you're hurt," he said, seeing the blood on both of them.

"No, sir," Hooker replied, "but this lady—I gotta take care of her."

Hooker's daddy was so unnerved that he never came back to the race track to watch his son after that. But if it was too much of a scare for Daddy, it wasn't so for the young couple. "She had that baby, and the family turned out to be the best sprint car spectators I ever met in my life," Hooker marveled. "Every night, they were right there with me. The little lady sure didn't go around the end of the race track anymore, though."

That's the thing about sprint cars flipping through the air: The results are often unanticipated. For example, there was a night when Missourian Perry Tripp went off the embankment right where the wooden backstretch wall started at Godfrey Speedway, a quarter-mile track just north of St. Louis and now gone. In this instance, it seemed Tripp was going for distance rather than height, although he got plenty of both. A few minutes later, he walked back inside the track and approached photographers who had no idea that it had been as interesting from Tripp's vantage point as it had been shooting pictures of the flip from the infield. "Golly, guys," he said in his patented Ozark drawl, "did you know there's no roof on that rest room off the back stretch? I looked right down and somebody was in there takin' care of business when I went over the top of it."

Easily one of the most popular drivers in the history of West Riverside Speedway, Hooker Hood. (Courtesy Hooker Hood Collection)

But Tripp's aerial adventure didn't end there. "I hit a car some drunk was sitting in when I came down," he added.

"How did you know the guy was drunk?" someone asked him.

Turned out that track personnel towed away Tripp's race car, but the drunk had gotten out of his passenger car and was cussing to no one in particular that somebody had wrecked his vehicle. Tripp was still there, still in his firesuit, and he nodded agreeably, telling the guy, "Yeah, somebody must have really come through here and plowed your car. You better go in there and look for that guy."

And the fella, reeking of beer, stumbled right past Tripp to go find and whump the ass of the guy who caved in the side of his car.

❖   ❖   ❖   ❖   ❖

At Erie, Colorado, Lealand McSpadden did an end-over-end flip down the front straight. A few minutes later a rescue helicopter came in to land. Kenny Schrader was in a group standing beside the track watching, when he felt a tap on his shoulder.

"Who's that for?" he was asked.

Schrader turned around and saw who had tapped his shoulder. "Umm, it's for *you*," he told McSpadden.

Maybe because he's walked away from so many wrecks, Schrader, in spite of becoming a USAC national sprint car champion, loves to tell stories about crashes, especially when he's the unwitting victim. He has been known to talk about a particular race in 1985 when he was just getting his toes wet in NASCAR, driving for Elmo Langley in a limited number of races. Because only five NASCAR shows in a season hardly constituted a living (especially in the days when the circuit was still building appeal),

Perry Tripp in 1989. (Allen Horcher Photo)

Tom Stansberry creates sparks as he slides along the wall at Perris Speedway, Southern California, in 2000. (Allen Horcher Photo)

Schrader had to keep his "night job," driving short-track cars.

One weekend he raced at Michigan International Speedway during the afternoon, and then jumped in a rental car heading for Kokomo Speedway at a speed that would have ruined a state trooper's day. Although he missed hot laps, Schrader got to the track in time for time trials. He told a pal later on, "I'd been driving that stock car all afternoon around Michigan, which is really, really fast. Got in my car and drove my ass off, flying down the road to Kokomo. Got there, jumped in the sprint car and they pushed me off. Well, in those days they pushed you off in the pits, you came out turn two, go around and get the green for your lap. The problem is this thing's feeling really slow. I mean compared to what I'd been doing all day? So, I nailed it.

"Went down into turn three—and right into the wall. Flipped the damned thing just because it felt so slow, *and didn't even make it to the green*. Night was over. That was it."

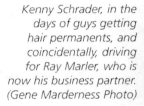

Kenny Schrader, in the days of guys getting hair permanents, and coincidentally, driving for Ray Marler, who is now his business partner. (Gene Marderness Photo)

Schrader's one of the most amusing guys in racing, but it's not from pratfalls and goofiness. In fact, his considerable wit rarely is dulled even when tested by a wreck. Consider that before he and his then-car owner Ray Marler bought I-55 Raceway in Pevely, Missouri, they raced there quite a few times. One event was a marathon still going on at four o'clock the following morning. A crash happened just off turn two and the umpteenth yellow light came on at this ridiculous hour—then went red because somebody had gone over. Schrader, observers say, was well ahead of this mess, entering turn four. However, he missed the red light and went sailing through turns one and two—and into the crash.

As the wrecker was loading what was left of the sprinter, Schrader asked his car owner, "Ray, what could I do?"

And the rather-unhappy Marler replied, "You went by the corner light in four, you went by the flagman, you went by the light in one, and you piled in! And there was nothing you could do? You want to know why I'm pissed? *You had to make almost a full lap to tear up my car!"*

But Schrader wasn't whipped yet. The officials decided to call it a race, since the sun was scheduled to come up in about an hour.

"Great!" said Schrader. "I'm the winner!"

"Huh?!" the stunned officials replied. "You wrecked!"

"The red light was on long before I was involved. I was leading, so I win," he said in all seriousness.

What the officials finally did to resolve Schrader's unshakable logic was re-start the race and run one lap under yellow. Since he couldn't restart with a race car in a thousand pieces, Schrader's argument was moot. But he wasn't happy about it. And neither were the half dozen fans still left in the grandstand.

Fans were far more entertained by a wreck that Jack Hewitt had at Angell Park Speedway on July 2, 2002. Although the track is better known as a midget facility, they have run some USAC sprint shows. And during the race Hewitt flipped so high he went over the billboards, landing in

During a USAC sprint race at Angell Park Speedway in Sun Prairie, Wisconsin, on July 7, 2002, Jack Hewitt flew over the billboard and out into the pit area. And after a few breathless moments, he reappeared at the top of a billboard to yell at the "dumb ass" who sent him flying. (Kevin Horcher Photos)

the pit area, reportedly just a few feet from his own trailer. As fans held their collective breath, a few moments later Hewitt popped up at the top of the billboard where he'd gone out. All anyone could see were his head and arms—kind of like a Muppet show. He scanned the field stopped on the track for the red flag.

And then he saw the guy.

"You!" he hollered, pointing toward one of the cars. "You are a DUMB ASS!"

It was so quiet all around the track and in the grandstand that all but the profoundly deaf could hear Hewitt's tirade. "You don't turn into anybody that late in the corner! You're a dumb ass! When you get outta that car, come to my pit. And if you're stupid enough to come out here, I'll prove that *you're a dumb ass!*"

No one at the track, including the guy to whom the diatribe was directed, doubted the man known as "Do It" Hewitt for a second.

There's no such thing as a cheap wreck. Only a less expensive one, and fans can be forgiven for thinking that racers are sometimes dogging it (not racing all-out) to avoid touching wheels or the wall. But, in spite of the best intentions, stuff happens.

Even veterans sometimes can't avoid problems. Fans recall the night that Bob Thoman hit the wall at Benton Race Park in southeast Missouri so hard he bounced back into another car, and the track crew had to walk some distance down the track to retrieve the motor. Onlookers say that the vehicle simply exploded in a thousand pieces. Yet Thoman had no more than a broken leg—and a hell of a story to tell his pals who weren't there that night.

Jimmy Sills had a similarly disintegrating experience: "At the time, the Western World race (at Manzanita) was probably the biggest race of the year, certainly for us from the region," explains Sills, a northern California native who became a champion in several types of racing, including sprint cars. "We qualified and we were going to be outside front row for the A Main on Saturday night. But on Friday night they have this invitational race. That's a race that the promoter got everybody to come and run for less money…"

Steve Kinser started the Friday night race on Jimmy's inside. As the field of cars picked up the throttle going into turn three for the green flag, Sills' motor stumbled a little. That meant Kinser pulled away a bit—but not as much as he thought. Sills came on strong again, running against the cushion with Kinser in the low groove.

"He doesn't know I'm out there and he drifts up," says Sills. "It gets me into the wall. Well, it flipped forever. It was just one of those wrecks that you think it's over because it gets quiet for a long time. Then I opened my eyes and I'm upside down, still going down the track fast. So, I closed my eyes again, and it flipped several more times."

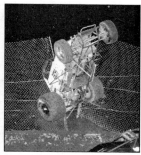

It's August 2008, and Donnie Gentry works on the altitude record at St. Francois County Raceway in Farmington, Missouri. (Kevin Horcher Photos)

After what seemed an eternity, the car came to a stop. Sills eased out of the car and sat on a tire, trying to focus. Someone came running up immediately and asked, "How ya doin'?"

"I think I'm all right, but how's the car?"

"Well, you see that yellow piece way back down the track there?"

Sills turned his head and squinted as he replied, "Yeah?"

"That's the front half of the car."

Qualified for the front row for Saturday night. Totaled the car on Friday night. No happy ending for Sunday morning.

Waking the next day following a bone-jarring crash creates a morning-after soreness that can leave a driver feeling worse than the worst hangover. A lot of guys choose to go off on their own and figuratively lick their wounds. Californian Brad Sweet did not get that luxury after flipping at Tri-State Speedway in Haubstadt, Indiana. Previously, no race car of any kind had ever gone over their wall in more than 30 years, mostly thanks to the billboards, which acted as an unofficial catch fence.

And then in July 2005, qualifying on soil that's among the best in the world for growing corn and slinging sprint cars around, Sweet found out what a Midwestern bite really was. Fortunately, neither Sweet—nor anyone in the pit area where he landed—got hurt as he hurtled above the boards. And then, the following morning, Sweet got to see himself flying through the air with the greatest of ease on ABC's *Good Morning America*. It was the talk of the sprint car world for a while, although Sweet probably would have enjoyed his 15 minutes of national fame getting a trophy and a kiss instead.

All these wrecks occurred at famous tracks and became part of lore. But if you wreck at an obscure, short-lived track the ground is no softer and you won't ache any less, nor will the repairs be any less expensive.

Consider such a place: For the briefest of time in the late 1980s and early 1990s, within spitting distance of Interstate 55 about 40 miles north of St. Louis there was a wicked-fast, half-mile track called White City Speedway. What made racers sit up and take notice there was the row of trees that lined the back stretch. While close-by trees had been a matter of concern at old tracks, especially Eastern and Midwestern fairgrounds, nobody built a brand new track anywhere close to a tree line for obvious reasons. A stock car was the first to demonstrate why they shouldn't have at White City.

During a day race, Lumpy Lowry ran his Mustang off the lip of the semi-banked track and launched. The only possible way for a car to avoid the trees was to get the car perpendicular and slide between them. Somehow, some way, Lumpy did exactly that. (In fact, it was a bit of luck that he was photographed in the process because no way would anyone ever believe it could happen otherwise.) It took a while to retrieve the uninjured driver and car because no one knew where the gate was to the farm field behind the trees. No one had ever needed to know that before.

So, when sprint cars ran White City, Lumpy's exploit was in the back of drivers' minds. It's probably incidental but when they crashed, it tended to be on the front stretch. Iowan Terry McCarl, in fact, didn't flip very high or very far coming off the fourth turn. He might have been better off if he had because the car bee-lined into the concrete Jersey barrier in front of the judge's stand. It was one of those instances of coming to an instantaneous stop. From 100 miles per hour to zero in .001 of a second. He wasn't badly injured—but his car was terminal.

It was "Fast Freddie" Rahmer, the hard-charging long-time member of the Pennsylvania Posse, who performed the most memorable disintegration in a wreck-strewn All-Stars race at White City. Rahmer got above the front stretch catch fence, but came back below the top before he started cart wheeling along the fence for a couple hundred feet. Parts flew off his car into the stands and infield, and by the time he stopped, rescue personnel hardly knew where to look first. No one was hurt, but the All-Stars never came back to White City in its short history, either.

Rodney Argo goes for a ride during a 1998 CRA event at Putnamville, Indiana. (Allen Horcher Photo)

Gary Wright encounters a little trouble at St. Francois County Raceway in Farmington, Missouri, 1995. (Kevin Horcher Photos)

At least Rahmer remained in the car. In the days before good harnesses and containment devices, that wasn't always the case. One of the more spectacular examples came at the Iowa State Fairgrounds in 1961, where future Hall of Fame driver Jerry Blundy lost the steering wheel off his car during the race. In the ensuing wreck, he actually *flew out of the race car* and onto the track surface, where he lay unconscious. As the grandstand fans watched in stunned disbelief, the rest of the competitors somehow managed to avoid running over him. Tough guy Blundy had a broken collarbone and bruises, probably from the original wreck itself. Proving that race-car crashes make no sense at all, he recovered, came back to racing and finished sixth in IMCA points that same year.

＊ ＊ ＊ ＊ ＊

Not all wrecks have the chipper tag line, "...*and he walked away.*"
Sometimes, he crawls away.

Or takes a ride in an ambulance, or doesn't remember how he got back to his hauler. Most race drivers admit that they don't remember their worst wreck—even if they were conscious.

Wrecking is as much a part of racing as winning, and nearly all drivers will do more of the former than the latter during a career. Good drivers learn from the experience—consider it valuable knowledge even. But racers also accept that there will be those rookies who keep coming along who figure they are bullet-proof. It's always been that way as Hall of Fame Pennsylvania driver Lynn Paxton notes: "I don't remember who it was, but somebody was really pulling some wild moves. And Ole Buzz Barton, one of the great early stars, said, 'You know the trouble with that boy? He ain't bled yet.'"

From an open-wheel racer who'd certainly *bled*, it was more than just a thoughtful observation. Paxton continues with his own judgment, "The mentality of a racer when he gets hurt is that all he wants is to get back in the race car. It's never a matter of, 'well, I might get hurt again,' unless it's a severe, severe injury."

Thinking about his broken back, Curt Michael reflects, "I guess I had some second thoughts when I came back. I started at the front my first race, but I kind of fell to the back. I was letting off going into the corners, which was rolling me up tight. But finally, I said to myself, 'You know what? If you're going to keep racing you gotta gas this thing up and go.' I finished sixth or seventh that night and then won the following week in Canada. I was over the wreck."

"Wrecking is just part of racing," says Gary Wright, a Texas ace who knows first hand. But after a particularly bad crash racing in Tulsa, he didn't heal as quickly as he thought he would. "I told my car owner, 'man, I'm hurting all over,' and he said, 'that's okay, we'll come back next year.' There were only a couple of races left, and when you're hurting and you can't sit up and drive like you need to, you better think twice. We came back the next year, and right off the bat we started winning. We had made the right decision. The wreck was forgotten."

Amnesia is a valuable tool to a sprint car driver.

Wright continues, "You know it's going to happen, so you don't worry about it, and you go ahead and do what you need to do to race and win."

He's right. If everybody thought about the *what-ifs* and *what-really-did-happens*, there would be no race drivers left.

Or the races would be 30 miles per hour.

2

Wins

Man, there is definitely a sense of relief in walking away from a savage wreck, but even that pales in comparison to the exhilaration of driving into the winner's circle. Even though the checkered flag flies through the air more often than a crashing car does, far more drivers experience a wreck than win a feature race. In fact, at any given track the number of guys with a reliable, predictable chance of winning typically numbers just five or six.

Even though Cinderella wins occasionally, within a few minutes of arriving at the track, with a quick peek at the pits and assuming you have some familiarity with the racers, you'll have zeroed in on about a half dozen potential winners. That's nearly always been the case, except in those few big races that draw drivers from all around the country. Even then, the pool isn't always deep.

So, why bother? Why run the races? Why do all those other guys even show up?

Beyond the pure pleasure of an unexpected victor there is also a deeply held enjoyment that comes from watching truly talented drivers coupled with good equipment take it to the track and compete with each other. Great races are savored long after the winner has wadded up the race car somewhere else on down the line.

So what about those drivers with little hope of winning? For them, there is such an incredible rush that comes from just being on the track, racing with good drivers, learning to trust one another, and finding out what they can do and how they can improve. Marquee drivers like Steve Kinser, Sammy Swindell, Doug Wolfgang and Donny Schatz all had a period of time, brief though it may have been, when nobody expected them to win. They were too inexperienced, their equipment wasn't all that great, and they simply hadn't won yet. Some Internet jockeys these days trash the drivers who don't win, or don't win regularly enough to suit. You would never see racers or true fans exposing such ignorance. The winner would look pretty

It's okay for Curt Michael to kiss Ms. Motorsports. She happened to be Jennifer Weaver Michael and they'd been married for just a few weeks. This was also only the second race back on the track for Curt following recuperation from a broken back. (Bill Hess Photo)

damned silly on the track with only another four or five cars. Furthermore, every driver, even the greatest, has gone through periods when wins simply wouldn't come, for whatever reason. Had they given up, some excellent racing and some stunning wins would have been lost to eternity.

Winner of a ton of events in a long, successful career, Jimmy Sills confirms, "In 1977, I didn't win a race at all. I had a few crashes [that year], and I thought, 'Man, what happened? Did I forget how to do this? I think I was better at this last year!' But we just had a car that wasn't very good and I didn't know the difference. I just thought it was me, so I drove it harder. As a result, my crash percentage went up and the wins really wouldn't come."

Jimmy Sills (#3) and George Snider at Sacramento's mile track. A few minutes later, they tangled. Jimmy won the race, George lost a car. Eventually, however, George got over it, they returned to being friends and Jimmy actually drove for A.J. Foyt and George later on. (Courtesy Jimmy Sills Collection)

Wins came by the hundreds for Hooker Hood and in a variety of racing divisions. But he always loved the sprint cars–and it showed in the results. (Courtesy Hooker Hood Collection)

Bottom line, there is a visceral thrill that comes from racing that is addictive and doesn't require winning to continue. Of course, every driver wants to believe he is a threat to win, but even for those who are realistic about their slim chances, just being on the track, being a part of the deal, is enough. Thank God for those people. Not only do they provide the measuring stick that marks the greats as great, they give hope to every individual who wants to pursue a dream of any kind.

The truth is that the driver who should be most admired at the race track is the one who has overcome the most obstacles to just be there. And that, truly, is "winning" in the best sense of the word.

All that said, the mission of every team in the pits is to leave at the end of the night with the trophy. Otherwise, it would just be Interstate traffic at rush hour. It's also natural that some wins are more memorable than others. Those instances are very, very rarely the race in which the winner came from the front row. The best races, many fans agree, are the ones in which the winner was unexpected, and especially when it's a charge from the back through the field. And sometimes, you don't even have to be the winner to be the winner. Think Doug Wolfgang.

America—and sprint fans especially—loves an underdog, although during much of his career it was hard to consider Wolfgang as even a distant relative of a disadvantaged canine. But during the 1990 Knoxville Nationals, the biggest race week of any sprint car year, Wolfie had mechanical woes and didn't automatically qualify for the A Main. Instead, he came close to "running the alphabet," the most romanticized accomplishment a sprint driver could hope to achieve, mainly because no one has ever done it in the long history of the Nationals. It involves starting at the back of the E Main and coming through to qualify for a transfer spot at the back of the D Main. From there to the C Main,

If you win the race, as Danny Lasoski did, but the trophy girl is pretty and the car owner at the time is Tony Stewart, and the race promoter is another terrific driver like Terry McCarl, you end up being only one of the folks in the photos afterwards. But it's still worth a grin. (Max Dolder Photo)

and B Main, and then into the most coveted race of the year, the A Main. Reciting the alphabet backwards is easy. Racing it forward—that's almost beyond comprehension in a race week that attracts the finest competitors from across the United States and, often, Australia.

When it appeared that Wolfie was going to come close to achieving the unachievable—just close, because he did not have to run the E Main— the crowd, the television audience, probably anyone on Planet Earth who had even a passing interest in sprint car racing, was entranced. If Burt Reynolds and Hal Needham were making it into a movie, Wolfie would have won. But it was reality television, unscripted and real, so Wolfgang finished fifth in the A Main—although maybe first in a lot of hearts that night. It's a drive of lore and still is discussed from coast to coast every year when Nationals time approaches.

So, how would you feel if you had *won* that particular race? And then been ignored or considered an upset victor by much of the media even though you were one of the premier drivers in the country?

Bobby Allen had won a lot of features in a lot of different states, but his Knoxville experience had been less than stellar to that point. However, that could be said of nearly everyone whose name wasn't Steve Kinser or Sammy Swindell. It wasn't a stretch to say that for many years the field was racing for second.

But in 1990, Bobby Allen knew—just knew—it was time for a new name on the trophy. "I thought when I went to the race track that day, 'Son-of-a-bitch, the race track's going to have a bottom groove on it! I'm going to win this race.'"

Considering how the track has nearly always had a high groove by A Main time, it was forgivable that it seemed nobody else sensed what Allen saw that morning. And while attention was riveted on Wolfgang's brilliant run through the field, there was also the fact that the usual suspects of Kinser and Swindell were starting up front for the big race with the little-noticed Allen.

It was a surprise when Kinser lost an engine early. Then Swindell

Daryn Pittman receives congratulations from Knoxville flagman Doug Clark after an August 2005 victory at the track. (Max Dolder Photo)

Daryn Pittman hadn't even been born yet when Lealand McSpadden was celebrating in Victory Lane during the late 1970s. However, his wins spanned several decades, the sure mark of one of sprint racing's most enduring and remarkable careers. (Win-Di Publishing Photo)

nipped at Allen's lead all race, and, finally, late in the event passed for the lead. "Sammy got by when I about spun out, and I thought, 'This ain't supposed to happen.' The next lap, he goes to the bottom, which I didn't blame him. That's what you do to protect it," Allen explains. "Well, then he kind of lost it. I think we had about four or five laps to go. The next lap, I saw him go to the top and as he did I knew that all I needed was one lap without him on the bottom groove. That's all I needed, I knew. He ran into the wall watching me, because I saw him look at me. I knew I was going by him and he was done. He wasn't going to get another chance."

One little slip had nearly cost Allen the most-sought-after victory in sprint car racing. One little slip did cost Swindell. And a week later, everybody went racing elsewhere. The Nationals had just become a part of history. But that's the way it is, and the way it should be, or we would never run another race.

If there was drama in the Nationals race that Wolfie almost won, there was humor in a race another driver almost won.

Ron Milton, the guy who trashed his helmet in the junkyard outside Manzy, was one of a fairly small but substantial sub-culture in sprint car racing who could win it, wear it—and get a fight started—all at once.

One night he literally danced on scorers' sheets to express his displeasure at the outcome of a close call. Another night he dumped the car coming to the finish line. "My tire crossed the line first," he insisted, and the officials agreed, but responded, "Had it been attached, we would give you the win. But the wheel wasn't attached, and we can't give the win for parts and pieces flying ahead of the car."

They did award his flip across the start-finish line second place since the majority of the car—with Milton riding it out—came across ahead of all but one (complete) car. Most people wouldn't have had any idea

Does winning at Knoxville matter? We'll let Shane Stewart's exuberance speak for itself. (Mike Campbell Photo)

Ron Milton flips, but at least this time all the wheels stay attached. (Kevin Horcher Photo, Courtesy Jeff Moe Collection)

of where a flying wheel was headed as they were going over and over. However, it was just the kind of splitting-hairs argument the colorful Milton thrived upon.

As hard as it has always been to win races anywhere, anytime, traveling adds the challenge of unknown tracks, added expense and competition with unfamiliar drivers. Rick Ferkel is one of those whose gypsy life got him many wins all across the country, and a race in Albuquerque, New Mexico back in the 1970s holds special resonance because it defined for him sportsmanship—and, possibly, its limits. This was a non-winged show, and without the extra down-force the already quirky sprint cars had minds of their own that night. That didn't slow down Ferkel in his #0 Kears Speed Shop-sponsored car or his chief rival during the event, Bubby Jones. Side-by-side, they were putting on the kind of show that delights fans—until there was contact.

"Bubby actually knocked me off the track," explains "The Zero Hero." "They didn't have a wall there, so I kept it going and got back on the track. Bubby realized what had happened and he allowed me to go back by him because he felt bad that he'd booted me. We both knew it was just a racing deal—no intent—but I thought it was real classy of him to let me go back ahead of him, and we picked up the fight from there."

The contact hadn't bent anything and Ferkel was as racy as he had been before the inadvertent tap. Come the checkered flag, and he had gone back into the lead for the win. At the pay window, the promoter gave Ferkel $2600, the winner's amount, as advertised.

Second place paid $600, which prompted Bubby to good-naturedly grumble, "I'd never have let you go back by me if I'd known that."

The experience didn't end either driver's habit of calling tracks to ask what it paid to win and nothing more. That's what the drivers who raced for a living did in the days before the Internet and easy access to information. If they didn't collect enough of those winner's shares, they wouldn't have been professionals for long.

Some drivers, whether long-haul travelers or weekend warriors, can remember every win, no matter how many that may be, while others can barely recall what happened last week. But not too many drivers get the chance to pull a fast one on the competition.

Very early in his career, Gary Wright ventured far from his East Texas home and ended up in Kankakee, Illinois, at an All-Stars Circuit of Champions race. About the only thing the youngster had going for him when he signed in at the gate was that Kankakee was acknowledged as mostly a late model track. None of that evening's stars had much familiarity with the facility. However, stars get to be stars by figuring out and adapting to strange tracks more quickly than the average jockey. There was no surprise, then, when the well-known drivers qualified well. However, when Wright qualified fourth, that prompted Jack Hewitt to walk over to Terry Gray's pit. The Memphis driver ran the same tracks and circuits that the unfamiliar Texan Wright did. "Who is that guy?" Hewitt asked.

If Gary Wright seems comfortable in the winner's interview, it may be that he learned as a sports-playing teenager how to be a gracious winner. (Steve Hardin Photo)

"You'll know his name after tonight," Gray assured him.

It was not surprising a little while later in the feature event to find Bobby Allen leading and Hewitt second. It was astonishing, however, when Wright came up and passed both. Then, as Wright was basking in the glow of a Victory Lane about a thousand miles from home, Gray walked over to Hewitt and grinned, "Do you know who he is now?"

The anonymity advantage was over at that point. So, too, could a hometown-track advantage swiftly pass. When a local star won the first night of a two-day special at an Illinois track, Hooker Hood's son Rickey, up from Memphis for the first time, told the local hero as he came out of the pay office, "You won't get that tomorrow night. You showed me the line [to race around the track]."

Steve Kinser has 12 A Main wins at the Knoxville Nationals, but Donny Schatz has taken home the trophy the past three years. (Mike Campbell Photo)

It wasn't an idle boast. The following evening, Hood took home the big bucks as the local guy just grinned and shook his head.

For season-long accomplishments in the win column, it's going to be very difficult for any gypsy to exceed what North Dakota's Donny Schatz managed in 2007. For the first time in racing history, a sprint car driver won the Knoxville Nationals, Kings Royal at Eldora, Williams Grove National Open in Pennsylvania and the Don Martin Memorial at Lernerville Speedway also in Pennsylvania, arguably the greatest and most prestigious races of this era. Not even "The King," Steve Kinser, has been able to win all four in a single year. The accomplishment netted Schatz the Economaki Champion of Champions award

On September 26, 1998, Jack Hewitt swept the 4-Crown, winning all the races. In Victory Lane are son Kody, wife Jody, Jack (with a broom), and promoters Berneice and Earl Baltes. (Allen Horcher Photo)

over the accomplishments of NASCAR champion Jimmie Johnson, NHRA top fueler Tony Schumacher, and Indy 500 winner Dario Franchitti. It was a sterling moment for sprint car racing, thanks to a little reflective glory flashing off Donny. Anyone who had ever beat Schatz under any circumstance felt just a smidgeon taller.

But for a single-day accomplishment it may be hard to ever surpass September 26, 1998, when the incomparable Jack Hewitt won all four feature events at the 4-Crown Nationals. Admittedly, Hewitt and Eldora Speedway have had a mutual admiration society of many seasons standing. Few people have ever mastered the legendary half-mile dirt track, and those who thought they had usually found themselves getting a personal, up-close inspection of the concrete wall when the track slapped them around. Hewitt is among those who've worn bits and pieces of wrecked race cars there, but on this particular date, the mighty Eldora had to bow down to him.

The 4-Crown Nationals have been around since 1981, combining four types of cars. On Jack's night he ran a 20-lap UMP Modified race, 25 laps in the midget, 30 laps in the sprinter, and 50 laps in the Silver Crown (dirt championship) car.

He credited third-turn ripples on the track in helping to preserve the longevity of his tires' grip. Many a racer's heart has been broken by Eldora's "bumps," as Jack called them. They have been less kindly called "craters," "sinkholes" and "freakin' pits of hell" by the many who've never won there. As even physically fit youngsters will attest, Eldora can wear out the best-prepared driver just during a single event. However, this was a guy who'd recovered more than once from life-threatening injuries, was flirting with 50 years of age, ran 125 grueling laps—and aimed for the "bumps" every one of those laps!

It would be hard to convince a lot of drivers that there's any such thing as a "bad" win, but for fans on rare occasions it happens. It could be when a driver wins by a full lap over the field or when a guy takes out the leader and goes on to win. Even when a driver just innocently inherits a lead from someone who worked hard to get to the front and then meets misfortune, it can take the awe factor out of the finish.

But unless your name is Steve Kinser, wins are always hard to come by, and these days even his wins are more difficult. Racers around the country who accumulate 100 or 200 wins in a career will admit that it's never enough to satisfy them, and it's always doubly frustrating to see a win slip through your fingers. Worse yet, sprint car careers being the frail and flimsy things they are, who knows when that final win will be chalked up?

At least one driver knew.

Chet Johnson was a journeyman racer, normally running on weekends but occasionally taking on the better-known, better-financed USAC teams. He always acquitted himself well, but, realistically, other drivers didn't walk through the gate of a major USAC show saying, "We gotta beat Johnson today."

Frankly, on May 10, 1982, it looked like the Hulman Classic was going to Ken Schrader, rather than Johnson or any of the other drivers in the pits. Driving the Blackie Fortune sprint car, Schrader was headed for victory in the 100-lapper when he realized going down the back stretch that he'd blown a radiator hose. Assuming the worst, that the engine would experience a meltdown if he stayed out, Schrader came through turn four and started to pull into the pits. But Blackie was down on the apron and he frantically motioned for Schrader to stay on the track—go on—DON'T PULL IN! The lead was huge, and paying for engines wasn't as big a deal for Blackie as for some of the other car owners, especially with the enormous prestige of the Hulman Classic on the line. So, Schrader gave it the giddy-up-and-go once more.

Unfortunately, his rhythm was shot. Racers, great and small, will tell you that rhythm is more critical to racing than it is to *Dancing With the Stars*. As a result of that, coupled with water spraying out the hose and onto the tires, Schrader ran down into the first turn—hit the wall—and flipped.

Rescue personnel hurried out on the track with the yellow flag, and one of them tried to help extricate Schrader from what was left of the car. But Schrader—normally about as

Roger Rager in the 7r cannot believe that Ken Schrader has gone out in the loose stuff to pass him. Look at Roger's head whipped around to the right. (Allen Horcher Photo)

Schrader has just crashed leading the Hulman Classic thanks to a radiator hose coming off the engine, and he's not really receptive to offers of assistance from the safety crew. He knew car owner Blackie Fortune would not be pleased. (Allen Horcher Photo)

Chet Johnson inherited the lead and went on to a surprise win in the 1982 Hulman Classic. And then he quit racing. (Kevin Horcher Photo)

nice a guy as has ever strapped into a race car—began flailing away at the would-be rescuer.

"Let me help you," the EMT insisted.

"I'm fine," Schrader replied, "but you have to leave me alone. I got to get out of here before the car owner shows up. He's gonna be so pissed!"

Meanwhile, Larry Nuber was calling the race for ESPN cable television, and reported that Chet Johnson was a lapped car. And then in one of those awkward moments the talking heads dread because they've been fed erroneous information, Nuber had to admit that he was wrong. Chet-Who?-Johnson, a Saturday Night hero not very many outside of Illinois and Indiana had ever heard about, not only was leading but proceeded to get the job done.

Johnson had said that if he won the Classic, he would quit racing. It's not clear how much previous Hulman Classic winners dying later in other races had to do with it, but Chet's casual observation about retirement seemed tied to a pipe dream anyway. Little guys just didn't waltz into USAC's huge race and take it away.

And then, Johnson did the most remarkable thing. He won—and he kept his word.

3

Push-Offs

As the sunset neared for a fabled track, there was just enough time left to be part of the beginning of an extraordinary racing career.

Springfield Speedway had long been a measuring stick for many drivers, which may have been why a youngster with great promise showed up at a time when it seemed like more and more racers were avoiding it. In those final years, beset by too many nights of car-swallowing ruts or rolling dust, a kind of grim determination seemed to mingle with the sweat. Racing was going to happen, dammit, no matter how much the glory seemed to be only an echo. So when a particular truck and trailer rolled into the pits there was an audible buzz in the joint.

It didn't require a Rhodes Scholar to figure out that sprint car racing was changing in a lot of elemental ways. The tire bill told you that. So did the appearance of Jeff Gordon at a track. If ever there was a time in his racing career that he wasn't a lightning rod for controversy, it had already passed when the teenaged sprint car phenom continued to add widespread track experience to an already impressive resume.

Memories are funny things, often less than accurate, especially as they add to lore, but there were a couple of observations from that night that hold remarkable clarity decades later. One was that stepfather John Bickford not only was propelling Gordon's career, but also keeping a close sentinel on the teenager. There was no shortage of people who would have liked to climb on the bandwagon or figure out how to make a buck off the kid, but that wasn't something Jeff had to worry about at sixteen.

How much would-be hangers-on had to do with Gordon's demeanor then and now is hard to say, but already, at a really young age, he had a kind of cloak about him. The smile was ready but said, "keep your distance." You have only to look at him today to see the shutters in his eyes that are, quite simply, a matter of self-defense. It wasn't his idea to be controversial, but he figured out how to cope with it at an age when he

*Not only does Jeff Gordon look impossibly young, he really **was** that young. (Gene Marderness Photo)*

should have been worrying about zits and dates for the prom instead of bloodsucking adults and boos from the grandstand.

Even before Gordon was a stock car superstar (instead of the Indy car champion we envisioned back then), it was clear that getting behind a steering wheel in the post-toddler years had a huge impact. He was a thoroughly experienced race driver when he was still designated a sprint car rookie. Whether he meant to or not, Gordon had effected a fundamental change in how careers are begun.

By the late 1980s Jeff Gordon(#6) was accomplished in many different classes of cars and on all surfaces, but even the better drivers occasionally jump the cushion, and it rarely turns out well. This was a rare USAC sprint cars-with-wings show at Tri-State Speedway in Haubstadt, Indiana. (Kevin Horcher Photo)

In the years since, nearly every driver who's raced Gordon at any level has stated—sometimes emphatically—that he is one of a kind. Unique. Truly blessed with extraordinary innate talent. "There will never be another Jeff Gordon," claims former teammate and longtime friend Ken Schrader. "There have been other drivers who make a name in some fashion, but all the dads out there who are trying to turn their little kids into 'the next Jeff Gordon' are wasting their time and probably hurting their relationship. 'The next Jeff Gordon' as a retirement plan is a good way to waste a lot of money and forget how much fun racing is."

Schrader's point, as many others have also observed, is that the primary goal of going quarter-midget racing or go-kart racing with the kids should be to share quality time. Maybe it's possible to get the skills that will help when or if the kid grows up and wants to get into full-sized race cars, but maybe not. And if it hasn't put the family in the Poor Farm, there just may be enough funds left to create even more memories.

Certainly there are plenty of accomplished drivers today who got started young, if not quite Jeff Gordon-esque early. For example, Curt Michael drove quarter midgets, following in the tire tracks of his two older brothers. "They say the family that races together stays together," he observes years later, and it certainly did theirs.

Curt's dad was really into the racing, sometimes taking the cars or motors to the firehouse where he worked and tinkering between calls. Not only did he get a little extra work done, but he drew in his co-workers and got them interested, too. Those extra hands were sometimes needed to ensure all three Michael boys got to race from week to week. "I can

Even though he showed promise at a very young age as the checkered flag demonstrates, Curt Michael ended up dropping out of driving for a while in order to help his older brothers' efforts. This was 1993 at Airport Speedway. The same year, Curt won the championship at Linda Speedway. (Joe Simpkins Photo)

remember him building motors on the kitchen table," Curt continues, "doing whatever he had to do to help us."

But they kept their perspective, too. "When I was five, I would get a big lead and then I would look over and see my mom. I would start waving to her and I'd end up getting passed. I would have to pass those cars all over again. Thankfully, I stopped doing that."

The Michael family saw Curt's action for what it was—a cute little story to savor. It was not a reason to excoriate him for failing to keep focused on the goal of winning. If you've ever been to a quarter-midget track, you've undoubtedly seen the father-from-hell screaming at his kids, apparently concerned about that retirement account.

Some very successful race drivers, in fact, have sometimes sacrificed for other family members' budding racing careers, including Curt. He dropped out of the quarter midget club when his oldest brother began racing seriously. On their fireman dad's budget, there wasn't enough money to cover all the expenses. The Michael family didn't create an impossibly stressful scenario by trying to do the unrealistic. Those few years off for Curt, turning wrenches for both his brothers and being their booster and fan, did absolutely nothing to hinder his long-term accomplishments. His five URC championships prove that point. Whether he could have been "the next Jeff Gordon" if he'd applied himself at a younger age isn't worth even considering. He is what he is: Curt Michael—talented artist with a successful graphics business, happily married and racing weekly and successfully.

Johnny Herrera is another poster boy for time off to be a kid. His early racing ended because his folks couldn't afford two race cars, and at the time his dad had a solid career as a sprint car driver in Albuquerque. Johnny's selflessness paid off when he did return to straddling an in-out box as his dad did everything he could to propel Johnny's career. After a couple of decades on the road, Johnny returned home and the Herreras have picked up where they left off, racing as a family.

Since "the next Jeff Gordon" hasn't happened in over two decades, you'd think kids would have easier beginnings, but there's no question that we're in an era in which sprint car drivers as well as NASCAR and Indy drivers are being groomed from a very, very early age. Sprint car racers these days come from families solidly in the upper middle class or higher incomes. It takes money to put even go-karts on the track, to develop public relations, travel to meet potential car owners and sponsors, and any number of stressful requirements that precede a racing career today.

It wasn't always that way.

Only in the past couple of decades have careers developed from kids racing. Previously, childhoods usually consisted of young noses pressed up against the fence, longing to enter what was then a forbidden zone—the pit area. No way could they go where spitting and swearing were casually accepted, and kids and women weren't allowed. For decades, no one would have thought to even question that fact.

Back then busted knuckles were a badge of belonging. Grease-smeared clothes were outnumbered only by greasy fingernails. It was no stretch, either, to say that a driver might be having his final conversation prior to the green flag. There was rarely any melodrama associated with death because it was all-too-common. Limping drivers were as frequent in sprint car ranks a half-century ago as they are now in motorcycle pits. It was a grown-up, macho world that little boys aspired to join in the future.

Which begat lies about age.

"They used to sneak me into the pits in the trunk of my brother's '34 Ford," explains Lenard McCarl, one of the Iowans who contributed so much to building sprint car racing in the 1960s and 1970s, and making Knoxville Raceway the legend it has become. "Once, they asked him if I was 21, which was the age you had to be at the time to be in the pits. And he said, 'Lenard must be—he's had the seven-year itch three times.'"

A sense of humor was a valuable tool in Lenard's childhood, since it had hardly been a comfortable road. A child of the Great Depression, Lenard had an especially difficult life, even by the standards of the time. Like many farm families of the period, the McCarls sought to escape the killing droughts and crippling debt that saw too many multi-generational farms mortgaged and eventually seized. Added to a *Grapes of Wrath* scenario, when Lenard was still a youngster his father lost his hand in a shotgun accident.

With the breadwinner sidelined, the children grew up even more quickly. Racing for fun wasn't

The first time Lenard McCarl drove a race car, it was in his brother's #24. He was hooked, so the next move was to build this modified. (Courtesy Lenard McCarl Collection)

even a small dream. And yet, some time after returning to their native Iowa, Lenard's older brother began stock car racing. The smuggled-in teenaged Lenard got into racing later, but through a long career he almost always stayed close to home. There were a few special shows in other parts of the Midwest, and a couple of trips to mid-winter Florida series, but essentially, the shadow of the Great Depression never freed Lenard to try his hand at something bigger. For those who lived during a period when help was so sparing, it's a reflection of the times that early sprint car generations remained more cautious with money than almost any who rode through the pit gate later.

Lenard took care of his home, his wife, their three kids, and then went racing with only what was left in the account. It would not have occurred to him—or most of his contemporaries—to spend on a race car based on anticipated winnings. Cautious thinking defined his career in a way that this age of the credit card has not. In fact, Lenard's son Terry has been far more daring in looking far afield and it has yielded dividends, with more than 200 race wins in 16 states and Australia. It's the difference of growing up in the 1930s and 1940s versus the 1960s and 1970s. And into the 2000s, where Lenard's teenaged grandchildren are successfully racing already.

If there weren't many races in Lenard McCarl's early years, there were other eventually successful drivers who never even saw a race when they were young. Considering how brilliantly he wheeled a sprint car through a long career, it's hard to imagine that one of those deprived youngsters was an original outlaw. Rick Ferkel was an excellent athlete in school, and that was the focus of his youth.

"I wanted to be a professional football player, and, of course you get in too much of a hurry," he admits. "I quit school and joined the Marine Corps. That took care of my football career."

In fact, quite a number of drivers were good team players in school, thereby shooting down the mainline press theorem that racers aren't athletes. Jimmy Sills and Lealand McSpadden also played high school football, but few people are aware that the late and legendary Pennsylvania star Dick "Toby"

Rodger Ward and Tommy Hinnershitz at the Eastern Museum of Motor Racing in York Springs, Pennsylvania. Hinnershitz ranks at the top of many lists of the all-time great sprint car drivers. (Courtesy Lynn Paxton Collection and EMMR)

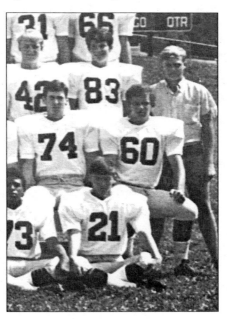

Jimmy Sills is thought of as a Californian, but he actually went to high school in North Carolina after the family relocated to Asheville when stepfather Dick Johnson got a NASCAR ride. (Jim Sr., also a good driver, had passed away at age 30 when Jimmy Jr. was only 3 years old.) During this period, Jimmy took his stepfather's name for a while, and the 1970 Roberson High Rams featured #60, Jim Johnson, a 5'10", 165-pound senior who played Guard. (Courtesy Jimmy Sills Collection)

Rick Ferkel, U.S. Marine Corp. (Courtesy Rick Ferkel Collection)

Tobias was offered a football scholarship to Wyomissing Polytechnic (now part of Penn State). Even with scholarship aid, however, Toby couldn't get enough money together, so the Pittsburgh Steelers' future loss was sprint car racing's gain.

Among the many excelling at other sports pre-Nomex is Gary Wright, who gave up baseball because he figured out that it was costing him too much money when he had to be at a game instead of the race track. Hall of Fame driver Kenny Jacobs was a high school wrestler—when he wasn't driving the water truck at his family's Ohio dirt track. One of the very best of the current crop of youngsters tearing up the World of Outlaws is Daryn Pittman, who played soccer and basketball throughout school. His brother was so good, in fact, that he ended up playing soccer professionally in Europe while Daryn pursued—with their parents' blessing—the race car route.

His football career over before it began, Ferkel served in the Marine Corps during a relatively quiet period. He chose not to be a "lifer," or 20-year veteran, and when he came out of the service, he was very much at loose ends. "I definitely didn't want to have a job. I wanted to be a professional *something*, but I didn't want to be a professional factory worker."

It was happenstance that he ended up at a local race in northern Ohio and he decided, "Well, shoot! I'll just become a racer."

If the decision was that easy, the execution was not. Ferkel concedes that he had no mechanical ability at the time. Today, if a guy can write a big enough check to hire a mechanic, it's not such a huge deal to get behind the wheel, but in the 1960s racers automatically had to turn their own wrenches. Only the very top echelon of drivers at Indy didn't work on their cars—and some, like A.J. Foyt, still preferred to bust knuckles so they would know what was in the car and understand how it was put together.

Maybe Hooker Hood should have been a movie star on the side. He's better looking than Clark Gable, who got to star in a racing movie! (Courtesy Hooker Hood Collection)

"I was raised on a farm. Milked cows, drove tractors since I was six or seven years old. But as far as working on them, I had no idea. And so, I probably set myself back five years just from lack of knowledge. Then you add that to the fact that I didn't start until I was 26 years old." Ferkel laughs. "Of course, nowadays that's almost retirement age."

The military also resulted in Hooker Hood getting a late start in racing. He dropped out of school in 1945 to join the Navy, and although he never saw combat he did get to see the first post-World War II race in Los Angeles. That experience totally and thoroughly hooked him on the sport. Nobody, including the Hood family's many fans, was happier that Hooker's son didn't have to follow in his dad's wake and wait until he was in his twenties.

"Rickey come up to me one day and said, 'Daddy, I'm ready to drive race cars,' and I tell you what—chill bumps jumped up on me an inch tall all over," says Hooker.

Understanding the temptation, he told his son to round up his friends. The following day at least a dozen teenagers showed up in the back yard, all clamoring for a place in the pick-up truck headed for nearby Milan, Tennessee. That afternoon at the dirt track, after telling Rickey to take it easy as he warmed up the car, Hooker pushed off the sprint car with his son aboard for the first time. Each lap, following the instructions to the letter, Rickey cautiously came down the straightaway and looked over at his dad, waiting for the signal to open it up.

"I finally give him the 'go' sign, and I tell you what, he jumped off that first corner and was throwing rooster tails plumb back over the fence. Wasn't but a few minutes and the promoter came up to me and said, 'Hooker, I thought you said this was the first time he ever drove a car.' I said, 'As far as I know it is.' And from that day on, the boy never looked back."

Rickey Hood was 14 years old.

Like many sprint car drivers, Rickey Hood had first learned to be fearless and trust his instincts while running a motorcycle. Two wheels have often led to four, but Bubby Jones is among very few who think he would have been happy with a career on bikes. However, he had family members concerned about the potential for serious injury, even as they realized that he would never be satisfied without an outlet for derring-do. In Bubby's case, the family convinced him to go racing with driver (and fellow barber in Danville, Illinois), Larry "Boom Boom" Cannon.

Larry "Boom Boom" Cannon with one of his earliest modified rides, mid-1960s. (Courtesy Jeff Moe Collection)

In 1969 Bubby Jones received one of several sprint car championship trophies from Springfield Speedway. (Courtesy Mary Standridge Collection)

Boom Boom was a little older and set a path leading to the Indianapolis Motor Speedway that Jones would follow. The crew-cut, straight-laced Cannon fit the USAC mold better, but as far as driving careers are concerned the hippie-fied Jones became a legend among the outlaws and eventually surpassed his pal in overall sprint car racing fame. "I'm sure he didn't like it when I started outrunning him," remembers Jones, "but anybody that's got any gumption at all, they don't like to get outrun. I never did begrudge anybody doing good. It just gave me an incentive to try harder."

Shane Carson is on the way to a two-wheel championship. (Courtesy Mar-Car Collection)

Most sprint car drivers who've messed with motorcycles did so when they were youngsters. Not Jimmy Sills. He calls it his last "adventure" with racing, but he had to give it up because of a broken ankle, two broken collarbones and six–yes, six–rib fractures. (Courtesy Jimmy Sills Collection)

While Jones had never made any secret of his affection for motorcycles, Shane Carson did.

He had to.

Carson's father Bud was very successful as an Oklahoma track promoter, in part because the whole family was involved, including Shane, who started selling programs at the age of eight. Still, there was always an assumption within the family—and certainly in Shane—that he would race someday. They just didn't realize that he wasn't willing to wait.

"You had to be 18 to race in Oklahoma at that time," he explains. "All my buddies could race because they just lied to the officials and said they were 18. I couldn't get by with that. My dad knew better."

But nothing is more ingenious than a teenager on a mission. "I had a 1950 Chevy panel truck and I kept the motocross bike in there," he explains. "It had curtains on it, so Dad didn't even know I had the thing. But then it came out in the paper that I had won the Oklahoma championship, so obviously, he figured out how I'd done it."

Bud then offered the teenager a choice: Shane could continue racing the bikes—or he could continue to live in the family home. He couldn't do both, and there it was again—that anti-bike feeling from people who love four-wheeled vehicles that have been known to bite a driver every bit as nastily as the two-wheelers. But in this instance, the pot was sweetened when Bud agreed to let Shane move into cars.

Not that it necessarily was easy, thanks to being the promoter's son. "Dad definitely made an example out of me most of the time. He said that if it's a close call between someone else and me regarding what happened on the track, I should know that I was going to lose the decision. I understood he had to do that as the track promoter, to make sure the other racers didn't think I was getting a break."

At the time, the Oklahoma City quarter-mile track was getting over 100 cars a night in the six-cylinder modified class in which Shane started.

Fourteen-year-old Scott Carson gives his auto a last-minute check under the inspecting eye of his brother Shane, 7. Scott is co-owner of the new sportsman class auto which will be entered in Friday's weekly race program at Taft Stadium.

Because their dad Bud was a Hall of Fame promoter, it's not surprising that Shane and Scott Carson were involved in racing from very young ages. They became close, even while competing with each other. Shane (above in Western hat) helped Scott on the latter's modified in 1973, and then went on to join him on the track, here at Oskaloosa, Iowa, in 1978. (Shane is in the low groove, Scott on the high line.) Scott passed away in 1998. Shane still races when his schedule allows and says he wishes he was as good a driver as his brother. But it is likely that if he could be asked, Scott would say the same thing about Shane. (Courtesy Mar-Car Collection)

So, it was more than a month before he accumulated enough points just to get into a heat race! Several weeks later, when he progressed to making the feature event, Shane won from the git-go. On the heels of immediate success, he figured he would just as quickly move up to the eight-cylinder class.

"I assumed I would get my brother's old super, but it never happened," he laughs. "I got lucky enough to be running at Tulsa where [well-known and highly regarded chassis builder] LaVern Nance watched quite a bit. He thought I was doing a good job in the Sixxer, so he gave me a shot in his sprint car. That was 1976, and by that time I was 22, so it certainly didn't happen overnight."

There are drivers who are basically a law unto themselves.

Not that there is anything wrong with that. On the contrary, sprint car racing, with its history of minimal rules and encouragement of individualism, is the ideal destination for those who don't expect others to open doors and smooth the path. Work hard. Depend upon yourself.

These are the tenets of many sprint car drivers. Especially, Bobby Allen.

Bobby Allen at the Knoxville Nationals, five years before he won the race, but more than 20 years removed from his Florida childhood where he was raised around some huge racing stars. (Gene Marderness Photo)

Superficially, it might seem that he had a golden childhood, growing up in Florida with the likes of Fireball Roberts, Marshall Teague, Bobby, Donnie and Eddie Allison around the Allen family's garage. Another friend of Allen's race-driving dad was a service station owner by the name of Big Bill France, although this was a time before these men had carved out legends in stock car racing.

Not even Big Bill, however, could convince Eastern Airlines—then one of the major air carriers—to allow Bobby's dad to continue the very dangerous business of racing while working as one of their pilots. But the absence of a full-sized race car in the garage was eclipsed by a miniature car and later go-karts for the boy. Only die-hard Allen fans are aware that Bobby was a world champion in the karts and traveled Europe racing them while still a youngster. During times back home, he also was allowed to hang out at the shop of Indy 500 star Jim Rathmann.

With puberty came rather wild ways. Allen was only 16 years old when he traded his car for a 1946 Ford street vehicle that happened to have a Lincoln engine in it. And within hours a cop showed up at the Allens' home to tell his parents that Bobby was due in court the following day. Seems the cop had clocked the teenager running in excess of 100 mph.

Instead of the Florida courtroom, Allen took off for Pennsylvania. "I went over and got my girl friend—who eventually ended up being my wife—and headed out of town because I had to. Along with a buddy of mine, we lived out of the truck for quite a while."

While residing in that mobile forwarding address, Allen and cohorts got themselves kicked out of a farmer's barn where they had their rig stored because they had been throwing bottles at the house. "We were just being kids," he insists.

Meanwhile, brash as a blonde James Dean, Bobby talked his way into driving race cars. After all, he had already established that he could run in excess of 100 mph.

Shortly thereafter he crashed, and the car owner said that he didn't care about blown engines but he didn't want to crash. Rather than be without a ride, Allen contacted his grandmother, who promptly wired enough money to buy the racer. Allen went on to win the Lincoln Speedway championship that year, "but I hated the fact that I won the championship, because I didn't win a race. I ran a couple of seconds. That burned me. I didn't deserve it, so that made me hate points. I couldn't stand that if they had 30 races and the guy who won 20 but fell out of a few could lose the points. I thought it should be the guy who won the most. I lost a lot of money in later years, chasing points, going to races that ended up rained out. Sponsors and people around you care about them, so it's important, but I don't care about points—and never have back to that championship."

So, for all those Bobby Allen fans through the many years of his career who wondered why he didn't chase World of Outlaws or All-Stars championships, the answer is rooted in success—even if he doesn't technically view it as such—in his teen years.

Lynn Paxton in 1968 demonstrating a little of the high, wide and hard Hall of Fame style that earned him so many fans. (Al Consoli Photo)

No matter how old a racer was when he first contracted Incurable Speed Fever, what era it was or how many detours there have been on the way to a career, there came a time—probably very early for those who have demonstrable talent—in which they realized what it was all about. Few have articulated that epiphany better than Lynn Paxton, whose family ran an auto-court (forerunner of motels) just down the road from Williams Grove Speedway immediately after World War II in the years before Lynn built a Hall-of-Fame sprint car career.

"The first sprint race I ever ran was an IMCA car with no roll cage," he says. "They came to Allentown in '68 or '69, and I had been running a super-modified. I climbed in that sprint car and the sun's out—I'm sitting there in the middle of the car and I'm looking around, thinking, *this is different*. But you know what? When the green flag dropped, the job is to pass the guy in front of you and I don't care what class of car you are in, that's what you're paid to do. I found out that it didn't matter what type of thing I was in. I took it out and I used it to the best of my ability to get by the guy in front of me."

Race drivers could do worse than borrow Paxton's simple, clear philosophy.

4

Rules

Before stock car racing had Dale Earnhardt, sprint car racing had Jud Larson. Just as Earnhardt would be later, Larson was a law unto himself, a unique individual in the 1950s and 1960s era that produced so many characters.

Larson was a poster boy for racers as tough guys with hearts of gold. The Texan loved everyone—maybe some females a little too much—and had as much as anyone to do with the evolving image of sprint car racers as outlaws. Flamboyant to an excess, Larson was as likely to show up at a tiny bullring paying $50 to win—as long as a post-race party was planned—as racing at a track paying big bucks that had no sure promise of fun. As his career advanced it seemed the party that was his life tended to follow wherever his tire tracks took him.

Jud Larson was unlikely to have had an introspective period where he thought through the development of his own personal creed. Instead, he simply lived it, and it didn't take a rocket scientist to figure out this much: He absolutely loathed rules and organizations. It didn't mean he avoided sanctioned races—in fact, his career included many International Motor Contest Association (IMCA) and United States Auto Club (USAC) sprint wins. But Larson was not impressed with the two biggest organizations of his time. In fact, he made that point quite vocally. Even when he got a shot at Indianapolis it did nothing to alter his opinion. It's said that he walked through Indy's gates observing something like, "Ain't nothin' wrong with this joint that a little dirt couldn't fix."

Yup, he disliked pavement tracks almost as much as rules and organizations.

Maybe it was his nomadic childhood in Texas that shaped Larson's disdain. Quite possibly it was a matter of being absolutely fearless on-track during the age of wickedly fast sprint cars with no roll cages. Whatever bug was in his brain, the actions of USAC following the running of the 1959 Dirt Champ race at Springfield only cemented Larson's contempt. During that race Larson apparently suffered a heart attack. In the aftermath, he made a few concessions to his condition, and he briefly disappeared from the tracks in order to heal. Once he felt he was ready to return to the track, however, USAC wouldn't release him to drive in their organization—for nearly five years.

The damned rules made no sense to Larson's legion of fans either. He was willing to climb into a vehicle that could very well kill him, and, in fact, had beaten the hell out of him in some outrageous crashes in the past,

It must have been a tough track because Jud Larson has both goggles and a shield for his eyes. But notice that he is wearing a tee-shirt. He was one of the original tough guys of sprint car racing. (Dick Wallen Photo)

and yet the pencil-pushers in their little cubicles on 16th Street in Speedway, Indiana, determined it wasn't in his best interest to race!

For all that Larson nursed a grudge about the ban, he eventually recognized that there was more power in the cubicles than within the fiercest Offy he'd ever driven. Jud complied with the requirements set down by USAC and eventually passed a physical that allowed him back on-track in the spring of 1964. What followed was quintessential Larson. He proceeded to engage in one of the all-time great duels for the championship with Don Branson, who was exactly the type of driver USAC was encouraging at the time. The Illinoisan was a family man, clean-cut and quietly brilliant behind the wheel. He was the kind of guy they could point to with pride as a role model for children, well-spoken and polite even though he was as tough on the track as anyone.

Meanwhile, Larson kept the throwback image alive. Most of the time he drove an Offenhauser-powered car in an age when the small-block Chevy was taking over. And when the races were over, he'd climb out of

Don Branson, a gentle family man, was the antithesis of Jud Larson. On the track, the two waged some of the most exciting matches in sprint car history. (Courtesy Jeannie Hinnershitz Craig, National Sprint Car Hall of Fame Collection)

the race car, get the party started and tell anybody who didn't like it they could kiss his ruby red…well, nothing had really changed with Larson beyond the addition of some scar tissue in his pericardium.

One imagines it was to USAC's great relief that Branson narrowly edged Larson for the championship, with the duo finishing just ahead of a young man beginning to develop his own unique reputation—Mario Andretti. But here's the most remarkable tidbit to come from that incredible title fight: Branson, a.k.a. "Grandpa Don," suffered a broken arm at Reading—and had to sit out nearly two months of the season! These days, title fights

During the running of the Don Branson/Jud Larson Classic at Eldora in 2008, Brady Bacon, Jesse Hockett and Brad Sweet tangle. (Mike Campbell Photo)

are so intense that it is unthinkable for a title contender to sit out even a single race and remain in the battle for the points.

Ironically, both Larson and Branson died in separate on-track wrecks in 1966—Larson in June at Reading, Pennsylvania, and Branson at Ascot Park in November. Two enormously different men's careers were tied forever by the epic points battle of '64, and perhaps it is appropriate that the rules-appreciating Branson came out on top. Had Larson won, he would have had to spend the rest of his life explaining to his fans why he hadn't thumbed his nose at the Suits.

While Larson was possibly the most extraordinary example of his era's independent thinkers, he was actually just the front man for scores, possibly hundreds, of racers who shared his disdain for rules. Conformists weren't particularly attracted to racing, especially the genuinely dangerous world of sprint car racing, and that's probably still true today.

Lenard McCarl, a contemporary from the same era, explains, "One of the reasons I raced supermodified and sprint cars—and that sort of thing—was that we didn't have any rules. That's why I liked it. You could do whatever you wanted and whatever you could come up with in your mind. If you worked harder and made your car better, it was to your advantage. I used to work on my race cars an awful lot. I think that's probably why I won the races that I did."

The modifieds of the early 1960s were really modified. Look at the gas tank on #18, not to mention the lack of body panels. (Courtesy Jeff Moe Collection)

Innovative thinking worked to the advantage of many guys whose names are listed as race winners from post-World War II through the 1970s. There were certain parameters that nearly everybody accepted, like wheel-base length and the use of in-out boxes (sans transmission and starter). But if you moved the engine back an inch, or you used a lighter-weight alloy wheel, well, you were just smarter than the next guy.

The problem was that the thinking got a little *too* innovative. Costs went up as everybody tried to keep pace. Disagreements arose over what was legal and what wasn't, and guys who despised rules got aggravated, especially the ones who traveled around a region or the country. What you could do in Iowa wasn't necessarily allowed in Ohio, but you didn't always know that until you'd towed all night to get to the track.

This Bob Davis-owned car launched Jimmy Sills' sprint car career back in the 1970s. It was the period when everyone was experimenting with aerodynamics and getting pretty wild. Note the side pod in addition to the wings. (Courtesy Jimmy Sills Collection)

About 2,300 miles east of Sills' burgeoning career, Rick Ferkel was getting attention, too, and note how similar the cars look in spite of the distance. Rick loved the side wings: "They really worked, but they were outlawed quite fast." With this car, Rick set three track records in three days: 15.26 seconds at Atomic Speedway in Tennessee, 17.30 seconds at Eldora, and 18.25 seconds at Millstream Speedway in Ohio. (Courtesy Rick Ferkel Collection)

At a season-ending race in 1984, competitors were allowed to make any modifications they wanted–EXCEPT no wings. You can see Lexan modifications to the car on the left. The drivers for McGonigal this day are unknown–but what's obvious is that they got together coming off the turn. (Allen Horcher Photo)

The irony is that as rules expanded, so did cost. Purses went up, but never as much as the cost. It became clear that cost containment was the greatest oxymoron of racing, and racing with sanctioning groups (and their rules) has continually gotten only more expensive.

Whatever rules are written in the future, the truly individualistic approach to racing is as dead as Jud Larson. And he would have found it unimaginable that independence, to a degree, went with him to the grave.

Rules have been an attempt at sanity and fairness, but for at least a half-century the playing field's base has been elevated by thick wallets. Even well-to-do teams decry the ever-escalating costs, but the answer—so far—hasn't been found in sanctioning groups.

Nonetheless, the organizational bodies have been the back-drop for some extraordinary racing—and they've been equipped to record and save some of the best racing tales ever—no matter the cost.

To the average racing fan today who knows anything beyond NASCAR, the acronym IMCA is synonymous with modifieds. Actually, IMCA, which stands for International Motor Contest Association, sanctions a variety of racing divisions, including sprint cars, and has done so longer than anyone. J. Alex Sloan set up IMCA in 1915 with a single division, mostly because there weren't enough racing cars to warrant multiple groups.

Considering that American drivers have been mostly squeezed out of the top open wheel racing division by foreign drivers these days (as well as a lack of rear-engine racing experience), it's somewhat ironic that IMCA's first superstar was a transplanted Norwegian speed skater—who eventually was edged out of the spotlight by a native Iowan. Go figure.

IMCA's first superstar, Sig Haugdahl, opened a machine shop shortly after emigrating to Minnesota in his late teens. That mechanical ability led him to a wide-ranging career setting speed records and becoming

The earliest IMCA stars: (above) Norwegian-born immigrant Sig Haugdahl, the first champion from 1927-1932; Canadian Emory Collins (#7), 1938 champion and frequent points runner-up; and Gus Schrader (#3), champ 1934-37 and 1939-1940, who lost his life racing in 1941. (Sigdahl and Collins photos: Courtesy Jeannie Hinnershitz Craig, National Sprint Car Hall of Fame Collection); Schrader: Bob Sheldon Photo, National Sprint Car Hall of Fame Collection)

the IMCA champ from 1927 through 1932. He retired two years later, in some part because the "King of the Dirt Tracks," Gus Schrader (no known relationship to Kenny) had taken control of the championship. He was often challenged by Canadian Emory Collins in what became the modus operandi of racing—top drivers got top cars. In this case, the two aces drove cars worth about $15,000 each—the equivalent of about $300,000 today.

And Schrader was probably the first high-profile racer to experience what would become a fairly common occurrence for the next half-century—the efforts of sanctioning bodies to ensure the biggest stars raced exclusively within their own organization. Schrader had first made his name in the American Automobile Association (AAA). That forerunner to USAC was engaged in a fierce off-track battle to retain the name drivers who sold tickets, so anytime a licensee raced with another sanctioning group he got fined—unless he was smart enough to race under an assumed name, hoping that no one recognized him. That was considerably easier in the age before *Speedway Illustrated* and *National Speed Sport News* printed racers' photos.

When Schrader jumped to IMCA, it cost him a $2,500 fine (about $40,000 today), but he chased Haugdahl into retirement. Gus went on to cop the national title from 1934-1937, took it back from Collins in

1939 and 1940, then tragically lost his life in 1941 at a Louisiana State Fairgrounds race.

Schrader's death left a huge void in IMCA racing, and it's been argued that the association was never as highly regarded thereafter. Nonetheless, some of the best racing in America continued, even as it was done by blue-collar, working stiffs who showed up at the track after punching a time clock. In spite of the handicap of having to work in the real world, a number of astonishingly good drivers came out of the post-World War II IMCA period, including Jerry Blundy, Gene Gennetten, Ray Lee Goodwin, and the Weld brothers. But to summarize what it was like on the IMCA circuit, one has to look no farther than three-time champion Bill Utz.

Utz was a farrier, and the "Flying Blacksmith" as he became known, needed 15 years experience in local racing before he became a regular on the IMCA circuit. That was not uncommon at the time. It was always a challenge to tow to enough races on the far-flung circuit to be a competitor for the national title. In fact, in 1973, it was mid-season before Utz had a secure enough ride to go for the title—and then he finished third, barely missing the top two spots. The following year he captured that long-sought championship, and then followed it up with another title the next year. To get an idea of the type of competition at the time, second place in 1975 went to Jan Opperman.

Utz's final championship in 1977 was also IMCA's last national title. While he continued to race for a few more years, and IMCA continues to sanction sprint races today, the spotlight faded, even as IMCA secured a spot in sprint car history as the prime destination for racing in February.

While NASCAR was just building a reputation with Speed Weeks, IMCA had long been entrenched with racing just a three-hour drive

Bill Utz, three-time IMCA champion. (Rocky Rhodes Photo, Courtesy St. Louis Building Arts Foundation Collection)

Rick Ferkel emerges from his race car. That's Jan Opperman in the hat behind the car and Bobby Allen in the driver's suit. This was Plant Field in Tampa during the IMCA Winternationals—note the University of South Florida minarets in the background. (Joyce Standridge Photo)

across the peninsula from Daytona. In fact, Tampa's Plant Field served as a multi-function facility for much of the 20th century and was the site of a 528-foot Babe Ruth home run, the longest of his storied career.

Auto racing began there in 1921, and later races were held in conjunction with the South Florida Fair. While Floridians took pride in the IMCA championships of local drivers Pete Folse and Frank Luptow, it's arguable how well local fans understood the quality of talent that showed up for the Winternationals. It was far more than simply a bunch of Yankees pulling out of snow banks and heading for palm-tree country.

"IMCA ran that thing with an iron fist," recalls Rick Ferkel. "They would send out only so many entries, maybe 60 or 70 of them, and I had a terrible, terrible time getting accepted."

Ferkel finally got in as driver in someone else's sprinter in 1968. He continues, "That experience was the story of my career: I drew a really bad number to go out to qualify. And then the car had no brakes. Those were really good guys on that team, but not real good mechanics."

Ferkel proceeded to back the car into the fence during qualifying, among other things bending the fancy fin on the tail. For a team that had spent the winter painting the wing nuts with hand brushes so they would be pretty enough to be acceptable to IMCA, the twisted tail and bars were especially upsetting.

Although drivers sometimes got fired for less, the team kept the young driver and literally slunk off into the night to race at Sunshine Speedway in nearby St. Petersburg. They had managed to fix the brakes, and Ferkel finished third there.

"I can't remember what my 'name' was," he says, "but it wasn't *Rick Ferkel* that night because Sunshine wasn't an IMCA-sanctioned track, and *Rick Ferkel's* IMCA license meant that he couldn't race elsewhere during the period there was a sanctioned event nearby. Never mind I had failed to qualify for the sanctioned event."

Unfortunately, finishing third got the team a little more attention than they had bargained for. Maybe it was because Ferkel was too tall to hide behind the winner and second place. In any event, he was recognized.

"I mean, they threw us right out," he chuckles. "They suspended us for a year. And they fined us. And I never got accepted again until 1975, which was the last year they ran Plant Field."

Even without the great USAC stars of the era, such as Gary Bettenhausen and Larry Dickson, the Winternationals were well-attended by superstar outlaws such as Ferkel, Opperman, Bubby Jones, the Welds and every IMCA master of the time. They could hardly keep out the guys whose names sold tickets, but a lot of the invitations were also extended to less-well-known drivers who supported IMCA the rest of the year. That was somewhat controversial as it meant some major stars, such as Ferkel for a while, didn't get to race or work on their mid-winter tans. But all those so-called little guys, who sweated their way through July fairgrounds races in the Midwest each year with the thought that it would yield an invitation to Florida, really appreciated it.

Even after IMCA stopped sanctioning the Winternationals, there was no keeping drivers up North in February. This is Shane Carson in 1982. (Gene Marderness Photo)

And just when it seemed that IMCA could ride on the reputation of its winter racing—it stopped. There's still plenty of sprint car action in Florida each February, but it's not the same and never will be. There's no state fair on the other side of the fence, no minarets on the college buildings in the background, no Flying Blacksmith or Opp to create an unmistakable aura.

And racing is poorer for that fact.

For a significant period of time, if you wanted to go to the Indianapolis 500, the road ran down 16th Street and through the offices of the United

Richard "The Gas Man" Griffin at Bloomington Speedway on July 24, 1998, during the USAC Indiana Sprint Week. As have many drivers in recent years, Richard dropped in and out of USAC racing with impunity, unlike his predecessors who got fined for racing elsewhere. (Keith Wendel Photo)

States Auto Club (USAC). Even though sprint car drivers had far more fun at the dusty outlaw fairgrounds events, there is something inside nearly every driver that seeks approval and respect. Just as many drivers today feel that their place in racing history is secure only after racing in the NASCAR Cup series, until circa 1980, racers—particularly those in open wheel cars—sought the stamp of approval that came with an Indy career. And Indy was the big stick that USAC used to keep its sometimes-restless troops in line.

USAC was formed by Indianapolis Motor Speedway owner Tony Hulman in 1955 when AAA pulled out of race sanctioning, following an horrendous wreck at Le Mans, in which 82 spectators were killed and at least 76 others were seriously injured. The other USAC divisions, including the sprint cars, were viewed as feeder or development series with the goal of Indianapolis racing in time.

Even with the lure of the Brickyard, some USAC drivers, like their IMCA counterparts, just plain had occasional wanderlust. Even if there was no USAC show scheduled concurrent with another race, these guys also had to race under assumed names. Wanda Knepper, whose late husband Arnie was successful in sprint, midget and Indy cars, recalls that a lot of guys would use the name "Danny Burke."

There really was a Danny Burke. She recalls, "Burke was an old-time racer who lived in Texas. Arnie figured he would never turn up in the Midwest again, so Arnie and several other drivers in the area used the name. I wonder who was most surprised when Burke's boys began racing and found out that their 'dad' had been running in the Midwest for some time, and occasionally managed to be at two different tracks on the same night."

Over the years, the list of sprint car champions was also a who's-who of Indy car racing, including A.J. Foyt, Parnelli Jones, Roger McCluskey and Johnny Rutherford in the early years. A regional champion, Elmer George, is particularly notable as he married Hulman's daughter and sired a son, Tony, who would one day play a pivotal role in trying to renew interest in Indy car racing.

Rich Vogler gets enough altitude at Terre Haute to clear the fence. (Allen Horcher Photos)

Later champions included Rickey Hood, Sheldon Kinser, Ken Schrader, Jack Hewitt, Tony Stewart and Tom Bigelow, the latter holding the record for most total USAC sprint car feature wins with 52. Two now-deceased champions also stand out: Rich Vogler, possibly the most intense, hardnosed racer in USAC history and Sammy Sessions, who survived his share of sprint car tumbles only to pass away when he was decapitated in an off-season snowmobile race.

But of all the champions, perhaps none better demonstrated USAC sprint racing at its pinnacle than the "Larry and Gary Show," in the persons of Larry Dickson (champion in 1968, 1970 and 1975, and 45 total wins) and Gary Bettenhausen (1969 and 1971, with 40 total wins).

Few families have paid a higher price to go racing than the Bettenhausen family of Tinley Park, Illinois, and yet fewer people have given more and stayed so tenaciously involved. That's Merle standing beside the car, talking with Gary who is in the cockpit. (Allen Horcher Photo)

Bettenhausen arrived on the scene with the better-known—if star-crossed—name.

His father Tony had won two national championships and participated in 14 Indy 500s before losing his life during a shakedown run in an unfamiliar car at Indy in 1961. Youngest brother Tony Jr. and his wife Shirley, daughter of Indy driver Jim McElreath, were killed in a 2000 airplane crash. Middle brother Merle survived an Indy car crash at Michigan in 1972, but suffered serious burns and lost his right arm—and his career.

Gary was not immune. A bad wreck on the one-mile dirt at the Syracuse fairgrounds in 1974 took away the use of his left arm—and yet he didn't quit. "Gritty determination" in the dictionary could be illustrated with Gary's photo as he not only continued in the Thunder and Lightning division (which was how USAC marketed the sprint cars), but also ran Indy cars in the 1980s, too.

Larry Dickson came into USAC as a regional champ from Marietta, Ohio. Not many know that he had won the Williams Grove National Open in 1964—one of the top events in sprint car racing throughout

Larry Dickson, 1980. (Allen Horcher Photo)

Gary Bettenhausen at the Copper Classic in Phoenix, February 4, 1996. (Bill Taylor Photo)

history. A decade later, he added the Little 500, a mind-boggling 500-lap race in Anderson, Indiana, complete with occasionally disastrous pit stops and held the night before the big 500 down the road.

As is often the case in describing actual racing, it's difficult to explain the magic that occurred. Observers from the time saw and felt it, and still recall it. "It was a privilege to watch Gary and Larry race," says a contemporary. "This was a time of USAC dominance in just about all forms of racing, and there was nobody more dominant than Bettenhausen and Dickson. A lot of times, you felt you were just racing for third place— and in awe of the show ahead of you. I don't think they were ever pals—the stakes were too high—but I doubt they respected anybody else on the track more than they did each other. And it showed. They were relentless with each other, but always fair. There was nobody they wanted to beat more than each other— even after I think they realized that their names were going to be forever linked in racing. But you could never feel bad about losing to them because you'd been beaten by the best."

Nothing lasts forever. After Bettenhausen and Dickson were out of the limelight, USAC's place as the preeminent sprint car sanctioning body waned to a degree. For a long while they rode on the Thunder and Lightning reputation and some televised races. But when the USAC sprint division stopped being the primary feed to the Indy cars, mostly because of the lack of rear-end experience, a lot of drivers no longer felt the need to run with an organization that seldom welcomed newcomers. This slide may also have been hastened by the rise of the World of Outlaws and All-Star Circuit of Champions as viable career choices.

At the time that the only road to Indy was through USAC, however, both Bubby Jones and Jan Opperman trimmed their hair and tucked the love beads inside their uniforms. "They didn't really take to me and Opperman too well. I think they had respect for us when we first came out, but we were outsiders, and you come in as an outsider, you're coming into their territory," recalls Bubby. "If I ran a place regularly like I did Springfield and Ascot, I didn't want anybody coming in from the outside and beating me, so I understood."

Both Jones and Opperman would make it to the elite level—a few more haircuts and shorter sideburns later—but it was Jones who adapted really well, nearly winning the 1979 sprint car title. After dominating the season, he had only to get a good finish at Eldora during the penultimate event. Instead, he wrecked on the first lap. "It was a big let-down, but it really didn't demoralize me or anything. It was just one of them deals where we had it won, and I screwed up and had a wreck."

USAC regular Greg Leffler slipped past and took the title, but the outsiders weren't done yet. Bobby Allen also tried USAC for a while. "I went to run USAC and I couldn't get the car to go real good, and I thought it was because I was used to running a wing. I had $13,000 saved and I spent it all, right away," he remembers. It was part of the boyhood dream of having wanted to someday race in the Indy 500. "I couldn't make a living at it, so I thought, 'The heck with USAC. I'll just go do what I do—be a rebel.'"

Not a lot of fans know that Rick Ferkel won the 1994 USAC sprint title—as chief mechanic for Doug Kalitta, who is probably better known as one of the world's premiere drag racers. Even through a dream season, Ferkel and Kalitta were never quite allowed to forget their tenuous footing in the series.

Doug Kalitta may be better-known these days as an NHRA Top Fuel star, but once upon a time he was a USAC sprint champion with Rick Ferkel as his crew chief. And in 1996, he took the scenic route at Terre Haute. (Allen Horcher Photo)

"We were at Marne, Michigan, and Tony Elliott, a long-time USAC regular, was leading the race," Ferkel remembers. "Doug and him got together and Elliott slipped off the track. USAC put Doug on probation, and I didn't feel they were justified in doing that. But I didn't argue with them, because there ain't no sense in arguing with them."

Ferkel understood what it was like to be an official, having been one for the World of Outlaws prior to this time. But that wasn't why he didn't argue. This is the reason: "If the officials for USAC come up and tell you your car is black, and you know your car is white—it's black. Man, them guys have got it made! Because you come up and tell a World of Outlaw guys something, he's going to argue like a son-of-a-gun. Whether you're right or wrong, he's going to argue about it. But USAC runs that thing with an iron fist."

Ferkel grins. "Doug ended up winning the championship anyhow. I realized then that I was really happy I didn't go USAC during my driving career. It was such a huge hassle, we just went off and did other things after that."

It's still possible to encounter that attitude from the occasional official, driver or fan, but the truth is that USAC has not fined a licensee for racing elsewhere in many years. They simply don't have the power, and the insular attitude they nursed may actually have sped up the demotion of USAC from its exalted status.

Bubby Jones racing at Imperial Speedway in 1987. He gave up on USAC and headed West, which turned out to be a personally satisfying decision as he and rival Dean Thompson thrilled fans with their duels for years, and Bubby met his wife. (Bill Taylor Photo)

Whatever the argument about USAC's rightful place in sprint car racing today, at least one former outsider-turned-USAC-record holder found a silver lining. "If I'd won that championship in 1979, I would probably have stayed around Indy, and I never would have gone to California," muses Bubby Jones. "I never would have met my wife, and I don't think I'd have what I've got today."

5

Dark Horses and the Posse

It probably had seemed like a good idea back in the winter months when the racing schedule was drawn up. But the reality of an afternoon race at Granite City, Illinois, was a nightmare of finger-pointing proportions. What ever possessed people to think the race would be anything but a diabolical assault on equipment?

Yellow flag after yellow flag flew as the sun broiled the track and everyone there. The black loam dirt that loved sprint cars after dark was merciless in mid-afternoon. Adding to the misery, almost every lap a car blasted down into one of the corners and limped out a three-tire survivor with right-rear failure.

And pretty soon, somebody who hadn't torn the last fistful of hair off his head figured out there was no way the cars would be able to finish the race unless a National Guard tanker plane effected mid-air refueling. That wasn't happening, so the field was stopped—*but for fuel only.*

On the red, however, Jack Hewitt's crew took a long look at the right rear tire and decided that its probable remaining life span was another half lap—full lap, if they were lucky. Sensibly, one guy grabbed a jack and another ran for a spare tire.

In the meantime, the activity caught the notice of a crew member from another team. You may recognize the type: minimally helpful. Nearly every team has had such a guy. Loud enough to aggravate other teams, but either good-hearted enough you don't want to run him off—or a relative you can't run off.

This individual started yelling, "They go to the back! Hewitt goes to the back! He's changing a tire! *He goes to the back!*"

The only sound at the track had been the gurgling of the fuel being poured into tanks, a few hurried comments, and the drip of sweat plopping on the track. So, the sound of this guy, who was now moving from car to car, hunting either support from other teams or seeking an official, might well have reached the Mississippi River a couple of miles away. Apparently, he was really getting himself pumped up, because long after everybody in the joint had heard him, the crew man was still pointing over his shoulder and trying to focus attention on the Hewitt team's activities.

Finally, he turned around. And Jack Hewitt was right there.

In his face.

Hewitt grabbed him—by his cheeks—and squeezed until the guy looked like a goldfish in a vise. About the same color, too.

"*I know I go to the back*. I'm not disputing that I go to the back," Hewitt ground out between his teeth. "And if you say it one more time, you're gonna be laying on this race track."

The only sound that followed was Hewitt's footsteps back to his car. Nobody had the courage to walk over and check to see if there was a fresh puddle under the crew man's feet.

Just another day with the All-Stars.

Jack Hewitt bails out of his car after wrecking at Tri-City Speedway. This wasn't the night that another team's pit man was worried about Jack gaining an unfair advantage during a refueling red flag. (Kevin Horcher Photo)

For years, the All Star Circuit of Champions (ASCoC) have labored in the shadow of the World of Outlaws, but seemingly content with that position. Considering how many organizations have formed and folded over the years, long-term survival has been unquestionably a measure of success.

The series started in 1970 and was headed by Bud Miller, but lasted only until the national gas crisis a few years later, with the attendant negative publicity about racing's waste of the precious commodity Average Joes had to wait in line to purchase. A group of promoters, including Eldora's Earl Baltes, then ran the All-Star Super Sprints for several years, although some observers argue about whether it was the same organization or just nearly the same name.

"That series ran on Wednesday nights," remembers Rick Ferkel. "It ran pretty much local tracks in Ohio, but great talent like Bobby Allen,

Kenny Weld was one of the Pennsylvania Posse even though he'd come from Kansas City originally. In the early 1970s his duels with Opperman were so incredible that they were renowned from coast to coast. (Al Consoli Photo)

The All-Stars paid a call at Atomic Speedway in Oak Ridge, Tennessee, in the late 1990s. Although that was stock-car country, the sprinters were well-received and posted some wicked fast times on the super-sticky red clay. They should have come back–Atomic has joined the tracks now gone forever. (Joyce Standridge Photo)

Lynn Paxton, Dub and Van May, Kramer Williamson, Opperman and Weld— those guys would come to the shows. It made for a pretty good little series."

Fans who liked some laps in their races loved it. "That's the thing that's amazing," Ferkel continues. "I mean any race that paid more than $300-$400 to win was always a minimum—*a minimum*—of 75 laps. Normally, they were 100 laps. The guys of today, they can't even fathom that. They bitch at 40 laps. But we were on a mission—we were going to go Indy car racing, and it didn't matter how many laps we had to run to get there."

By 1980, it was clear there was a renewed market for a modest, well-run sprint car group. Miller, Baltes and the rest all had other interests and obligations, and they began to look for someone new to run ASCoC. Bert Emick had formed and run the Midwest Outlaw Sprint Series (MOSS) with some success, which made him a good candidate, especially since it meant also getting his wife Brigette. The couple was popular with the racers, who regarded them as trustworthy and highly

This is a very unusual sight–Frankie Kerr going over at Jacksonville (IL) Raceway during hot laps. Kerr is now a NASCAR crew chief, but as a driver didn't make many mistakes.
(Kevin Horcher Photo)

Bert and Brigette Emick traveled thousands of miles with the All-Star Circuit of Champions. After many years of improving the sport, the Emicks have retired to Florida. (Joyce Standridge Photo)

A big mess during a 1992 race in Indianapolis. Dave Blaney is at the left rear, Aaron Berryhill is in the 97B, and "Oklahoma" Andy Hillenburg is in the #21. That's Blaney's detached wing after he had cleared the fence. (Allen Horcher Photos)

capable of molding the organization into something lasting. Indeed, for nearly 20 years the Emicks ran up and down Mid-America's highways, sometimes flush with success, sometimes worried about making the gate stretch to pay the purse. It was a heady time for them and the racers who followed the All Stars circuit, admittedly dealing with the fall-out from the World of Outlaws. The Emicks and their traveling band of racers also had to contend with unique, individual track rules since the All Stars always needed some local guys to fill the field.

While the biggest stars occasionally ran ASCoC races—still do, in fact—they tended to go to the big shows and Florida in February. But some genuine Class A talent has been at home with the All-Stars and their more limited traveling schedule. Dave and Dale Blaney, Frankie Kerr, Chad Kemenah, Kenny Jacobs, Rocky Hodges, and Joe Gaerte were just a few of the champions and top dogs. Above all it was the All Stars first champion, Jan Opperman, who put them on the map and secured the series' credibility. He certainly wrote his name in their records for all time with his 44 wins in 1972 alone.

The All Stars have always been viewed as the working man's series. Many local heroes who would never attempt to race against the high-dollar World of Outlaws would—and still do—bring out their cars to test their mettle against the All Stars. As a result, the All Stars win list is dotted with many names of local hot shoes essentially unknown outside their own area who, nonetheless, for one or two evenings of their career outran the second-best traveling group in America.

And that was never anything to be sneezed at.

Auto racing in the Keystone state began at the Allentown Fairgrounds in July 1915, within a few weeks of IMCA's birth farther west. Unlike IMCA or other successful organizations that have been well-received through the years, the Pennsylvania racing has always been a loose confederation of teams rather than a tightly organized body. Nearly a century later, arguably some of the most solid, enduring racing is held at several tracks in the middle of a single state, and without benefit of an acronym. This loose gang of racers has been known for years as The Pennsylvania Posse, although you'll never find any card-carrying, licensed members.

"The name 'Pennsylvania Posse' was media hype," says Lynn Paxton, one of the earliest designees. "It had nothing to do with the racers. The racers all respected one another, but the media needed a name. It was something that was built by the media and the fans—and it was good for the sport."

A name was necessary because very early on, the All Stars and World of Outlaws found themselves in Pennsylvania each year, and unlike most other parts of the country where the feature field was filled out by different outsider racers on any given night, in Pennsy, there was a pack of guys who traveled to all those shows. And, somehow, even after participating in several All Stars or WoO shows, these guys never thought of themselves as All Stars or WoO drivers. Somehow, some way, it became a matter of *Them-Versus-Us*—and that required a name.

"Even though All Stars was a second-tier group to the Outlaws, it was only by a little bit," Paxton continues. "I'm going to put the Outlaws on top, but I'm going to put central Pennsylvania next and then I'm going to put the All Stars. That's just the pecking order. I mean, there have been years that things change, but all in all, that's where it's been."

The Pennsy drivers have always believed their tracks belonged to them— not to be taken for even one night by a bunch of outsiders. Of course, drivers everywhere can relate to Bubby Jones' comments about how he felt when so-called outsiders came into the tracks he felt he "owned." But in central Pennsylvania, it was more than just one or two drivers per track who could back up the feeling with a strong finish. At Williams Grove, Lincoln, Selinsgrove, Port Royal and others, there was nearly a full feature field of local drivers. And they often won.

Al Hamilton's race cars have always been among the best on the race track. A wheel disengaging was a real rarity, even back in 1990. (Allen Horcher Photo)

There are several famous tracks in central Pennsylvania but probably none more than Williams Grove, which opened in 1939 with the first win going to the legendary Tommy Hinnershitz. Weekly sprint car racing began in 1967. The bridge across the back straightaway is among the most recognizable landmarks of any track in America. (Photos www. stevehardin.com)

That's why, over the years, many aspiring drivers have first apprenticed in central Pennsylvania. Lealand McSpadden is one of them, and he came all the way from Arizona. "Those guys get to race at least three nights a week, where on the West Coast if you raced two nights you were lucky, and usually it's 300 miles apart. That's why I would go East, so I could meet car owners and find rides, and get to do other things. Going to Pennsylvania—it was so tough to try to get into it with those guys. They were like the traveling outlaws long before World of Outlaws. They were running three-four-five-six nights a week, long before anyone else was."

The appeal of all that extra racing extends around the world, in fact, luring Australia's Skip Jackson for a season after he'd settled near Knoxville but then got the opportunity for a good Pennsy ride. "When I went to Pennsylvania to race with Lance [Dewease], Fred [Rahmer], Todd [Schaffer] and Keith [Kauffman], I found out fast how really good they are and how great it is to race with them. Definitely, they won't give you an inch, but at the same time, they don't *take* your inch.

"I won a race at Port Royal one night and after the race, Lance and Todd—and all those guys—came down and said, 'That was great. We're

Curt Michael with Walt Dyer at Williams Grove in 2000. Talk about smart marketing, Walt Dyer's #461 "brickmobile" has long presented an instant visual connection between his highly sought-after sprint car ride and the Dyer Masonry business. (Barry and Mike Skelly Photo, Courtesy Curt Michael Collection)

Another very famous central Pennsy ride is the Weikert Livestock #29. Just about every great driver from the area has driven the car at some time. It's always been fast, no matter who was behind the wheel. Here it's Doug Wolfgang at Grandview (PA) Speedway in 1986, with the legendary Davy Brown turning wrenches. (Ray Masser Photo)

It's hard to believe that hard-charging Mitch Smith (right) drove only one time for the results-loving Bob Weikert (left), but it happened near the end of Mitch's career. (Courtesy Lynn Paxton Collection)

happy that you won.' And that made me feel good.'"

Daryn Pittman, one of the top WoO drivers today, is among those who spent some time in Pennsylvania first. It was a special time for him because as a child in Oklahoma, he had heard the legend and lore about the Pennsylvania Posse. "I grew up reading about Lance, Fred and Keith. It's obviously neat to still see them around and running good. Those are the guys I came to look up to, not that I ever had seen them, but just because I'd always read about them. The way racing is—so intense, I mean—racing there was everything I hoped it would be because it's still, by far, the toughest local place to go in and win. And the great thing is that with still a lot of race tracks close by each other, those guys manage to make a living, not even traveling out of their own state."

Although the Pennsylvania crowd has always been closely aligned and tended to treat one another more like club racers do, it's clear that the skyrocketing costs of going fast are taking their toll and impacting the racing. Curt Michael, who raced in central Pennsylvania before turning his attention to pursuing URC championships seriously, notes that, "In Pennsylvania there is no screwing around. They do it for a living. If you're running 14th, the guy running 15th will put a slide job on you if he can because it's money in their pocket so they can eat. There's a whole lot more money involved compared to URC, but it's kind of like URC in that it's changed. Everybody used to go hang out and have a picnic—but it's real business now."

Curt Michael ran with the Pennsylvania Posse for a while but has found a more comfortable home as multi-time champion with URC. In September 2006 Curt won the Bully Hill Nationals at Black Rock Speedway in Dundee, New York. (Guy Fortier Photo)

Two of the reasons the media had to come up with "Pennsylvania Posse" as a name for the brilliant racing there: Lynn Paxton (#1) and Smokey Snellbaker (#5), 1976 at Williams Grove. (Courtesy Lynn Paxton Collection)

Even so, the Pennsylvania tracks actually appear to be at least somewhat less affected by economic issues than many others in far-flung parts of the country. As individual tracks that have dotted the landscape either turn to other classes or close their gates altogether, any racer will tell you that sprint car racing continues to be healthy and strong in Knoxville and Eldora—and central Pennsylvania. Much of the credit, people believe, is due to a fan base like almost no other. If sprint car fans are fanatics, then the Pennsylvania fans are *certifiable*. The quality and quantity of support sets the standard for fans of all other types of racing—and other sports—to emulate.

That is not to say that the Pennsylvania Posse isn't impacted by costs and rules, but they are brothers of a different gang. You can take this to the bank: If sprint car racing ever folds in that region, it's not likely to be replaced by anything else. It'll be Saturday night at the tavern instead.

Whether it's the 50-year-plus United Racing Club (URC), American Sprint Car Series (ASCS), Northern Auto Racing Club (NARC), California Racing Association (CRA), or small regional organizations like the Empire Sprint Series (ESS) and the Cajun Racing Association (another CRA), the performers on the national stage started out in one of these organizations. Rarely does a driver jump into the deep end with World of Outlaws (WoO) like Johnny Herrera did. The vast majority paid dues—sometimes literally—to a club or local organization. It's there, among the other eager youngsters and tested veterans, that character is shaped and experience gained. It is where they figure out how badly they want to chase a bigger prize, or if they are content to stay close to home, something every bit as honorable as going for the brass ring.

When Bobby Allen derided that championship he'd taken without a feature event win, he spoke to the eternal argument at every level

Ron Shuman (#2), Billy Boat (#6) and Lealand McSpadden (#91) during a CRA race at Manzanita in 1991. McSpadden is driving Frank Lewis' car and together they enjoyed tremendous success. (Bill Taylor Photo)

of the sport: How much weight should wins have in the battle for a championship? That's been discussed and dissected among the drivers and fans of every one of those organizations. It's at least as big a deal within the smallest regional group as the largest, and it has meaning, as individually as the individual driver.

"I drove for guys who were pretty points-driven, so if we had to sacrifice some other big races to go after a championship, we did," says Richard Griffin. "You have to be consistent and finish races to be a champion, but really I struggled with just focusing on points because I saw a lot of champions who didn't win a race, and I think that isn't really right. You see guys who win ten races and they don't win the championship because they might crash ten times, too. I think you have to have an equal balance of consistency along with an equal desire to win to deserve a championship."

For younger race fans who don't understand the concept behind points and declaring a champion at the end of a season, it was originally a way for track operators and sanctioning groups to increase the number of drivers who would be loyal and return to race again and again. Fidelity was bought via a point fund. The more points awarded for simply showing up every night, or the closer the point spread for each succeeding finish position, the more it was a matter of getting competitors to come back again and again. Declaring the person with the most points accumulated at the end of the year as "champion" was, essentially, a bonus. It has never necessarily meant that the champion was the best, most talented, most accomplished racer. Rather, it meant he or she had accumulated the most points. Period. Quite often, the champion has been the unquestionably best performer that year, but there have been enough no-win, or few-win, champions to fuel bench racing arguments for an entire winter.

"I didn't really run a full season very often, but we got toward the end of my career and I hooked up with Frank Lewis. I started running CRA full-time because he was president of the organization," remembers

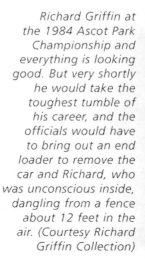

Richard Griffin at the 1984 Ascot Park Championship and everything is looking good. But very shortly he would take the toughest tumble of his career, and the officials would have to bring out an end loader to remove the car and Richard, who was unconscious inside, dangling from a fence about 12 feet in the air. (Courtesy Richard Griffin Collection)

Lealand McSpadden in the famous Brake-O car. (Gene Marderness Photo)

Lealand McSpadden. "At that time, the biggest rivalry was with Ronnie Shuman. He had won five or six championships in a row. If you look at the record I had won close to his number of races, if not more, in CRA than what Ronnie had. But I'd be second, third or fourth in points because I'd take off and go do something else."

Sometimes, going after a championship is like flirting with voodoo. Ask Griffin: "Nobody sat me down and said, 'Look, we don't have to win the race, we just have to run 10th or whatever,'" he recalls of the 1997 season, chasing a title in the Southern California Racing Association non-winged series. "So, in qualifying I go out and flip out of the park. Hurt me pretty bad. A doctor there said I couldn't race anymore that night. So, I ended up losing the championship to Ron Shuman. We came back the next year and going into the last race we were leading the points, but not by much of a margin. We knew we had to finish within two spots of Ronnie. Well,

Doin' it slideways! Jimmy Sills in Don Berry's 1996 non-winged sprinter at Kings Speedway in Hanford, California. (Steve Turnross Photo, Courtesy Jimmy Sills Collection)

on the last lap he was behind us, but he passed three other cars—and won the championship by one point. That was really heartbreaking. We won it five times after that—and always before the last night."

McSpadden adds another thought: "That year, when I stuck with CRA, Ronnie and I traded the points lead back and forth a number of times, and Mike Kirby and Cory Kruseman were involved in it, too. We were all right there in the battle to the end. Man, that meant we had to do our very best every time out—and that made it fun!"

As a result, the fans were richly rewarded, while the organization garnered some well-deserved appreciation. In the midst of a great championship run, drivers have done more than just show up and drive their cars. They've had to think about just how badly they really wanted a championship. Buddy Taylor and McSpadden were trading the points lead at Manzanita Speedway in 1973, and Lealand's long-held philosophy about loyalty collided with pragmatic reality: "Buddy had broken a couple of times and got in another car," explains McSpadden. "I had broken a couple of times and crashed, but I wouldn't get in anybody else's car. I had offers, but I said, 'No, I got in this deal with a good car owner, and I'll go out with this car owner.' By doing that I ended up second, but my car owner won the championship—and I was fine with that. To me, I was pretty loyal to people if they were loyal to me."

Not everyone is seduced by the prospect of being the local champion, as McSpadden had already proven in '73. Sharing a similar outlook to that of Bobby Allen, Rick Ferkel, Opperman and Jones, Lealand made the conscious decision to be a road warrior much of his career. "For me it was a job," he says. "Like all the guys who race for a living, you look at how much it pays and what areas you are going to. I would follow the money. If I could run three nights in northern California, but I could run CRA only one night, then I was better off to go to northern California. If I had to do it today, I'd go broke. But at that time, you could get cheap flights. My wife Janet and I laugh now, because when you really get down to it, all the money I made racing—80 or 90 percent of what I earned I probably spent getting to where I was going! But it was all worth it."

6

The Big Dog

I f NASCAR has become the 800-pound gorilla of racing, then the World of Outlaws is the 200-pound Big Dog. In the very beginning, however, a lot of observers thought WoO looked about the size of a three-pound Chihuahua.

"Ted Johnson, World of Outlaws founder, was just kind of winging it, really," observes Shane Carson, formerly a bona fide star driver in WoO and now one of its executives. "He was not sure where it was gonna go, and he just wanted it to bring him in enough tee-shirt revenue—what he was doing at the time—to make a living."

Although Johnson had a very brief midget racing career in his youth, it was during his years as a traveling salesman enjoying races around the country that he began to contemplate the potential for a traveling sprint car group. The difference, to his way of thinking, was that his version would be colorful and more reflective of the loosey-goosey, free-spirited times. Already there were gypsies—guys like Opperman, Jones, Ferkel, Allen and more—who eschewed the rigid, unbending rules of USAC and similar touring groups, choosing instead to run all over the country at the best-paying independent races.

"Ted thought he could get about six or eight guys to follow his circuit," Carson continues. "He thought he could bring them to each track and then they could beat the locals."

It was an audacious plan in the world of 1970s racing. In a kind of Catch-22 loop, tracks would have to charge more at the pit and also at the front gates so that higher purses could be paid out to the Outlaws, who were going to spend a lot more money traveling and fielding the kind of cars that could routinely beat the locals at their own tracks. This meant full-time, professional drivers, making their living by immediately figuring out unfamiliar surfaces. And, in the beginning, it even meant a few paved tracks and a split between winged and non-winged shows because wings were nowhere near as pervasive then as they are now.

The very first World of Outlaws banquet in Tampa, Florida, February 1978. Front Row: (from left): Bobby Marshall, Shane Carson, Ted Johnson, Johnny Beaber, and Sammy Swindell. Back row: Doug Wolfgang, Rick Nichols, Dub May, Bobby Allen, Steve Kinser, Danny Smith, Rick Ferkel, Terry Gray and WoO executive Don Mack. (Gene Marderness Photo)

Lealand McSpadden won one of the non-winged WoO races in those early days, and it is indicative of how versatile the drivers had to be at that time. They were running all types of surfaces, with and without wings, and towing trailers with three or four racks full of different types of tires. Decisions, decisions, every night, made quickly and a bit wildly, truth be known. That's why guys who won one night might find themselves missing the A Main at the next track.

"I was really starting to travel then," Lealand notes. "I would go East and run a lot of wing, but then back to non-wing stuff in the California Racing Association. Basically, I would just kinda go wing or non-wing, wherever I could make the most money for the time frame of being off work."

Few drivers of the era could afford to cast their lot with WoO. Lealand, for example, held down a full-time job in the real world, and as much as he lived to climb in a sprint car, the reality was that come Monday morning, he had to be back in Phoenix. The perception of sprint car drivers as part-timers was only starting to change, and it didn't happen overnight. No individual or group did as much as WoO to attract the sponsorship necessary to make it happen for more racers, but it took time.

Nobody was thinking about that in the beginning.

Heck, WoO was just in *survival mode* back then.

On March 18, 1978, at Devil's Bowl Speedway in Mesquite, Texas, Lanny Edwards demonstrated either the foresight that has made him a Hall of Fame promoter or a daring gamble on a totally unknown china salesman, because Johnson didn't even have a band of merry gypsies to call solely his own at the time.

"I went to a lot of Outlaw shows when they first started," notes Hooker Hood. "In fact, the first one I ever hit was Devil's Bowl. I was leading that one and a cat took me out. So, I should have won the first one ever instead of them people from California that won it."

The winning Californian was Jimmy Boyd, a driver of sufficient stature that his victory gave the World of Outlaws some reflective glory for its launch. But that alone couldn't be expected to be enough. Lots of would-be sanctioning groups have attracted talent during ambitious, hopeful launches. WoO didn't have enough power to dictate much of anything early on, but Ted and those who advised him seemed to hit all the right notes over the years. Whether it was luck or smarts—or both—by the 1990s WoO was cooking, turning away requests for races and leaving some of the early tracks because they could no longer support the large purses required. This remarkable success story was built in those first few years when Ted's waking hours were consumed with chain smoking, nail biting—and innumerable telephone calls to promoters, trying to line up shows.

Jimmy Boyd, winner of the first-ever World of Outlaws race, Devil's Bowl, 1978. (Courtesy Brian Eaves Collection)

It's never gotten any easier—and it's certainly gotten more expensive—but some of those early races could have been construed as down right discouraging. At another Texas track that first season, a rainy spring made for Texas-sized ruts. "Everybody was blowing tires," remembers Gary Wright. "I had a steel block, which was weighing my front end down and I could go over the holes, but Steve Kinser and Doug Wolfgang were battling for the lead in light cars, and they both had flats. Back then, we had tires that just screwed on, so you'd pull in and change—and go back out and bust a new one."

Wright continues, "Wolfgang took over the lead, and I'm second. We had passed Sammy Swindell and Ron Shuman, and I'm like, 'Wow, we're doing good!' Wolfgang had a flat in the fourth turn and I got the lead. But then I went down into one—and we had a flat. In fact, we knocked our tire off."

Even though "we were actually running pretty decent for no more than we knew," Wright chose to stay home when WoO exited the South Central states. Costs were lower and the tracks known. "I made a couple of mistakes in racing. That was probably one of them."

Among those who did hit the road with WoO was Ferkel. "We ended up second in points that first year. When my car would break—and it did quite a bit back then—other drivers like Lee Osborne would offer their cars so I could stay up in points. But I'd never raced for points before so it didn't mean that much. In fact, I didn't realize it meant anything. Well now—looking back—it would have been neat to win it."

While the championship is now worth a substantial amount of money, prestige and potential sponsorship appeal, 30 years ago it was basically a few dollars and nice trophy. So, Ferkel and Wright, and everybody else who didn't share Ted Johnson's vision, could be forgiven for not seeing where this was all leading.

"At that time we just went by the ads in *National Speed Sport News*," Ferkel continues. "Anything that paid $800 or more—it didn't matter if it was on the West Coast, we were going to go. At that time, $800 was quite a bit of money in your pocket and gas was 30 or 35 cents a gallon. And then we would stay out and find something else, even if it was a $400-$500 show. When the World of Outlaws came about, it just sort of fit right into our thing. It was there for anybody to pick up the ball and carry it, and Ted Johnson was the one who did."

Johnson succeeded in spite of conventional thinking—then and now. The kinds of things that would kill a short-track on its own—and is hurting Saturday Night car racing of all types—somehow worked for him, and did so better than all the other would-be sanction heads who tried the same thing. These were some of the tenets that should have killed the Outlaws long ago:

- Pit passes are sometimes twice what is the normal amount— including for the guys in the support divisions.
- Ticket prices at the front gate are double or more the regular admission price.
- Theses are the most expensive short-track cars to field, with the possible exception of the World of Outlaws Late Models.
- The circuit hits 80-90 tracks a year, requires a rolling garage that costs $1,000 per fill-up at the gas station.
- The regulars are away from their homes 200-250 days a year.

- Races get the green with straight-up or slightly inverted line-ups.
- One driver has so thoroughly dominated the record book that it will take decades—if ever—for anybody to tie him.

It looks like Steve Kinser can't possibly miss a flipping Johnny Herrera during a 1990 World of Outlaws race in Pevely, Missouri–but sure enough, quick reflexes take him outside and around. (Allen Horcher Photos)

That last is a big one. Many observers will argue that WoO's reputation was built on the brilliant driving of Steve Kinser, enhanced by the unquestioned skill and challenge of Sammy Swindell and Doug Wolfgang. The Big Three. WoO succeeded where others failed, in considerable part, because of the dazzling performance of three guys who previously had never really been heard of outside their respective regions. All three epitomized a marketing dream. They were what sprint car racing needed at that time—hard-nosed, determined, unbelievably talented, macho men more than willing to engage in a rivalry for the ages.

When all is said and done, however, one name will stand out from all the rest, appearing on the list for record after record after record. It's a variation on the old conundrum, which came first: the chicken or the egg? *Who made who: the World of Outlaws or Steve Kinser?*

The two faces of Steve Kinser: incredibly intense, and enjoying life as a King ought to. (Mike Campbell Photos)

Actually, it's impossible to think of one without the other. The bench-racing discussion has to be whether WoO would have become the premier sprint car organization it did without having a 20-time champion. Or whether Kinser would have become a motorsports icon without WoO as the framework.

Even the ever-talented bunch in central Pennsylvania developed a sense of awe at Kinser's talent. "When WoO came in here in 1979 and 1980 we kind of put it on them," recalls Lynn Paxton. "Then, I think it was '81 or '82 there were seven or eight races here, and damned if Kinser didn't come in and win every one of them. He came in and just cleaned everybody's clock—not only us but the other Outlaws. I was supposed to be the guy to beat him, but he was clearly better than us.

"People came up and said, 'What's wrong, why did he beat you?' I said, ''Cause he's faster!' Then they would say, 'What's wrong?' And I said, 'What's wrong with the rest of the Outlaws? He made all of us look like fools.' Every dog has his day, but Kinser's has just lasted an incredibly long time."

While Kinser's enormous success has been tied to WoO, including 46 A Feature wins in one season (1987) and more than 500 A Feature wins by the time the organization was only a quarter-century old, to go with those championships and wins over simply the best sprint car talent *in the world*—he's not always been WoO's biggest cheerleader. In fact, in

Doug Wolfgang, one of the Big Three who created enthusiasm for so many years for the World of Outlaws. (Courtesy Brian Eaves Collection)

1988 and 1989, Kinser and several other top stars left WoO for the United Sprint Association. In 2006, he and Danny Lasoski were among the WoO notables who departed for the National Sprint Tour, again dissatisfied with the status quo. Neither rival group survived, but NST could well have been a threat if not for a freak accident.

Richard Petty (far left) anchors the National Sprint Car League press conference on September 23, 2005. Some of the top WoO stars were expected to join, but the NSCL folded before it ever ran a race.

It all began when Richard Petty's motorsports company developed plans for the National Sprint Car League in 2005, but with the misreading of the situation that might be expected from a stock car-oriented group of people, never actually put on a single race. Just as it appeared that the brief threat to WoO supremacy had sunk without a hurrah, former WoO Promoter of the Year Fred Brownfield resurrected the embers and re-named it slightly.

WoO had the history and the tracks signed up. NST had some of the top drivers and only about 45 events, but enough to mount a potentially serious challenge. And then in 2006, Brownfield, making a chalk line on his own Grays Harbor Raceway track in Elma, Washington, during a yellow flag for a non-NST event, was fatally run over by a race car. NST was thrown into disarray. Steve Kinser joined several other heavy hitters in purchasing the assets from Brownfield's survivors. Without a strong administrator, however, NST quietly vanished and became the answer to a trivia question that will likely become more obscure with time.

Danny Lasoski won the NST race at Davenport (IA) Speedway on May 2, 2006. The flagman is Justin Clark, son of Knoxville's famed flagger Doug Clark. (Steve Hardin Photo)

An entire book could be written on how and why WoO succeeded where others failed. Ted Johnson hadn't invented the wheel—or the concept—but he certainly was in the right place at the right time. And within a remarkably few years—without the carrot of the Indy 500 or Daytona 500 he had the destination for sprint car drivers, even if they could afford to stay with the circuit for only a year or two.

That included West Coast ace Jimmy Sills. "The team I drove for thought we could just win the World of Outlaws championship, and I knew that we were going to a lot of tracks that I'd never been to, and they hadn't been to either. I knew it would take at least a year to learn the ropes and set-up for different tracks. It was tough when you knew you could win every night, but you actually had a good night if you just finished in the top ten."

As so often happens when teams don't perform to expectations—no matter how unrealistic—Sills found himself on the outside looking in as another driver was installed in the car. Meanwhile, Sills picked up the ride

They've been dueling–and thrilling–fans for over 30 years in the World of Outlaws. This is Steve Kinser and Sammy Swindell at Huset's (SD) Speedway in June 2003. (Doug Johnson Photo)

Jimmy Sills calls it his favorite win ever, and not just because he had beautiful company in Victory Lane. This was the Indianapolis State Fairgrounds mile track in 1986. He was driving for Lenard McCarl and beat the best in the business. (Courtesy Jimmy Sills Collection)

in the Cahill Brothers-Lenard McCarl car, and as luck would have it, they found the winner's circle quickly. Shortly thereafter, he added possibly the favorite win of his long and fabled career.

"We started on the pole at the Indy Mile, with Steve Kinser on the outside and Sammy Swindell right behind me. Heavy hitters from the start. I still wasn't used to going that fast, but you ran wide open around there. You didn't let up at all. We were probably running 165 mph around the corners, and that was way faster than I really wanted to be thinking about flipping!

"Lenard had that car perfect, so I'm pretty comfortable and I come up on three lapped cars running side-by-side down the straightaway. I figure these guys are all probably gonna tuck to the bottom and I'm gonna drive wide-open on the outside of them. I wasn't going to follow them in and let Steve and Sammy drive by me and make me look like a fool. I kept the throttle down and drove on the outside. Went by the first two cars getting in and then the last one coming off. Steve had followed them so by the time he got by I had half a straightaway lead. Well, I'm feeling cocky and then *I ended up lapping my old car.* That was the most fun race of my career, I think. Winning with the World of Outlaws, lapping the ride I was fired from, and doing it in style!"

Gary Wright also managed to put together parts of several years with the WoO circuit—winning, too—but his memories include how difficult it was to stay with the series. "Everybody said, 'You need to run the Outlaws full-time,' but I had only one good motor and one good car. After a week on the road with them, I was all out of stuff. When they came to Dallas or Little Rock where I could have my fresh motor and all new tires, I could compete with them for a weekend. That was the '90s. Now I don't even have a motor to compete with them."

Wright's observation mirrors that of the scores of sprint car drivers who have aspired to the current full-time WoO tour but have never been able to quite pull together all the financing necessary. They are the majority of WoO competitors. So, then, what is it like for the envied minority, those who do get on the circuit and stay there?

In 2002 at Eagle Raceway, Craig Dollansky demonstrates one of the reasons WoO is so popular—those sideways slides! (Doug Johnson Photo)

"As long as you're spending someone else's money, it's a lot more enjoyable," jokes current WoO star Daryn Pittman. "To be honest, it's great only as long as you're running well. It's 100 percent the opposite when you're struggling. You feel like you're ready to quit, you're ready to go home, if you get on a bad streak and don't know how to fix it. It can be the most humbling and frustrating sport."

That can be just as true for the corporation as for a low-buck racing team. After more than two decades of dominance in the sprint car world, a few seasons back there were some rumblings from within about WoO's financial shape. Rumors were sparked that Johnson was in personal financial trouble—and that it might very well extend to his now-grown-up baby.

"Ted was perfect for what we wanted in the beginning, but he wasn't perfect in the end," opines Bobby Allen. "If you said, 'Ted, I think I've got this sponsor,' well, he'd go get the sponsor for himself. He did that to several people. He didn't have to keep lying to me. I don't know if he thought I could make it or something…but I lived day-by-day. So, it mattered."

If money matters were murky to some, what was abundantly clear to all by the 2000s was that Johnson was aging. He was also ill.

Boundless Motorsports was in a dizzying spell of buying racing organizations in 2005, and the offer to take the financial burden off Johnson must have seemed

Another reason fans flock to WoO races–Tim Shaffer walked away from this May 3, 2008, wreck. (Doug Johnson Photo)

perfect timing, especially since they left most of the existing staff in place, including members of Johnson's family. Ted was kept on as a consultant, a kindness, really, as the man who had successfully beaten cancer in 1979 succumbed to the disease in late 2006.

There's no good time to lose a centerpiece of the sport, but it was particularly difficult, given some of what was happening with Boundless. The company had renamed itself DIRT Motorsports (and now is known on NASDAQ as World Racing Group, Inc.). As one of very few auto racing series to be publicly traded, anyone could nose into their business, and the buying spree had led to concerns about the company being overleveraged.

In spite of encouraging television ratings since coming under the SPEEDtv umbrella, the company had a net loss of nearly $13 million in 2007, down considerably from the $22 million-plus loss in 2006. (These figures cover all the WRGI holdings, not just WoO sprints.) In its SEC-filed report for the period ending in 2007, WRGI's auditor gave an "unqualified opinion expressing doubt that the company can continue as a going concern." That's a big caution flag for investors who play the stock market.

Even as racers, fans, staff and shareholders look to the future with at least some trepidation, it's important to remember that there is clearly still a market for high-quality sprint car racing. Says Shane Carson, now head of Industry Relations for WoO, "I think that the World of Outlaws has always concentrated on a certain clientele, certain facilities…and you may have the same car that can run all the series, but they come to us to attract attention. I felt like we were the ones that would be successful with the high-end sprint events. I still feel like we are doing that."

"There are guys who say they won't go race the Outlaws," observes Paxton. "I say, 'My friend, if I'm going to go out and play golf—and I shoot 80 and the guy that shoots 90 is there—I expect to win. But if I

The World of Outlaws signature four-abreast salute to the fans at Eagle Raceway on June 29, 2003. (Doug Johnson Photo)

think I really have my shit together, I want to play golf against the best guy I can.' And as far as I'm concerned the best guys were—and are—the Outlaws. That's where you want to prove it. I think the better quality opponent you run against, the better it makes you."

For all time, people will think of (and appreciate) the World of Outlaws whenever a sprint race starts with the four-abreast salute to the fans—a brilliant ploy conceived by Johnson as a signature statement. It's "often imitated but never duplicated," as WoO announcer Johnny Gibson intones before each feature.

As to whether WoO's behind-the-scenes issues should be worrisome to sprint car fans, think about Samuel Clemens, a.k.a., Mark Twain. Upon being told a London newspaper had run speculation about his ill health, he noted ironically, "The report of my death was an exaggeration."

Twain lived 13 more years.

7

Knoxville

Knoxville Raceway, which is located on the Marion County (Iowa) Fairgrounds, is the most famous publicly owned race track in sprint car racing history. (Tailwind Aerial Photography)

I t's not just about the racing.

While there are people who maintain a serious and intense demeanor about the racing, it doesn't take a lot of time in the midst of a grandstand full of sprint car fans to realize that many, if not most, regard it as their civic duty to ensure that racing never takes itself too seriously.

Let the good times roll, man.

Nowhere is that more evident than at the Knoxville Nationals, sprint car racing's equivalent of the World Series. The *racing* begins on a steamy Wednesday evening in early August and doesn't conclude until Saturday night. The *partying* out in the nearby campgrounds starts on Tuesday night and doesn't conclude until sometime on Sunday. If it's a little tamer in recent years, it's not for lack of juvenile-inspired tomfoolery.

There are a lot of hours to fill between checkered flags. You can discuss last night's racing only so long, and then wander through the vendors' trailers buying tee-shirts for everybody you know so they won't forget that you got to go to Knoxville and they didn't. You can also drink only so many beers before you're watching tonight's races from the disadvantage of an alcoholic stupor. So, what do you do?

The entrance to Knoxville's infamous north campgrounds, which includes an ambush alley where practical jokes abound. There is some appreciation for beverages here, with a preference for domestic brews. And then there is the nearly non-stop poker match involving fans from Nebraska and Colorado. All in all, it's a great time! (Steve Hardin Photos)

Water balloon fights across a small basin in the campground got to be such an anticipated annual event that military-precision planning escalated the "war" to the point that one army actually developed launchers. When the water balloons started making hail-like dents in the campers, security guards stopped that fun. If the missiles could create a permanent crease in aluminum, imagine what they could do to humans— even anesthetized drunks. Next thing you know, ambulance chasers would be roaming through the campground trying to sign up class-action lawsuit participants. In the middle of a 95-degree afternoon just this side of corn fields, with thunderheads on the horizon and not a lot else to distract, a class-action lawsuit might start to sound pretty good.

A little less destructive were the antics of a group of fans just looking for a laugh at others' expense. It was born when one of them rode a bicycle through the grounds and spied a $5 bill on the ground.

Only a rich car owner or driver would ride past that. But, when the fan stopped and leaned over to pick it up, suddenly the fiver sailed through the air and came to rest several feet away. When chased, it kept moving another few feet each time. Even though he was sober, the fan tried several times before he realized that Lincoln's portrait was attached to a rod-and-reel and he was the afternoon entertainment for a group who had managed to keep it going by rolling around on the ground, red-faced with suppressed laughter.

"Well," this fan figures, "That was funny, but did they go far enough?"

And the answer was, "Of course not."

That trick led to a toy skunk attached to a remote-control car that not only disrupted many a campfire, but was also used to ornery effect in chasing poor, defenseless dogs. But it was the shenanigan that really cemented the deal, ensuring a glut of stories for the following winter's bench racing:

"You remember how Schatz blew everybody away in the A Main?"

"Oh, yeah, but he wasn't half as fast as that woman on the way to the showers in the campgrounds when she almost stepped on The Snake."

It was just a rubber snake, but a particularly well-crafted one. You didn't have to be half-blind or half-in-your-cups to mistake it for the real thing. Pulled on nearly invisible fishing line, it appeared to be slithering down the path, and the trick was to make sure that the unsuspecting didn't see it until they were upon it.

Then the fun began.

People tossed drinks in the air.

Guys screamed like women.

Girls would beat on their boy friend's chests like *they* were at fault.

Some would say, "Oh, shoot, you got me last year—I can't believe I fell for it again!"

A few said, *"Stay right there! I'm going to go get my wife—make sure she doesn't see it until we're right on it!"*

But it wasn't security or an angry victim—or even boredom—that ended the silly game. One afternoon as the snake was being reeled in, a guy didn't see it until he nearly

With a little time on their hands, Earl Baltes (left), former owner of Eldora, and Ralph Capitani, race director at Knoxville, trade hats. (Mike Campbell Photo)

Knoxville flag man Doug Clark (left in cart) and announcer Tony Bokhoven enjoy a little down time with some fans prior to the 2003 Nationals. (Steve Hardin Photo)

This is the side of Donny Schatz's car that many competitors have seen over the past few years, including during the Nationals. (Doug Johnson Photo)

stepped on it. Surprised, he jumped straight up in the air. Nothing unusual in that—no different than the gang had seen before, really. But then the guy fell down on the ground.

To one and all, it became immediately clear that he was having something like an epileptic seizure. One of the girls watching began to scream. Another pleaded with the guys to *do something!* Camp chairs were overturned in the haste to go find first aid or an EMT. Beer was spilled. The gang had gone from mildly amused to genuinely alarmed in record time.

And then the guy jumped up off the ground.

"Gotcha!" he laughed. Dusted himself off and strolled away.

A retaining wall outside the track features an exceptional insert. This is at the corner of Route 14 and Sprint Capital Place, and Skip Jackson, who has been accused by his wife of driving like an old grandmother on the highway, will confirm that the Knoxville police enforce that speed limit you see posted. How many other communities embrace racing like this? And how many grocery stores like the Knoxville HyVee get in the spirit? Would you like a little Valvoline with your cole slaw? (Steve Hardin Photos)

The fans' silliness aside, Knoxville Raceway, 45 miles southeast of Des Moines and one could argue another planet away, is often considered to be the Mecca of sprint car racing—for the quality of racing, as well as the fun. Some fans would vote in favor of Eldora Speedway, and a few others would contend the title belongs to Williams Grove or Manzanita or any of a number of other famous tracks. But the Knoxville Nationals have achieved such stature that it's hard to argue against it.

Knoxville did not reach that pinnacle overnight. It actually took many years just to be thought of as a race track first and foremost because it was—and is—a county fairgrounds. There's bunny rabbit judging every summer, along with hogs and roosters and heifers, and all manner of critters.

The Marion County Fairgrounds dates back to the 1800s, and a 1901 auto race there was the first in the state of Iowa. There was some fairly regular auto racing prior to World War II, but the facility was more frequently utilized as the locale for high school football games and Ku Klux Klan rallies. Seriously.

After the War, like so many places in the country but especially fairgrounds in the Midwest and East, Saturday Night racing was the entertainment

of choice. While sports like professional baseball, football and basketball grew in large urban areas, taking advantage of taxpayer-financed stadiums, racing grew on the backs of individuals and groups in rural America willing to gamble on the popularity of something that didn't have to fight other sports for attention. Certainly, having fewer neighbors to complain about the noise and dust was an advantage. But, in fact, throughout much of the country, racing grew with the blessings of the taxpayer-supported county fairgrounds. Taxes weren't raised in the millions as they were for the ball sports, but Saturday Night racing wouldn't have happened quite the way it has without contributions from the tax base. Many of the great racing facilities—well beyond Knoxville—have been constructed or improved, at least in part, thanks to tax breaks and incentives.

The main grandstand at Knoxville with the famous black-loam dirt track. From that seating, it's a great view of Victory Lane, the pits and the National Sprint Car Hall of Fame outside turn two. (Steve Hardin Photos)

There's nothing wrong with this as it can be argued that professional sports bring back far more dollars into the community than they cost, something the Marion County Fair Board recognized long ago. They got serious about racing in 1956 when they hired Marion Robinson as the Racing Director for a then-2,000-seat facility. An already experienced promoter, Robinson was as rough-hewn as the racers of the era. Through the week he ran a machine shop and garage, which made him a down-to-earth, grease-under-the-nails kind of guy. Nonetheless, it's said that he succeeded in attracting some of the best racers in the country, mostly by just not leaving them alone. He was relentless. No one was going to get a break until they showed up and proved they could race at Knoxville. And then he would leave them alone until he decided that they needed to come back again—which was usually right after they'd been there.

It's further recorded that Robinson sent out upwards of 150 press releases in a single week in an age when they had to be written, typed, copied and mailed. Among many early accomplishments, Robinson brought in IMCA and USAC for races. Then, in 1961, Robinson added to the track's growing stature with a race that featured a $5,000 total purse! This First Annual Super-Modified Nationals was so successful that within a few years it had evolved into the premier summer sprint car event in the entire country.

If you have ever served on a committee or worked in some manner with a group that included 24 people from the community, all of whom had a somewhat proprietary notion about their obligations on behalf of the public, then you have some sense of what it was like for Robinson. He had 24 bosses on the Marion County Fair Board. They all believed they had another 30,000 bosses, the residents of the county. In the end, a dispute with a Fair Board member escalated in 1974, and Robinson, Father of the Nationals, resigned in disgust. The next Race Director, P. Ray Grimes, was sidelined by a snowmobiling accident after just three years, and Ralph Capitani was hired.

Capitani's racing résumé wasn't especially impressive, considering he was then the local high school football coach. Yet the Fair Board has been proven wise several hundred times over in the 30 years since, because "Cappy" has polished the track's reputation to a sheen attained by very few race tracks in America. Not only has he survived having to deal with a Board all these years, he has done it with grace and style. And, along the way, he has convinced the ever-conservative Midwesterners that investing in the infrastructure was the smart thing to do.

If a race fan had dropped by the track in the 1950s, and then didn't come back until the 2000s, he might well think Jules Verne was his guide. There is a state-of-the-art grandstand that swells Knoxville's population the second week of August from its normal 7,500 to nearly 25,000. Off Knoxville Raceway's second turn, the highly regarded National Sprint Car Hall of Fame was constructed and thrives.

That vision has worked for the town as well. Many smaller places in the Midwest have become a little tattered around the edges as jobs and young people emigrate to urban areas. Yet driving through the town of Knoxville it's abundantly clear that there's still some pep. The red carpet is always out for the four-wheeled, fuel-injected visitors who've contributed so much to making it so.

Knoxville's success has made it famous among racing fans world-wide. English race driver Phil Smith and his wife arrived in America a few years ago for a vacation. They just wanted to meander around and struck out on the Interstates with no particular plan. A couple of days later, they saw a sign that said *Knoxville 175* miles.

The vacation suddenly had purpose. They took the turn, determined to see the Sprint Car Capital of the World. But 175 miles later, they were a bit puzzled. There was a lot of traffic, multiple Interstate highways, and a big university just off the main road. Phil and Terry stopped at a gas station, where the people talked *funny*—even for Americans, and asked for directions to the race track.

"Race track?" the attendant scratched his head and asked. "Do you mean Atomic or Bulls Gap?"

That didn't ring a bell.

"The one where the sprint cars race," Phil said.

"Sprint cars? Man, they don't run no sprint cars in these parts. This is

(Left) Knoxville, Tennessee, home to a World's Fair in 1982 and some of the most rabid college football fans in America. (Right) Knoxville, Iowa, home to a world-renowned sprint car track and some of the most rabid racing fans anywhere. You can see how foreigners would get them mixed up... (TN Dept of Tourist Development Photo and Steve Hardin Photo)

stock car country!"

The Smiths were 800 miles off course. They had found Knoxville, *Tennessee*, rather than Knoxville, *Iowa*, but as Phil observed years later, "We just figured that any place that famous had to be unique. Never occurred to us that there was more than one Knoxville in America."

For many years, Australians have also made the pilgrimage to the big ole half-mile dirt track. There certainly are several famous race tracks Down Under, but not much anywhere else can prepare you for the awe-inspiring experience of going into Knoxville's first turn full-bore for the first time. Once you do, it's so addictive that most Aussies who come over try to figure out a way to stay, at least through racing season.

One of them has managed to stay permanently. Skip Jackson married a local girl, and "over the years the people of Knoxville have made me feel very welcome." Even living elsewhere in the States didn't have the same appeal. The Jacksons returned and continue to live a few blocks from the

The weekly show at Knoxville rivals the best racing in the country. The appeal of being one of the best there is a lure for drivers from all over the world. (Steve Hardin Photo)

Saturday night racing at Knoxville. That's Skip Jackson on April 23, 2005. (Doug Johnson Photo)

The pits at Knoxville fill up quickly. (Steve Hardin Photo)

track that is the literal driving force of the community.

Not everyone across the country realizes that Knoxville's weekly show is also one of the best in the country, with both 410-cubic-inch and 360-cubic-inch engine sprint cars. Conventional thinking would be that a class or two of similar cars couldn't survive, especially with one-night-a-week racing. There are other sprint car tracks in Iowa and surrounding states, of course, but a lot of guys who run Knoxville go nowhere else. The quality of competition is so extraordinary that winning the track title is highly sought after and, as a result, many drivers choose to stay close and pursue racing just there. There is genuine status in saying you race Knoxville regularly, and it has been so for quite a number of years.

"When I was driving for LaVern Nance, we went up there in 1977 and ran a couple of races," says Shane Carson, whose career took a major turn the following year as he became one of the Knoxville regulars. "I looked forward to running every week. The very first race there, though, I went out and the car started shaking. Really bad. I pulled it in because I thought the thing was blowing up."

Well-known Des Moines car builder Bob Trostle walked over to help analyze the problem. It wasn't at all unusual for drivers—even talented, accomplished guys—to come in to the track and struggle at first. But it took just one quick circuit around the car for Trostle to figure out the problem. Carson had packed the right rear wheel full of mud by roaring into the turns too hard and smacking the cushion.

Trostle just shook his head and muttered, "*rookie,*" as he ambled away.

"I learned how to run the cushion a little bit better," Carson notes, "and that's what you do, no matter where you are racing. You learn that stuff and usually the hard way."

"I had won some races, but I wasn't doing good enough to put my name up there and get a decent World of Outlaws ride," notes Johnny Herrera. "Then I got hooked up with [successful car owner and mechanic] Guy Forbrook in 1995 and we decided to race Knoxville every Saturday night, plus whatever else we could find. He was—and still is—a good friend who jump-started my career, which had gotten kind of stagnant at that point. I had fallen back to running in the pack, and then you beat yourself up—wondering, 'Can I win?' and start doubting yourself. It's hard on everybody involved with the car, but when I realized I could win races at Knoxville, I got confidence in myself and realized I could win anywhere."

Steve and Kraig Kinser are the only father-son duo to have won the Knoxville Nationals. Their cousin Mark has also won the biggest race in sprint cars. (Doug Johnson Photo)

Herrera enjoyed later success on the WoO circuit, as have a lot of champions who called Knoxville their home track, at least for a while in their careers. Among the champs who also went on to national fame and success are Carson, Jackson, Terry McCarl, Doug Wolfgang and Danny Lasoski, who leads with seven championships and the all-time feature wins.

But it is the Nationals that cemented Knoxville in sprint car history. Most drivers confirm that they would give up all other successes and wins combined to see their names engraved on the winner's trophy. "We should have approached it as just another race," notes Rick Ferkel, "but we always tried to have everything so much better prepared—and it backfired on us almost every time.

The people of the Knoxville community who deserve far more credit than they ever receive: the rescue squad. (Steve Hardin Photo)

"The only time we had the car to beat in the Nationals, we broke a rocker arm in the B Main. But this was back in the non-winged days, and you didn't have to be as hooked up. So, I taped the spark plug wire to the frame so it wouldn't kill the magneto and took off the rocker arms from that piston's valves. That meant we were on only seven cylinders, but *we were awesome!* By the 12th lap we had come from the back up to fifth and we were coming like a son-of-a-gun—when we broke the rear end. The car had chattered so bad coming off the corner that it broke the ring-and-pinion.

"Later we finished a winged Nationals third, and we won some other races there at times, but that was the night we were not only gonna win the Nationals, we were gonna put it to them all on *seven* cylinders! And— *bam*—the engine was fine, but the rear end broke!"

There are a thousand more heartbreaking stories than winners' tales unless your name is Steve Kinser, winner of 12 Nationals. Still, youngsters (and oldsters) follow the dream by pulling through the gates each August.

Above, Wayne Johnson celebrates a preliminary victory during Nationals week 2008, and then, at right, shares a tender moment with his wife and baby. (Mike Campbell Photos)

"If you think about it when you're at the driver's meeting with 100 drivers, and knowing who all's there, it can be intimidating," says Daryn Pittman. "People ask me what it's like to race Knoxville, and to be honest with you, I think it's the easiest race track that we race. I mean, you can put anybody who's never been in a sprint car out there, and they'll probably go around there pretty decent. It's a flat, big half-mile and you just pretty much hold it flat out."

Pittman continues, "But that being said, it's so easy to drive that you have to do everything perfect to be better than the next guy. The people who are able to fine tune and then make the fewest mistakes on the track are the ones who succeed. It's really hard to get better than everybody else. It's pretty simple to drive around there—but to get *better* is a lot more difficult than it is at most places because the line is so fine between *fast* and *fast enough to win.*"

8

Eldora

Eldora Speedway as few ever see it. (Courtesy www. stevehardin.com)

If Knoxville is Mecca, then Eldora Speedway must be Medinah, the other sacred site. And while it is another Midwestern, half-mile track with 20,000-plus seating, that's approximately where the similarities end.

Knoxville has its century-plus history, perpetual emphasis on sprint cars (only in the past few years have major late model races been added to the schedule), and a long-time peacemaking Race Director. Eldora, on the other hand is just over 50 years old, with a great mix of car types and a history of feisty owner/promoters.

Eldora was built in 1954 next to the Eldora Ballroom, which was owned and run by musician Earl Baltes, who had fallen under racing's spell after seeing his first race in nearby New Bremen a short time before. Carved out of the hillside, Eldora wasn't a showplace for many years in terms of facilities. Walk up to the front gate 40 years ago, and it looked like a lot of other short tracks with whitewash attempting to disguise the flaws. The grandstand splinters were legendary and allegedly almost

The Eldora Ballroom, site of Saturday night dances where that well-known musician Earl Baltes played back in the 1950s. (Steve Hardin Photo)

lethal. The food was over-priced and greasy, the rest rooms the gag line for a host of jokes. Beer was sold in the pits during the races. Only a few tenacious weeds grew in the infield and those were trampled when the pick-ups and open trailers were parked.

But the second—*the very second*—they dropped the green flag, all was forgiven. There is no simple explanation for why this particular track has been so conducive to memorable racing—wonderful dirt tracks are sprinkled all across the country—but the racing gods have surely blessed these few acres.

"Running two inches off the wall at Eldora thrilled me to death," says Lealand McSpadden. "I managed to smile the whole time. It's a high that no drug will give you."

Up by the wall is the preferred line most of the time, and the closer the better. After a breathless encounter with that tiny, hair's-breadth width between car and wall, another driver pulled in after a race and sat for a moment. One of his crew people ran up and said, "Man, you almost hit the wall!"

Well, a rock had been kicked up off the track surface and torn the right sleeve of his firesuit, adding to the thrill. He was the only one who knew what had happened to the suit and just how close he really did get to the wall, so he decided to see if he could take away the crew's breath, too. "Yup. I scraped my elbow on the wall," he said, holding up the torn sleeve as the crew's eyes got big as humper tires.

Watching the races, no matter what line the drivers choose, is only minutely less exciting for the fans, who have endured mud baths and dust storms, sometimes during the same race. Where Knoxville's is a fairly consistent surface that only recent rain seems to alter to any real degree, Eldora is Sybil. You never know which personality will appear, and even with the brilliant Baltes touch through the years, who knew what they would find.

Possibly that's the secret. Knoxville is so wickedly fast and smooth, as Daryn Pittman alluded to, that the primary ingredients for success are the purest courage to run cheek-sucking fast, coupled with fine tuning the set-up. Eldora, on the other hand, requires adaptability. Even the great Jack Hewitt was occasionally fooled by the surface. Talent and mashin' the gas are not nearly enough to be successful at Eldora. Drivers have to be prepared to change their mind-set, often within the context of a single event.

"I've been there when there was a huge downpour right before the races," recalls photographer Kevin Horcher, who's been there many times. "They would get 20 trucks out and run it in. In 45 minutes they're ready to go. And three laps into the race—*it's dusty!* How do you do that?"

The ever-changing track surface challenges racers to make the right compromise in the car set-up to be quick, if not always rocket fast. Sometimes the guy who is fastest at the beginning of the race is also the fastest at the end, but you can't count on that. It's not any change in the car or driver, but rather that elusive surface.

Then there are the times when it is just plain *mean* to drivers. Ruts, berms, cushions, whatever can jar the fillings in teeth and jump-start a future case of arthritis. "I went there in 1979 and got upside down twice in three nights at the Eldora Nationals—and that's a nasty place to get upside down at," says Jimmy Sills. "By the final night I was pretty sore. It was slick but it had a hole right in the middle between three and four. That hole had a lot of grip if you hit it just right, and so I ran through there once. But the car really porpoised on me and so I moved up.

"Well, the red flag came out later—for somebody else, thank goodness—and my car owner came out and said, 'I know you're pretty sore, but if you're gonna go forward you are gonna have to run through them holes.'

"I said okay, I would give it a shot. So, the green came out and I ran through the holes—and the car bounced a couple of times. Well, the frame rail hit the race track and the car took off—and we were flipping again."

Jan Opperman and Steve Kinser share the Eldora pit wall. It's a wonder it doesn't just crumble under the weight of so much talent in such a small space. (Gene Marderness Photo)

Bubby Jones at Eldora in 1978. (Allen Horcher Photo)

Score: Eldora 3, Jimmy Sills 0.

"The first time I went there I was with these guys from Columbia, Missouri, and it was a day race," Sills continues. "They had never been to a high-banked track and they hadn't run many wing shows so they said, 'Well, if we were at home we would put a pair of those double diamonds on.'"

Jimmy Sills in a Gary Stanton Mopar sprinter at the 1996 4-Crown race. (Allen Horcher Photo)

Double diamonds were manufactured by Firestone and the most stagger—or difference in size between tires—was maybe two inches.

"You needed at least six or eight inches, just to turn the car through the turns. So, we started on the pole but when I got to the first corner, that thing goes from the bottom of the track clear to the fence. It won't turn! So, then I go down to the other end and I tried to turn it sideways, and that only makes it worse. After the races Doug Wolfgang said, 'Man, that was the worst push I've ever seen on any race car.'"

Daryn Pittman's first time at Eldora wasn't just any race either: It was the Kings Royal, the biggest single sprint race of the year. "I'd heard so many horror stories about how fast it was and how you're supposed to knock the fence down running around there. I was a little nervous, and it was worse because I was filling in for Lance Blevins. I remember I walked up to the fence with the crew and my first thought was, 'Oh, this place isn't very big.' Well, I'd just imagined it to such big proportions, it couldn't be as big, could it? I said something like, 'It's not going to be that bad.'

Some of the oversized winner's checks, including Jac Haudenschild's for winning the Historical Big One, end up on the wall at the track. (Steve Hardin Photo)

"And I remember both of those guys just looking at me and one said, 'Oh, no, we're going to *crash*!'"

The result was somewhere in between Pittman's insouciance and the crew's terror. They didn't set the world on fire in the prelims but the night of the Kings Royal, Pittman won the heat, the dash and started on the pole for the feature. "We wound up ninth or something," he remembers. "We backed up, but for being the first time there we still ran decent."

They continued to do so for several years, right through winning the Historical Big One (another big-paying race that was run from 1993-2003), after which reality set in for the next little while. "There's times I think we've figured it out, and the next time we show up, we can't even make the race. I wish we knew why we were so good or why we were so bad at times. A lot of it is confidence. That's a place that, no matter what, you know it's an intimidating experience."

(Left) Before the 2008 Kings Royal race, Daryn Pittman was second from left (#21) in the four-abreast salute to the fans. (Lower left) Forty laps later it begins to sink in that he's just won the 25th running of the most prestigious single-day race. And then he gets to pose in Victory Lane with a big check, big crown and his gorgeous wife Mandy! (Mike Campbell Photos)

Obviously, Daryn has learned a lot since that first stroll to the fence to look over the joint. He may have tasted a bit of Eldora humble pie along the way, but in 2008, he won the Kings Royal, one of the greatest highlights of his career, just as it has been for all who accomplished that before him.

No matter how much the track slaps around the drivers, they keep coming back. Adding your name to the list of previous winners is a high, as McSpadden noted, but so is pocketing a big share of the purse. And Eldora has always been noted for paying the winner very well. For everybody else—well, they hope to cover the tire bill. The term "Dolly Parton Purse," was coined to describe the Eldora prize money.

(Above left) Rick Ferkel, one of the earliest winners of the Eldora Nationals, with Ted Johnson. (Courtesy Rick Ferkel Collection). (Above right) Johnson with Steve Kinser, who also won the Eldora Nationals early in his career. In fact, Kinser has won nearly one-third of all A Main races he's run at Eldora. (Courtesy Brian Eaves Collection)

"Now it's called the Kings Royal, but the biggest sprint race was called the Eldora Nationals when I won it," remembers Rick Ferkel. "It paid $5,000 cash. That ain't nothin' now, but back then it was real money."

Over the years some zeroes were added, and the winner now takes home $50,000. Among those who have walked out the gate a little wealthier was Johnny Herrera in 1996. "From the way the track conditions were, we thought we would be in a good position," he recalls. "The track dried out and ended up taking rubber from the cars' tires right in the middle of the race track. But I knew that if I didn't make mistakes I would

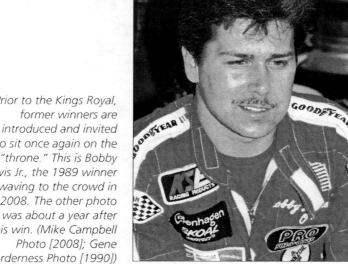

Prior to the Kings Royal, former winners are introduced and invited to sit once again on the "throne." This is Bobby Davis Jr., the 1989 winner waving to the crowd in 2008. The other photo was about a year after his win. (Mike Campbell Photo [2008]; Gene Marderness Photo [1990])

be okay. I almost made one, though. I was lapping a car, and I got myself in a position where I didn't want to be. I had to twist the car and just about spun out. Andy Hillenburg passed me, but a yellow came out and he had to go back behind me.

"The commentators were saying that the top wing on my car was falling down and I had my hands full—that I had to make adjustments. To tell you the honest truth, I had no idea my wing blew a sideboard. I just kept going. That's what you do in the Kings Royal. No way are you going to pull it in or give up!"

At the conclusion, as all winners before and since, Herrera went to the stage where he was "crowned." Now, to any racing outsider, the photos from the Kings Royal look a little...well, silly. There appear to be friars, girls in lamé, and the winner—usually in a firesuit that looks like he's been mud wrestling, with helmet-flattened hair and sweat rivulets through the dust on his face. He inevitable grins hugely as a large red robe and a big crown similar to Queen Elizabeth's Crown Jewels is placed on his head. So did Herrera mind wearing the over-the-top royal garb?

"Absolutely *not!* And I was the 13th winner, too," he insists, debunking the old superstition about that number. To win the Kings Royal, most sprint drivers would kiss a black cat, dance under a ladder and eat peanuts in the pits until they puked.

The indomitable Earl Baltes with his very own bobblehead. (Steve Hardin Photo)

Earl Baltes is also in many of those photos, and justifiably so. These races were his brain child, just as the track cut into the hillside 50 years earlier had been. Even after he sold it in 2004 to the equally feisty Tony Stewart, Earl has continued to be involved, as have many members of his family.

While Capitani at Knoxville has always figured out how to be low-key and work with so many people, Eldora was Earl's kingdom. If you didn't like that fact, it didn't matter your name or perceived fame or whether you were the sanctioning body bringing in the racers and putting on the show. In fact, Earl threw out USAC for a while in 1978, and later nearly did the same with the World of Outlaws. He got away with that, quite simply, *because he could.*

He was no less intractable in later years than he was when the track was still relatively new. "Earl kicked me out twice," says Ferkel. "We're still friends—and we were at the time, but that didn't stop him from throwing me out."

The first instance was nearly 40 years ago after Eldora held a race that paid $300 for first place. "I wasn't going to run for $300 to win. And that's all I said. No threats, no demands—just said, 'I'm not running for $300 to win.'"

A little later Ferkel's team was in Hartford, South Dakota, and they heard that Baltes was having a $1500-to-win race, so they drove all the way back. When they pulled in at Eldora and went up to the pit gate, Earl's brother-in-law Joe Schmitmeyer, who ran the sign-in window, said, "Earl wants to talk to you."

Ferkel cooled his heels for a few minutes, but it wasn't long until Earl showed up at the gate. He immediately launched into a tirade, "There ain't no way you are gonna race if I ain't paying enough money. You just get out. *Get out!* I'm serious."

And that was it. Ferkel was barred from the track.

A few years and a lot of races later, Ferkel was at the track following a race elsewhere during which he had blown a motor. Gypsies rarely had time to go home and change engines in those days. They didn't have the rolling garages that are today's haulers, so they were literally shade-tree mechanics, working on the cars wherever and whenever they could. In this instance, Ferkel's team had pulled just inside the pit gate and begun to work when Earl came up from the track.

"Get that thing out of here," he barked at Ferkel. "Get back out in the parking lot."

Ferkel said, "I can't move it, Earl. I got the motor and the rear end out, and I just can't move it."

Earl got off his tractor so that he could make his point a little plainer. Or maybe to chuck the motor parts over the pit gate. As always, the bill on Earl's signature baseball cap was turned up and he appeared ready to go nose-to-nose with Ferkel. Whatever his intentions, they were lost in the pandemonium that followed—*because the tractor started rolling.* And it didn't stop until it backed into a race fan's parked van.

Earl threw Ferkel out for a few more months, because he rationalized that it was clearly *Rick's* fault.

Earl was not the only colorful Baltes in the group, all of whom worked at the track. Because his wife Berneice was considerably lower-key, she often was the go-to person for a saner perspective. Son Terry, however, is pretty much a chip off the old block, making him a lively track announcer and some-time official.

The following story may be apocryphal, but it's classic Baltes, and a late model driver who was there swears it's true. One time during the

The main grandstand at Eldora, and (below) the grassy area between turns one and two, where, as you can see, it pays to get your lawn chair placed early before the big shows. (Steve Hardin Photos)

driver's meeting prior to the World 100, by far the most prestigious late model race of the year, a bit of belly-aching got started and was feeding on itself, as often happens in such gatherings. Terry Baltes is reputed to have brought the griping to a quick halt by saying, "Shut up! You guys are only here to make us money so we can run *sprint cars!*"

No matter how truth and fiction intermingle, it's inarguable that there is anywhere else quite like Eldora. Its history is as richly detailed as any track anywhere, with any type of racing. When so many drivers say that it "separates the men from the boys," it is simply no exaggeration. Folks in the grandstand on the right night were just plain privileged to see Steve Kinser, Rich Vogler or Jack Hewitt come from the back of the pack to win. There are no tougher drivers in sprint car history, and it took every bit of that hardiness to win that way.

Fans also had grooved on the smooth-as-silk Brad Doty before the racing turned so cruelly on him. Jac Haudenschild stopped hearts as he

The pits at Eldora are always busy and full. (Steve Hardin Photo)

roared inches from the wall. A.J. Foyt and Mario Andretti added luster to their incomparable résumés. And Johnny Rutherford proved that being a defending USAC sprint car champion is no protection against disaster as he flipped completely out of the track in 1966, breaking both arms.

"You'll see a lot of drivers run harder—almost to the point like you're really racing—in hot laps," says Daryn Pittman. "Hot laps don't pay anything. But hot-lapping at Eldora is just so that you try to get your nerves under control. If you get behind somebody and you misjudge what they're going to do, it messes with you mentally for the rest of the night. So, it's a place to definitely go in headstrong and make sure you feel like you conquer it real early. That way you can just focus on your racing the rest of the night."

As hundreds of drivers will attest, that's easier said than done.

9

Innovation

One of the more than 200 wins accumulated in Jerry Blundy's career came in California back in the 1960s when officials stopped the race prematurely because three drivers had been killed.

As this is written, Blundy is 80-plus years old and in relatively good shape at a Galesburg, Illinois, assisted-living facility. Consider that most of his races were run in the era of no roll cage and no more restraint than possibly—*possibly*—a lap belt. Just surviving was a huge career

Jerry Blundy racing. (Courtesy Jeff Moe Collection)

accomplishment. Having accumulated 10 championships, including the 1970 and 1971 IMCA sprint crowns, as Jerry did, and then being around to talk about them is nothing short of amazing.

Those who watched Blundy race recall that he was as smart as he was brave. Drivers accepted that those attributes weren't always enough, as a number of really bright individuals got caught up in fatal wrecks. Competitors did some really dumb things to increase their odds of winning before the sanctioning bodies implemented rules changing cars in ways that weren't always obvious to the fans, but certainly reduced the body count.

"I would have been further ahead if I would have just went out and bought an old car when I was starting out," recalls Rick Ferkel. "I probably could have bought an old car for $500 or something like that. But money was really, really scarce and $500 seemed like an awful, awful bunch of money at that time at the beginning of my career. And so, I decided to try to build my own car. I probably wasted five years because I didn't have any mechanical ability. I mean, I couldn't even figure out how you could sit in the center of the car and it would steer out the left side."

Because he couldn't afford much engine and its attendant horsepower, innovation ruled. And not always wisely, he admits. Ferkel decided that part of the answer was to make the car as light as possible. "There was a lot of hole drilling, which was wrong, too, because you drill the holes in the wrong places...I drilled holes in the roll cage. And my roll cage was made out of pipe."

The car was fitted with a regular carburetor such as those on passenger cars at the time rather than fuel injectors. The car had a 1950 Mercury rear end, pulled out of a junkyard car instead of an open-tube rear end. Instead of a driver's seat, Ferkel sat on a wooden board.

His very first night on the track the drive line broke, but Ferkel managed to cobble it back together to run again. "And then I flipped the car, and the roll cage came down on top of me. I probably wasn't going very fast—but it *seemed* terribly fast. Somehow, though, we were able to survive. We just didn't have any idea, and I wanted to race so bad."

Few drivers have driven as many different types of cars over the decades as Hooker Hood. Not only did he participate in the evolution, he mastered every type. (Courtesy Hooker Hood Collection)

Ferkel admits to a couple more questionable building decisions. Because he couldn't afford an in-and-out gear box, Ferkel bought an arc welder and taught himself how to weld. Then he took a shaft and welded it into the crankshaft flange. A rear end coupler was slipped over the driveshaft onto a small stub shaft he had welded into the crankshaft flange.

"Unbeknownst to me at the time, you had to have a U-joint," he adds. "I didn't have any U-joint at all. So there was no way that I could put the car in gear or take it out."

To test his creation, Ferkel took the car out into the country to a friend's home and put it on a circular driveway. "Honest to God's truth, I would drive real slow around the driveway, and they would *catch* the car and put it on jack stands. But that was the only way I could have the motor running because I couldn't pull the car out of gear once it was fired up." He laughs, "It was a sort of a crude beginning."

Later in his rookie season, Ferkel bought a genuine racing frame, available only because Jimmy Smith had been killed driving it. But Ferkel crashed the car a short time later and finished it off. Now he really was broke. Still the fire in his belly wouldn't be soothed. Poverty dictated a radical approach, so he built himself another race car, and this time it was constructed from a *children's swing set*.

"We had a swing set and I thought, 'Well, shoot, I'll just use that tubing out there.' I took that thing and tried to arc weld it. I don't know if you realize how light swing sets are, but it was not my best idea," Ferkel admits.

He took the car to the Eldora 500. This was one of the very few racing concepts Earl Baltes had that wasn't such a great idea. The 500-lap race ran only a couple of years in the 1960s, but Ferkel ran the first one. "And I made the show," he says, "but the only reason was because they didn't have enough cars."

During the race, the front end came off. Ferkel had used a crossframe instead of torsion bars. The cross spring and cross member simply couldn't

Rick Ferkel didn't get any photos of the car built from the swing set, but this was another of his special creations about the same time. Note that he also had a trick towing set-up–the 1955 Chevy station wagon, room for a couple of spare tires on the trailer, a tool box and a bowling bag (for the helmet). It's also a tandem-axle trailer with some pretty slick-looking hubcaps. The man has always understood "presentation." (Courtesy Rick Ferkel Collection)

handle the stress of racing and broke off. Since it was a very, *very* long event, Ferkel decided to "repair" the car. There weren't a lot of spare parts. Heck, there weren't *any* spare parts, so they used wire and tape—and a borrowed belt. A man's *pants* belt.

"Well, to make a long story short, that didn't work either," Ferkel laughs. "I'm probably 40-50 miles an hour slower than them other guys, but even that was too much for that front end. But I got paid. I got $25. And that's what I made my first year: $25. Shoot, I figure, I got paid—I'm ready to be a professional race driver!"

Over the years, Ferkel drove much better, much safer equipment, although safety never appeared to be the primary consideration in the

construction of sprint cars for many drivers. For a short while in the 1970s there were all-aluminum cars, though not a lot of them. That was likely a good thing.

"George Gillespie and Fred Linder had a car at the end of 1976 that was a neat design and it was different from what LaVern Nance was building," recalls Shane Carson. "But then the three of them got together, combined ideas and the first car they built was all-aluminum. LaVern always liked to do stuff that nobody had tried. But it was brittle and something was always breaking on the car. One time the rear torsion tube twisted out of it. Overall, that thing probably wasn't too safe."

The next racing season, Carson was back in the all-aluminum Nance car as Gillespie and Linder returned to building with steel. At Devil's Bowl Speedway, however, former driver-turned-official Earl Wagner came up to the car and smacked the chassis with a wrench. Unlike the crisp *ping* of steel or chrome moly, the sound was the muffled tone of soft metal. He said, "This car's illegal."

Carson retorted, "You don't have any rules about tubing."

"Well, we do now," Wagner replied.

That was the last of the all-aluminum sprint car.

If the all-aluminum car had been successful it wouldn't necessarily have made cars any more expensive than the later usage of magnesium and titanium in parts. But wadding up a frame every few races would have meant that LaVern would have had to put on a second shift and hire a full-time banker.

Innovation has *always* been part of sprint car development. Originally, sprint cars evolved from passenger vehicles, in very uneven increments around the country, based on how creative the builder got. Frames were chopped, tubing substituted for heavy steel pieces, and the shape of the tail changed several times. The touring groups such as IMCA and USAC were probably as quick as anyone to have a car that was specifically a "sprint" car. In time, the specs brought about similarities, particularly through limits and measurements, and then the majority of the cars on the track resembled each other.

One of the things that hasn't changed on sprint cars over the past half century is that they need a push truck to get started. There has been talk at times about requiring on-board starters as a way to speed up the show. The push-off is such a quintessential part of sprint and other open wheel racing, however, that resistance to this is pretty well entrenched.

Even the most devoted sprint car fans rarely understand what a driver has to do to get the car started. Sprinters are direct drive with no transmission, so the car begins to be pushed with the car in gear. The fuel is turned on via a switch or valve. If the car was previously stopped after a spin or without clearing out the cylinders, there may be unburned

Eldora Speedway wisely has copious push trucks on hand for sprint car events. (Mike Campbell Photo)

Few fans ever get to see the tech process at the track. At Knoxville, an area is set aside where the cars are checked to be sure they meet the rule requirements and limitations. (Steve Hardin Photo)

fuel creating compression inside the engine. That's why it's not terribly unusual to see the rear tires not turning at first. The engine can't turn over until the methanol fuel clears out because when the tires are turning, so are the engine's internal parts.

At about 80 pounds per square inch of oil pressure, after also ensuring there is sufficient fuel, the driver can switch on the spark. But it takes some speed to get everything synchronized for a start. As an alternative to actually getting in a sprinter and trying to duplicate the start sequence, every sprint car fan ought to at least ride in a push truck to get a sense of how much speed is required—and how much fun it is, too, especially on a high-banked track.

Shutting down is also a process as the car needs to be taken out of gear, assuming you're not wrecking or spinning and can't control the circumstances. The fuel valve is turned off and as the engine gets lean, the ignition is switched off. That's why you'll usually hear a driver kick the throttle briefly as they come to a stop after it's out of gear.

❖   ❖   ❖   ❖   ❖

During the evolutionary period of the mid-1960s Rick Ferkel was running a chassis designed and built by Bobby Allen. No one could dispute how well Allen was doing, but Ferkel, frankly, was out to lunch. "In the early days at Eldora, I was horrible there. *Horrible,*" admits Ferkel. "To be honest, when we were supposed to run Eldora, I would hope it would rain out."

All that changed when a local driver who was running consistently well there looked over the car for Ferkel. "Rick, you just need to lengthen that frame," he said. "It's too square. It's as wide as it is long."

Ferkel extended the frame that week by five inches. Since sprint car wheelbases range from about 83 to 90 inches, variation is not unusual. Five inches, however, can be a significant difference depending on the rest of the car's design. "We went back there and we were awesome. And from then on, we actually started running really, really good. And not just at Eldora."

Herman Kluge (standing to right of the truck bed) built this modified sprinter in 1966, in part from steel he salvaged out of a huge communications tower. In those days, a single-axle trailer and a pick-up were all that were needed to get to the track. (Courtesy Mary Standridge Collection)

Jimmy Sills broke the stock car he drove at Asheville (NC) Speedway, ending that career the first night out. So, he packed up and went back to California where Ed Watson allowed Jimmy into a dirt supermodified– the forerunner of sprint car racing in many parts of the country. (Courtesy Jimmy Sills Collection)

Race car technology evolves all the time, but what don't change are the dirt tracks that have challenged drivers over the last century. This is the Indy Mile, a place that has bedeviled sprinters in the past. (Steve Hardin Photo)

Allen had begun building cars mostly as an economic move because, like so many of his contemporaries he faced tight purse strings. When he had success, not surprisingly, other drivers and car owners bugged him to build and sell cars. "I went to Hagerstown one time, and I was running about fifth. All the cars running in front of me are my cars," he recalls. "I said, 'Now, wait a minute here—this don't make sense. The money you made on the cars, you're losing in the racing.' I'll tell you what I noticed, though. Give the guys a month, and if they aren't making the same changes you are as you figure out things, well then in a month you're beating them again. You gotta know when to flow and change things."

There have been periods of time when race car technology was changing constantly, even within the limits of rules and specifications. Often changes are more subtle these days, but there are several areas in which evolution has been substantial over the past half century: tires, wings and engines.

"You started out racing with six- or seven-inch-wide tires, and then end up with 16-inch-wide tires," recalls Lynn Paxton, who raced through the changeover from modifieds to sprint cars, and who was so adept that he often raced a midget or a late model on the same nights he ran his sprinter.

Rarely do drivers cross over between dirt and pavement racing anymore, but there was a time when the sum-total difference was changing tires. And then, some of the racers started figuring out that it was an advantage to build a car specific to the track surface. In 1977, Rick Ferkel had an asphalt-only car that led over 200 laps of the Little 500 before blowing the motor. Then they won six of the next nine races with the car. (Ray's Racing Photos, Courtesy Rick Ferkel Collection)

Back when Paxton was in his prime, almost everyone pulled through the gate with a pick-up truck, maybe a camper shell and a single-axle trailer. A well-to-do team might have a rack for extra tires, but the rest just threw their stuff in the truck bed. There was plenty of room for the tool box, a couple of torsion bars, an air compressor and the helmet bag. Really, other than having a spare in case of a flat tire, there wasn't a reason to have a rack because the available tire compounds were so limited. If you ran a pavement track occasionally, you needed a few more. At that time the sum total difference between dirt and pavement was changing

Gary Irvin tries to dodge the Eldora wall back in the '80s. Note how the right rear tire tread is separating. He succeeded in keeping the car from going over, but the tire almost cost him a race car. (Kevin Horcher Photo)

Eddie Wirth driving the Tamale Wagon at Imperial Raceway in 1987 shows what often happens when a dirt track slicks over—you end up smoking the tire when you take the car hot into the corner. (Bill Taylor Photo)

the tires and maybe a torsion bar or two. The exact same car that took the checkered flag at Eldora on Saturday ran on the pavement at Winchester, Indiana, the next afternoon, often contending for the win yet again.

When the tire manufacturers woke up to the potential market, racers couldn't weld on tire racks fast enough or wide enough. And then the sanctioning bodies caught up again, resulting in tire rules.

"They've pretty much taken out 70 percent of our choices," notes Daryn Pittman. "It's three compounds now, and that really simplified things a lot. But that's one thing that I actually kind of miss about it. They did it for a cost savings, and to be honest with you, our bills did show that it saved us a little bit of money. It hurt us, sponsor-dollar-wise, but what I didn't like is that it did take that selection aspect out of it. Not all of the time did the tire make the difference, but out of 80 races last year, there were probably 10 to 15 where people went with different tires from anybody else, and they were hands down the best. Tire selection was a more important decision before tire rules, and it's always neat to win when you feel like you outsmarted other people."

About the time of the tire technology explosion, wings became an option, too. Initially, there was considerable resistance, and that's why the World of Outlaws in their early days ran shows that went both ways. There have been circuits that have been devoted solely to non-winged cars, particularly out West. Drivers from that region, such as Richard Griffin, have more experience in driving both winged and non-winged cars. "When we started running wings in the Phoenix area," Griffin says. "I was at the ground floor with a lot of the other guys. The wings were aluminum, but a lot heavier in comparison to today's standards."

(Above) Richard "The Gas Man" Griffin backin' 'er in at Godfrey Speedway, Illinois, during a wingless CRA show on August 14, 2002. (Allen Horcher Photo)

(Below) During one of the earliest WoO stops at Williams Grove, wing development was just beginning and they were smaller than they are today. What hasn't changed is how drivers are always looking ahead–even if that means turning the head sideways. (Ray Masser Photo)

(Left)They are still "open cockpit" cars, but just barely. Between side panels and wings, it's become increasingly difficult to see the driver at work. This is Curt Michael at Williams Grove in 2007. (Jason Walls Photo)

They also weren't adjustable during the race. You bolted it on and you lived with wherever it was set when the green flag fell. While Griffin began with aluminum, some of the earliest wings were made of plywood. Without restrictions on size, some resembled buildings on top of the cars. It became clear early on that lighter was better, however, and then the organizations added size limits, too.

The winged cars have proven to be wicked fast. Coupled with improved tire compounds the cars are turning laps that were unimaginable a half century ago. Lap speeds create G forces comparable to jet aircraft. Non-winged cars, on the other hand, are twitchier, less predictable in what they do. They are also great fun to watch, especially if you like your sprint car racing a little ragged now and then. There is more pack racing, too.

Whether winged or non-winged racing is your cup of tea, what prompts more squabbles these days is the 410-versus 360 engine size debate. Throw in the 358 for good measure. This is the ongoing determination of what size cubic-inch displacement should be in the engines.

The World of Outlaws is among the sanctioning bodies and individual tracks that allow a maximum of 410 cubic inches, although Shane Carson acknowledges that eventually the organization will have to take a closer look at the whole matter as the number of 410s continue to decline. The publisher of *Sprint Car Annual* says that there are only little more than 700 race teams in the entire U.S. still running strictly 410s.

What's with Jan Opperman's helmet? There's no visor, but there's a ton of duct tape. (Gene Marderness Photo)

The American Sprint Car Series specifies the 360-inch engine, and there are a number of tracks and groups in the East that offer divisions with 358-inch engines. Johnny Herrera sums up the dilemma as well as anyone: "It was a cost thing. Certain tracks and groups mandated the 360 because the cost of the 410 had gotten out of hand. You could get a decent 360 for $20,000 and race it for 30 nights, versus the 410 where you had $35,000 and you had to rebuild it every 10 nights or less.

"Well, that cost-saving trend isn't there anymore. It's about the same these days. Everybody wants to get a little bit more out of them so they start making internal pieces lighter to get more horsepower. Lighter parts turn more RPMs so you get off the corner, but the engine lasts half as long. You're lucky to get 15 races out of most 360s now—and they now cost $30,000, too."

Gary Wright ran both 410s and 360s in the same season for several years. In the early 1990s he won feature races in the Outlaws, All-Stars, ASCS and National Championship Racing Association (NCRA) in a single season. Considering how different the rules were and are, it's quite an accomplishment, but Wright says that all they had to do was "switch motors and put one extra turn in the front. That was it. I didn't even think about it, we were doing it so much."

But few people have garnered more experience in running varied engine sizes than Curt Michael. Within his own Eastern region, Curt has run 358s, 360s and 410s.

"I think anything you race is tough," is his opinion. "To win in anything is good because the competition is there. I think the biggest expense with the 410s is that there's just so much more money involved in the rigs and the spares. It's really crazy."

Give the 360s and 358s a little time, Curt. Crazy tends to be contagious in this business.

"The cars have gotten very expensive and very fast. They're brutally fast, and I don't think the racing is as good as a result," says Lynn Paxton. "I feel sorry for a lot of these guys today. There's a lot of great talent out there and there's a lot of talent that will never be shown because not

Warren Mockler is vaulting over Charlie Workman on his way out of Tri-City Speedway during a USAC race in 1985. The landing has never gotten softer but the ability of the cars to diffuse energy when a crash occurs has greatly improved driver survivability through the decades. (Kevin Horcher Photo)

everybody has enough money to get them shown. Youngsters ask for help these days and I hate to say it, but you can hardly overcome the money, even though desire has always counted for something.

"I remember the first time I went to Williams Grove. The advice I got was, 'Kid, you can't go there with that piece of shit. These guys have better equipment and they know what they're doing.' If I'd have listened to them, guess what? I'd have never gone. So, I took my inferior equipment and my stupidity—long on guts, short on smarts—and I went out and I found out at the end of the night that they were right.

"But you know what, instead of saying 'I'm not coming back,' I thought I learned something as a driver. I know that I can put this part on here and this one on here and make the car better, so the next week I came back to improve on what I did the week before. That was my approach. That's the progression."

Lynn has touched on the other part of the equation that is often overlooked. Yes, it takes a good chassis, tires, engines and more than a little luck, but it also takes the right driver and crew to make the complete combination happen.

"That's why Donny Schatz wins. He's sharp. He's a good driver, and you could put him in another car sitting right next to his and he'd still make them a winner right now," believes Bobby Allen. "I can remember having probably 10 different guys drive for me, and some would go into certain race tracks where they couldn't go good because they didn't know how to adapt to a race track. I used to let my crew guys go out and warm up at Lincoln Speedway sometimes. One guy would be pushing the front end and the other guy would be loose. It's how they drove the car. There is a difference in race drivers, no doubt about it. Also a difference in cars and knowing what to do with them."

However, if you are a quart low on talent, or haven't hooked up with the right car owner or simply can't figure out how to go fast, you can do what some drivers have done with flair and imagination for as many years as there have been race cars.

Cheat.

Even the best can have experiences that remind us of just how dangerous sprint car racing really is. During a preliminary Thursday event at the 2006 Gold Cup Race of Champions in Chico, California, Donny Schatz caught fire. As bad as it looked at the time, Donny came through it in relatively good shape, showing burns on his face two days later but otherwise mobile and ready to return to racing. (Tom Parker Photos)

Even when there's no chance of a tech inspector walking over to their cars and tossing them out for cheating, most guys just grin and shuffle their toes in the dirt when asked about...*ahem*...getting creative with the rules.

The following is indicative of the original thinking that has always been part of the sport, if perhaps a bit more so in years past. A certain driver, call him Bad Boy Smakyurhands to protect the guilty, has publicly proclaimed for years that you should always paint your car black so it's easier to hide what you're cheating. He doesn't have any statistics to back up this claim, but Bad Boy was in trouble so much over so many things that it's entirely likely he got some stuff past the inspectors because they couldn't catch it all. If he wants to believe it was the color of the car, well, so be it.

Bad Boy once built an entire frame out of thin-wall tubing, creating a substantially lighter car, though also substantially more dangerous. In those days entries were rarely ever weighed. In fairness it should also be said that Bad Boy didn't put other people in his cars. He took chances only with his own neck.

Early in the season, a rock got tossed up by a competitor's car and hit right at the front of the roll cage. The tubing was so weak that it actually pinched the tubing shut. "Well," he decided, "if USAC sees that they're going to be curious."

So, every race he went to after that, the first thing he did was walk to the track, get a handful of mud and plant it firmly in the dent.

His deception worked.

Toward the end of the racing season, Bad Boy was at the Indianapolis Fairgrounds on the one-mile track. There was a red flag because another driver had flipped badly and was killed. Bad Boy was sitting on the track waiting for the clean-up to be done and the race restarted. There was just enough time for a brief conversation with a crew member.

"Ummm, you weren't kiddin' around about using thin-wall tubing, were you?"

"No," Bad Boy squirmed in the seat. "Why?"

"Because the mud fell off the dent on the roll cage."

"Well, for Chrissakes, put some more on there!"

And then they restarted the race, Bad Boy finished, and he didn't win, in spite of the weight advantage. But that never stopped him from searching for a win by whatever means. He no longer drives, but he still builds cars. Lots of them. They're legal, or at least folks think they are.

Like all other race cars, eventually the thin-walled car died, even if the driver didn't. While most frames get cut up and taken to the recycling center, when Ken Schrader was racing sprint cars with sturdy frames he had a novel method of dealing with busted-up cars.

"I have a luxury at my house," Schrader told a friend at the time. "When I make a mistake, I bury it."

Schrader lived in Fenton, Missouri, on the side of a hill with a substantial gulley at the bottom of the property.

"Sure enough, I walked over behind the garage," says the friend, "and you could see pieces of cars sticking out. And he was filling it in with dirt."

Hopefully, that was on the disclosure statement when Schrader sold the property a few years later.

It's not all that unusual for a rock kicked up by a tire to embed and bend an aluminum wing, but you don't want to see this kind of dent in a roll cage. And that's happened a few times. (Joyce Standridge Photo)

10

Wallets, and Those Who Opened Them

Some racers don't drive.

Drivers drive but *racers* are people who add something of value to the sport, and it's not limited to the obvious. They are men and women possessed of as much passion for racing and determination as anyone with a heavy right foot and half a brain but for whatever reason don't climb into the cockpit. In no way does this diminish the contributions they make. On the contrary, many noteworthy driving careers would have slipped into obscurity without the folks who could wallpaper the interior of the hauler with tire bill receipts.

By February 1983, at Jacksonville, Florida, Bobby Allen had long since felt he'd earned the right to wear a driver's uniform. (Gene Marderness Photo)

The clear advantage of driving for oneself is control. It's a disadvantage as well. Even the most successful drivers who wheel their own mounts have experienced times money was so tight that they needed sympathetic track operators who didn't cash the pit-pass check for several days after the event, aware that the winnings were necessary to get the racer out of the red ink. It can be a career-long duel with looming bankruptcy, especially for youngsters without wealthy parents. Few drivers have ever crafted such a lasting career so peppered with wins and brilliant drives while nearly always flirting with financial disaster as Bobby Allen.

"I didn't want sympathy," he explains as the reason for keeping so much of his struggle to himself. In the early days of his career, Allen wore only a jacket rather than a firesuit. "I didn't want a uniform until I felt like I'd earned it. I had to earn my way with everything."

Bobby Allen wasn't kidding about racers taking an indifferent approach to wearing fire-resistant suits in the early days. (Above) Hooker Hood was a frequent visitor to the winner's circle and his concession was to put on a thick jacket that cushioned the blow from mud clods kicked up by competitors' tires. (Right) Eventually, though, even the toughest guys figured out how much smarter— and sharper—the uniforms were. (Courtesy Hooker Hood Collection)

But as much as the wallet influenced how Allen's career progressed, so did the freedom to do whatever he wanted. As a result, nearly every race he ran was some kind of experiment. Because he knew that he couldn't outspend his competition, Allen had to always search for some new advantage. "Once, I had a car that was like a buckboard, it was so stiff," he recalls, "so I took all the torsion bars out and turned them down on a lathe. I lightened all the bars, and then we started winning about every race we finished with that car, and I had stock motors."

Prior to the 1974 National Open at Williams Grove, legendary car owner Shorty Emrich was presented with an award. Joining him were Lynn Paxton and Bobby Allen. In Shorty's team cars, they formed one of the first super teams Pennsylvania had seen. (Courtesy Lynn Paxton Collection)

Bobby was further challenged because most of the competition was looking over his shoulder and adapting what he was doing to their own cars, quickly eliminating whatever gain he'd found. His independence aside, there were also times that he drove for and with others. Even though it was never unusual for Allen to put other drivers in his spare cars to give them opportunities, for a while he drove a car for the well-regarded Shorty Emrich as a teammate to Lynn Paxton. "Emrich liked me because I worked hard on the car and did all this stuff. But this is what it was like. If Paxton was running second and fighting for the lead but didn't win the race, you knew who was going to get in trouble after the race, even if I was running dead last: Paxton, because he didn't win the race. Emrich knew—correctly—that the guy who was running in the back had trouble. That was acceptable. But the guy up front should have won. That was just as true if the circumstances were reversed. If I didn't do as well as he thought I should have, I got yelled at."

Emrich was the kind of forward-thinking guy who was also always looking for even the slightest advantage. "He used to yell at us about running too heavy-weight oil in the motor. If we ran 50-weight oil, he said, 'You need to run 20-weight.' And he used to push on the side of the tire. Said if you're stuck in mud, you let the air out of the tire. We used to laugh at him, but it was the truth. And what I liked about him being a

sponsor was that he would come to the shop and watch what I was doing. He was my errand runner. I loved it because he was part of it. I always wanted my sponsors to be part of the experience."

There have been many famous sponsors over the years. Probably the first national corporation to advertise on the side of a sprint car was FedEx on Sammy Swindell's sprint car shortly after the World of Outlaws was formed. These days, especially on WoO cars that compete all over the country, it's not so unusual to see well-known companies taking advantage of the captive audiences. However, the majority of sponsorship money still comes from local or regional companies—and friends. It's always been *who do you know*? But for a too-brief a period in the 1970s and 1980s, there was a marvelous human being who dropped in at many of the bigger sprint and late model races to spread around

J.W. Hunt often dropped into races and handed out money to drivers he thought had shown extra effort, but there were a handful he helped consistently. You'll see his signature strawberry on the cowling of Jack Hewitt's car because Hunt liked the more colorful drivers. And who could be more colorful than Do-It Hewitt? Here he's removing his steering wheel while underway and on purpose for the benefit of photographers. (Allen Horcher Photo)

a little extra money. J.W. Hunt did some normal deals where money was given up front, but the Florida truck farmer absolutely loved to show up at a track and then walk over after the race to hand a sizeable wad of cash to a guy he thought had done an outstanding job of racing that day. And it wasn't always the winner. That made it great fun for observers whenever J.W., as warm and gregarious as anybody who ever walked through the gate, showed up.

"I couldn't care less if he ever gave me a dime," remembers Lealand McSpadden. "He did so much for everybody in racing. It was unbelievable. He put up tons of money for the purses and he gave bonuses to people. I never got a dime as far as a steady check from J.W. But he would come up and hand me money for winning a heat race that he thought I did really good in, or come up and give me a hard time because I didn't pass somebody. He was just fun to be around. He loved the sport and he loved the people, but he kinda had a soft spot for people like Hewitt and me who were flamboyant and different from the crowd."

When J.W. passed away in 1994, racing lost more than a generous wallet. It lost one of the truly great characters who made racing better by just being there.

There are hundreds, maybe thousands, of colorful and interesting men and women who have owned race cars through the years. It is impossible, of course, to even think about car owners and overlook Karl Kinser. What he has meant to sprint car racing cannot be overstated.

Born in 1938 in southern Indiana, Karl grew up amidst four brothers and a sister in a closely knit extended family. Cousins Steve, Sheldon, Bob, Randy and Kraig and son Mark have all made significant contributions. In the process, they have made the last name Kinser synonymous with sprint car racing. But it has been Karl and Steve who have made the most indelible mark.

Even before he graduated from high school, Karl was driving a car co-owned with his brothers. Then in 1970 he put Dick Gaines in his sprinter and wrote the first chapter as legendary car- and engine-building pacesetter. What an imposing team they were!

Few people have influenced sprint car racing more than master mechanic/car owner/innovator Karl Kinser.(Gordon O'Field Photo, Courtesy Mar-Car Collection)

The burly Gaines intimidated other drivers just by his size and steely countenance (which belied a genuinely engaging personality). Karl had a less-daunting appearance but never suffered fools gladly. He could send the nosy rubberneckers scurrying away with tail between legs even more quickly than Gaines.

During this period the Kinser brothers had as many as three cars at any given time, with such talent as Ron Fisher, Butch Wilkerson and their Kinser cousins, Bob and Sheldon. The list of accomplishments continued right up to Gaines' serious injuries at Champaign, Illinois, in 1977. The vacancy in the primary car led to Karl offering the ride to Steve, then just 22 years old. They proceeded to rewrite the history books during nearly two decades together and produced racing that is no exaggeration to call

"magic." The lucky fans who watched them race still shake their heads in awe and amazement. When they were done blistering the record books together, they went on to additional success separately—Karl with son Mark and Steve as an owner/driver.

Though Karl is no longer active, his contributions are still being felt today. Among the advancements developed in the Kinser garage are the hydraulic wing and lightweight fuel tank. Many observers feel that Karl also did more than anyone to advance the lightweight frames found in cars today. Others were significant in the development, but Karl was at the vanguard.

Some other car owners have garnered fame, in significant part, because of the great careers they launched or nurtured. An example would be A.J. Watson, whose sprint cars found Victory Lane with such luminaries as A.J. Foyt, Bobby Unser and

Mario Andretti at the wheel. Other owners are remembered because of loyalty and kindness, such as "Boston" Louie Seymour. It is telling that he didn't move to a more central location, but stayed solidly rooted in Massachusetts. As a result, he is said to have towed a million miles with his sprinters. Seymour also stuck with drivers who crashed his cars or blew up engines at times when others in similar circumstances might have fired the wheelman. And when encouraged to put on a wing and go chase the Outlaws, where he would have probably been as successful as anyone, Boston danced with the date who brought him prominence. He stayed vociferously with USAC through the long years of his career.

Who is that kid? It's Tony Stewart, September 3, 1995, beside and then driving Glen Niebel's V-6 sprinter–and they won the feature on this evening. (Allen Horcher Photos)

Other car owners were innovators. Glen Niebel was a self-made man noted for engine development as a significant part of his legacy. Niebel built a competitive V6 Chevy racing engine in the 1980s. The little 265-cubic-inch engine that debuted at Winchester Speedway in 1984 was created with almost no assistance from Chevrolet, which stood to gain substantially if the V6 was successful. Driven by Bob Frey in an International Championship Auto Racing (ICAR) event designed to save pavement racing after USAC had given up on the hard surface for sprinters, the car was going up against not only traditional sprint cars but also the monstrously powerful supermodifieds. Not surprisingly, one of the supers made a charge at the beginning of the race, but Frey got the lead back, and in classic David-versus-Goliath fashion won the event to the enthusiastic cheers of the crowd.

Over time, there were too many instances where the V6 was truly short on horsepower and the innovative engine faded away, but the clever Niebel had not placed all his eggs in one basket. During this time, he and

Bob Frey, who was instrumental in helping Glen Niebel develop the V6 as a viable racing engine for a while. (Gene Marderness Photo)

Frey had also been experimenting with handling and found combinations that worked brilliantly. When the low-key, smooth-as-silk Frey cut back on racing, Niebel was able to team up with the hard-charging Bentley Warren, the ageless veteran from Gloucester, Massachusetts. They focused on Niebel's beloved Little 500 race at Anderson, Indiana. This pre-Indy 500 annual show is unlike nearly any other sprint race in that the wins often go to the turtle rather than the hare, simply because of the marathon length. In spite of Warren's on-the-hammer style that many considered more suitable for a typical 25-lap feature, they found success. Niebel's car ground out over 4,600 laps without a mechanical failure, earning five wins and four runners-up with Bentley and a couple of other drivers behind the wheel.

If he had done nothing else in his career, Niebel should be revered for the 1995 USAC season, in which he teamed up with an up-and-coming youngster by the name of Tony Stewart. Even though the weight break for the now-315-cubic-inch V6 had been legislated away, they won the sprint title. They also teamed for the Silver Crown title, while Stewart swept USAC by capturing the midget championship in Steve Lewis' car. The unprecedented triple crown vaulted Stewart to well-deserved national stardom.

What these and so many other very successful car owners often had in common were humble roots. Niebel died in 1999 in the same home in which he had been born. Watson built race cars for years before he had any success at all. Boston—like so many others, was self-made, never sacrificing his family comfort in pursuit of racing success. Louie passed away September 13, 1996, and his sons Bob and Mike, both exceptional midget drivers, continue to host the Boston Louie Seymour Classic Memorial Race in his honor.

While to an outsider it may have appeared that some car owners threw money at sprint car racing willy-nilly, in fact, most people with unlimited funds have been drawn to other types of racing. It is often the man with blue-collar roots who finds the appeal of sprint car racing

Lance Dewease on his way to victory, May 31, 2003, in Al Hamilton's car. (Allen Horcher Photo)

irresistible. Probably no one illustrates that more than Pennsylvanian Al Hamilton, whose career began in the 1970s and continues to the present.

"Al's a very demanding person but a very fair person," says Lynn Paxton, who drove for Hamilton twice in his career, including a storied final season in 1983 when they won 13 feature events and dominated the National Open at Williams Grove. "He doesn't have a lot of patience, and that's sometimes to his detriment. He would buy the best equipment but he wouldn't always give it time to gel and he would move on to something else. He'd get rid of the equipment he felt was inferior, and then the guy that he dumped it on for half price comes back and makes a winner out of it sometime later on. But he's a very determined, self-made man. He started up in Clearfield in the coal business. He has a sixth- or seventh-grade education, but his horse-sense is phenomenal."

Hamilton has fielded cars for dozens of top drivers over the last four decades. Many people feel that he propelled the legendary Opperman to fame he might not otherwise have achieved—or at least not as quickly. It's fair to note that a few of the other brilliant stars besides Paxton and Opp have included Kramer Williamson, Lee Osborne, Smokey Snellbaker, Lance Dewease, Stevie Smith, Keith Kauffman and Fast Fred Rahmer. They're just the tip of the iceberg. Hamilton has accumulated more than 20 track championships in addition to winning almost every major show in the country. Starting out as a guy who bought scrap coal and then became the man who owned the coal mines, Hamilton brought the same approach to racing. Initially he bought a car simply to find out what it was all about, but he became the car owner with a bounty on his head because his car was winning so many races.

"Al and I have always been friends, and we'll always be friends," continues Paxton. "He did everything he ever said he was going to do for me. And that meant a lot."

You could take out Hamilton's name and insert others and the tale wouldn't be a great deal different. That's how important these people are, although guys like Hamilton made racing more expensive because everyone had to scramble to keep up. Nonetheless,

(Above) When Al Hamilton was honored by the National Sprint Car Hall of Fame, he was joined by Lance Dewease and Lynn Paxton, two of the great drivers who wheeled the famous #77. (Courtesy Lynn Paxton Collection)

(Below) Among the legion of genuine stars who drove Al Hamilton's cars is Smokey Snellbaker, a legend of Pennsylvania racing in his own right. (Gene Marderness Photo)

they led with their heart and they helped create the superstars.

"I think a lot of times we probably had better stuff than most of the guys we were racing against," notes Bubby Jones. "That's just the way it was. I learned a long time ago to pay attention. A lot of people called me to drive for them, but if they couldn't afford to do it, I wouldn't drive for them because you have to have the good stuff to do it. A lot of people would spend money they didn't have, and I didn't want to drive for people like that because, hell, they could go broke. A lot of people did."

Most car owners are not looking for the limelight. In a few instances, even in the days before motorsports marketing, individual cars developed reputations that probably ought to belong to the builder or owner. While there have been several cars variously called "Twister" or "Tornado" or some such colorful name, there are at least three rides that still conjure memories of success, no matter who drove the cars.

One such car was "The Tank," designed and built by Taylor "Pappy" Weld. The patriarch of the very successful Weld family that included sons Jerry, Greg, Kenny and Rick, all of whom drove The Tank for him, Pappy was famous for pushing the envelope without spending record amounts of cash. In an era when rules were less restrictive, a free-thinker like Weld could develop advantages in his mind that translated to on-track success. With son Kenny, they won the Knoxville Nationals with The Tank twice in the mid-1960s. Because the #94 car was so successful all the way from Knoxville to Texas and about everywhere in between, whenever the Welds had an internal family tussle there was no shortage of drivers with

helmet in hand, standing in line to drive the car. The list includes Ray Lee Goodwin, Jay Woodside, Eddie Leavitt and Roger Rager. Youngest son Rick won more races for Pappy than any other driver, and the string of victories began in 1971 when the venerable car was already over 10 years old.

Taylor "Pappy" Weld with "The Tank," one of the most storied cars to ever race throughout the Great Plains and Midwest. (Courtesy National Sprint Car Hall of Fame Collection)

Ron Shuman in the Tamale Wagon sprint car, 1995. (Allen Horcher Photo)

Alex Morales, whose race car has been one of the most sought-after rides in the history of Southwestern racing. (Courtesy Jeannie Hinnershitz Craig, National Sprint Car Hall of Fame Collection)

Another ride that garnered long-term fame was "The Tamale Wagon." The original car, owned by the Morales Brothers and sponsored by the family-owned Alex Foods, was built in the mid-1950s by Roger McCluskey, who later became a bona fide Indy star. Great drivers like Parnelli Jones, Jim Hurtubise, and A.J. Foyt added to the legendary status. Bob Hogle won two CRA driver championships in the 1960s while driving the car. Happily, The Tamale Wagon continued after Alex Morales' death, as son Andy carried on the tradition; the name has actually been used for several cars, including midgets and Silver Crown cars.

But for venerable individual cars, few rival "The Black Deuce." Between 1935 and 1967, Hector Honore criss-crossed America, racking up more than a million miles chasing races. Like most longstanding and successful teams, the driver's seat was coveted and occupied by superb talent, but it was with Bobby Grim on the IMCA circuit in the 1950s that the Black Deuce—always black, always #2, with "Bardahl Special"

Hector Honore (left) collected innumerable checkered flags with his Black Deuce, this time with Floridian Pete Folse. (Courtesy Jeannie Hinnershitz Craig, National Sprint Car Hall of Fame Collection)

The one and only Black Deuce. Note how the restraint harness was mounted. Bear in mind, too, that the car was run for many years before the advent of roll cages. (Courtesy Mary Standridge Collection)

emblazoned on the hood—created such a sensation.

Wanda Knepper tells a story of just how intense Honore (pronounced Hō-*nor*-ā) actually was: "Hector had packed the last of his parts and equipment into the back of his car and driven out of the track. He had not had a great day and evidently a lot of things were on his mind because the important thing he had forgotten to pack and take with him was his wife Olga. The poor lady was left standing in the pits. Hector had gotten a little ways down the road before someone caught up to him and told him that he left his wife at the race track."

In this age of throwaway frames when a car's life is often measured in weeks, it's amazing to realize that Honore ran that very same car for literally years! After his retirement, others bought, maintained and raced the car for another decade!

Perhaps because the history of some cars was as interesting as the drivers, certain ones have often been credited through the years with having a personality of their own. Unlike The Tank, Tamale Wagon or Black Deuce, which were defined by success, there are and have been cars that seemed as alive as a member of the crew.

"That's the funny thing about race cars," muses Jimmy Sills. "You can take two race cars out of the same jig, that were welded by the same guy, and they would work differently. Some of those cars wanted to win races, and some of them just wanted to make the night miserable."

Some cars perform so beautifully that the driver loves them more than a trophy girl with time on her hands. For Sills, it was a car owned by the Bailey Brothers Speedway Shop. "I drove for them for two years and the only time that car fell out of a race was because it broke a main web and block. That car was always ready to race and was always fast—even if it didn't have a wing. You couldn't do anything to screw up that car. You know what it does to your confidence level when you pull a car out of the hauler and everybody else is, 'Oh, gosh, we're gonna be running for second tonight.'"

"The real good guys—they got in tune with their cars a lot quicker than anybody else, so there was a comfort zone right away," adds Lynn Paxton. "It seems like every car, you have to tune in certain pieces and you know exactly how they react and what you could do to them."

Bub Dutton ran up onto Eric Gordon during hot laps at a 1993 weekly show at Bloomington, Indiana. So, was it driver error? Or did the car's personality take control? (Kevin Horcher Photo)

But personality is not always congeniality. A driver can ascribe certain traits to a car just as he would a person. Like people, some cars are thoroughly appreciated, some are basically ignored because there's nothing special about them, and some...well, some deserve the cutting torch.

"When I drove for Frank Lewis, we had three cars built that were all supposed to be identical," remembers Lealand McSpadden. "Right out of Gambler Chassis. One of the cars was like putting on a shoe. Another car was okay. And the other car was the most evil thing ever. I drove it three times, crashed all three times and flipped it twice. Five other drivers drove it and four of them flipped.

"The good one I called 'Bertha,' and that was the winningest car I ever drove. We ran it every time unless something was wrong with it. I finally crashed her at Bakersfield, they straightened the frame and sold it, and then she got crashed again, which was the end of her. But I ran her over 200 races."

Even as racers assign characteristics to a car, often they recognize that there is more going on here than an easy observation that "good" or "bad" was built into the car as surely as the tubing. "We called one of them 'Devil Car,'" notes Curt Michael. "We gave up on it and moved to a different car, but really, there's a lot of people who get it in their head, 'Oh, this car doesn't work.' I try to avoid that mindset for good reason. You can't always afford to go out and get another car, so I'd better learn to love it. I don't want to be one of those drivers telling the car owner who's spending all the money, 'You know, this car doesn't work.' I know drivers are head cases, but I try to control that."

Sometimes, it really *isn't* the car.

"I had a mental block about a car that I owned in 1976," Paxton continues. "I wasn't satisfied and I wasn't sure what the problem was. We were at a twin feature race at Reading, Pennsylvania, and one race was a rain-out makeup. Kramer Williamson was qualified for the first race but his car wasn't there. I asked him to run my car, even though he would be starting pretty far back. I said, 'I'm having trouble with it and I want to see how you feel about it.' So he took it out and gave it a hell of a ride. When I saw that, I thought, 'Well, hell, there ain't anything wrong with that thing.' And I think it helped me clear my head."

Even without help from another driver, sometimes the racer has to stop hating the car and take a different approach because there's no other choice. "We had a car we took to the start of the World Series in Western Australia and we'd not been having any success with it at all," recalls Skip Jackson. "So, my brother Paul and I decided that we had done everything we should do, so now we'll do the *opposite*. We totally changed everything on the car—and it was awesome!

"We didn't touch that car the rest of the year, and we were really, really good. Ever since, I'll think about that car and when I think my current car is set-up like it's supposed to be but I'm not going anywhere—well, let's try the opposite!"

Whether drivers ascribe personality traits or characteristics to individual cars or not, there's no question that they develop genuine affection for certain cars. In Rick Ferkel's case, it was this lovely car he drove later in his stellar career. (Courtesy Rick Ferkel Collection)

11

House Cars

When auto racing rebounded in America after World War II, most successful drivers had to learn how to build their own cars. Ingenuity flourished, and conformity floundered for a while. Just as street vehicles had found a mass market when production lines resulted in widespread availability, specific needs in racing dictated that, sooner or later and probably at the instigation of rules intended to level the playing field, entrepreneurs would find a market in racing, too. Not many people recall that as early as the 1930s, there were actually a few production companies, which made the building/rebuilding much easier on racers—if more expensive. Among the more notable was Floyd "Pop" Dreyer's business, one of the first to offer complete sprint cars and other open-cockpit rollers, along with aftermarket components. His most famous car was driven by Duke Nalon to the 1938 AAA championship. Well ahead of his time in conceptualizing the jig as a method for producing consistent parts, Dreyer is thought to have produced more cars than any of his contemporaries.

Costs and a lack of consistent technical rules limited the advantage of production sprint car frames for nearly three decades. In the late 1960s and early 1970s, thanks significantly to a couple of familiar names, Bob Trostle and LaVern Nance, production frames became a viable business and way for the Saturday Night racer to be competitive.

As with most car builders through the years, it took a while for Trostle to become well-known outside his Des Moines base. Trostle's first A feature win came at Knoxville in the late 1960s with Earl Wagner behind the wheel. Ongoing success with his home-built cars propelled Trostle from the security of a machinist's job to the ever-uneasy world of building and selling sprint car chassis. With partner Dave Van Patten, the team hired many of the great Midwestern drivers, including Dick Sutcliffe, Roger Larson, Larry Kirkpatrick and the ubiquitous Opperman in 1968. Of all the great stars who wheeled the Trostle "house car" itself or a race car that

It was a hot day at Sedalia, Missouri, but Shane Carson and car owner Bob Trostle (far right) don't care. It's always comfortable in Victory Lane. (Courtesy Mar-Car Collection)

It was success in LaVern Nance's house car that secured the ride in Bob Trostle's house car for Shane Carson. Among their many stops was Volusia County Speedway in Florida. (Gene Marderness Photo)

was based at the company shop, the greatest boon to Trostle's reputation came with Doug Wolfgang. The "South Dakota Wolf's" career, without question, was also boosted by the association with Trostle.

It's pretty remarkable that they worked together for several seasons, even as Wolfie was fired or quit, only to come back to Trostle more than once. Both have what could be called strong personalities. Both are also pretty sure they know what makes a car go fast—correctly, but not always in the same way. Butting heads was as inevitable as the splits, and sometimes success was not sufficient glue to hold the team together. Succeeding drivers were delighted to be hired for the always-competitive Trostle ride, but often found Wolfie's exhaust fumes pungent.

"He had won everything the year before, so I guess I didn't realize it going in, but there isn't anybody going to replace Doug," recalls Shane Carson. "I was certainly glad they gave me the chance. It got me on the map, for sure, and we won the championship at Knoxville that first year as well as the NFCA championship. I won 23 features, and obviously going into that hadn't really won anything big, so it was great for me. But it was half the features they had won the year before."

Trostle hired Carson after seeing him win at Phenix City, Alabama, in 1977, about the only time the house car with Wolfie had lost. Carson thinks they wanted a young kid to mold into the driver they wanted, and the experience helped Carson's career just as it did so many other drivers who were fortunate enough to spend time in the Trostle ride. "I learned how to balance the car and keep it from crashing because it was a handful," he remembers. "It was one of those cars that was really light and really powerful. Had a lot of bite. Those cars were hard to drive because they were just right on the edge of crashing all the time. Doug told me it took him weeks to figure it out, and he had three or four bad flips before he figured out what *not* to do."

Carson and Wolfgang also drove the Nance house car at different times in their careers, but Shane was one of the earliest to hit the road and help establish Nance's business. "LaVern was a great, home-taught, blacksmith-type sprint car builder," says Carson. "He built racing parts and started the business when there really weren't many production builders."

It had not been an easy progression. Eldest of eight children, LaVern left home at age 15, following the death of his father. The struggling family simply didn't need another mouth to feed. After several years as a drifter that included 14- to 15-hour days picking cotton by hand, LaVern met his future wife Marvell. That was the first smart thing he did. The next was hiring on at an aviation company during World War II. In time, he supervised over 800 employees and had accumulated a fair amount of income that was well-managed by Marvell. Restless for new challenges, he opened his own company, fabricating parts for the many aviation companies in the Wichita area. With his love of speed, however, Nance's family business soon provided parts and chassis for racers, too. Inevitably, he ended up chasing sprint car races over the road himself, if at a bit of a modest pace initially.

The Nance Speed Shop in Wichita, Kansas, 1983. (Rick Standridge Photo)

LaVern Nance with one of his cars. (Mike Evans Photo, Courtesy Warren Vincent Collection)

"We didn't crash a lot, which was a good thing," recalls Carson. "We'd go to a race series and he'd have just one of everything. Florida got us on one of those trips. We had won at Phenix City on the way down, which got me the attention that led to the Trostle ride later. That was my first sprint car win so we were on top, thinking we were gonna go down there and clean up. Then I turned over leading at Lake City, and then blew up hot-lapping at Golden Gate Speedway in Tampa. We were done for like three months because we had to get the motor re-done."

Unlike the sometimes prickly Trostle, Nance was blessed with an even-tempered personality that made him well-loved among the many drivers who turned laps in the Nance house car. Among those who struck gold driving for Nance were Eddie Leavitt, Jack Hewitt, Jimmy Sills, Jan Opperman, and a very young Al Unser Jr. They were just some of the racers who recognized LaVern's accumulated knowledge and appreciated his innovative approach. Working for and with the aviation industry, LaVern had learned a great deal about exotic metals and was the first to expand their use in a wide range of areas within the sprint car and engines.

Shane Carson prepares to go on the track during the period he drove the Nance house car. (Shane Carson Collection)

Although LaVern sold off the business in 1993 and his influence had ebbed somewhat by then, his name had been etched in sprint car history, and would have been even if he had done nothing else but team up with Sammy Swindell.

It's a wonder that these two very quiet men communicated enough to make the car always better. The sparsity of words might have been the secret of their success, as neither was known to waste air through the vocal chords. Undoubtedly, Sammy's background was key.

Sammy Swindell in the Nance house car races Steve Kinser at East Bay in 1981. (Woody Hampton Photo, courtesy Warren Vincent Collection)

A second-generation driver from the Memphis region that produced so many exceptional drivers, at least in part because they challenged each other so much, Sammy had already won many feature events in modifieds, late models, midgets and sprints before he came to LaVern's attention. Sammy had also studied engineering in college while racing. He has noted that he needed the income from racing to pay for college, but the time that studying required took away from his ability to prepare for racing. If postsecondary education is viewed as a means to a fulfilling career, then Sammy's decision to drop out of a recognized institution and enroll in the University of Dirt Tracks was the correct one. Certainly, the formal knowledge was beneficial in propelling him to the forefront of his chosen field.

While Steve Kinser dominated WoO from the start, Swindell took the 1981 championship and repeated the following year driving the #1N house car. Since Swindell and Nance often chased individual races rather than titles, it comes as no surprise that they succeeded. With Sammy and other drivers, Nance won the Western World, the Gold Cup at Chico (California), the Pacific Coast Championship at Ascot Park, and the highly sought-after Syracuse Super Nationals.

At the peak of the Nance influence, which coincided with Trostle's success, too, Nance was turning out in excess of a hundred chassis annually. Yet, with his family's assistance at the shop, he always seemed to have time for his customers. No one did more to advance the concept of feedback to the Saturday Night racer.

But there was another house car that combined with Trostle and Nance to change sprint car racing forever from home-built to production cars.

There are others who deserve credit for changing sprint car racing through the years: Names like Osborne, Stanton, King, Maxwell, Stapp, Tobias, J&J, Maxim and Eagle are just a handful that come quickly to mind. But from the moment the Gambler car appeared on touring circuits, sprint car racing was never the same. Just as Ted Johnson was in the right place at the right time to meet a need that had risen in racing, Gambler's timing in the late 1970s was ideal.

Nance had been ahead of his time in experimenting with new materials, but some ideas, such as the all-

Jeff Gordon at Eldora in 1988. He's driving a Gambler. (Allen Horcher Photo)

aluminum car, simply went too far for the average racer to accept. Karl Kinser was an innovator who reined in the lightweight concepts to more tolerable limits, although his creations gave his team such an advantage that he didn't seem especially anxious to rush his ideas out among the general population. Besides, Kinser didn't have the time, or seemingly the temperament, to run a major manufacturing and/ or distribution set-up such as Bill Smith's supply house Speedway Motors or the Nance Speed Shop were doing. The sprint car evolution needed an outlet.

Enter C. K. Spurlock.

A lifelong racing fan, Spurlock had just wrapped up a decade as a very successful entertainment promoter, with a client list that included several superstars. Having fattened his bank account, he could think about expanding his horizons, and at that time was fielding the Loretta Lynn Special sprinter along with Charlie Swartz.

Swartz has a well-deserved reputation for always being on the cutting edge, a thinker ahead of most of the competition, and he was already successful in both sprint cars and late models. In fact, Swartz's Wedge late model would revolutionize short track racing aerodynamics a few years later. With the financial backing from Spurlock, Swartz became a real force in sprinters, too.

Although Spurlock had bought from existing sprint car production companies, he got to thinking there was a better way to not only provide chassis and bolt-on, aftermarket pieces, but to do so in a way that spread the technology out to far more racers than Kinser or Nance or even Speedway Motors were doing at the time.

First, he had to develop a reputation that garnered attention and get the kind of standing that established the company as some sort of an authority. It also meant being competitive in pricing to ease the qualms among the ever-suspicious racing crowd, who know that there's always a line of people looking for ways to get into their wallets.

It was serendipity that Gambler and World of Outlaws started about the same time, but that's often the case with success in business and racing. Being in the right place at the right time is key. Spurlock cleverly glamorized his enterprise with a direct tie-in to his client Kenny Rogers, whose biggest hit song was "The Gambler." Although drivers of the house car say they never got to hang out with Rogers and only saw him at publicity photo shoots, there was something undeniably cool about driving the Kenny Rogers Special.

All this would never have been enough to make the company successful. The wins—especially the wins, accessibility for technical back-up, and competitive pricing shot Gambler to the top of the list. "He kind of started the Wal-Mart of car racing," muses Danny Smith, viewed by many as the first house-car driver for Gambler, even though Spurlock had earlier raced with notables like Swartz, Dub May and others.

"Part of what he saw as necessary was making cars, kits and parts that fit and you didn't have to fiddle around or do anything except bolt it together," recalls Smith. "That's what he wanted, and he didn't stop until he found the people who could make that happen. In a very short time, that's what he got."

Because Spurlock still had his hand in entertainment promotion and other business concerns, he was dependent upon good employees. He knew that in many ways they would be the daily face of Gambler Chassis. Probably no one fulfilled that role better or for a longer duration than Tommy Sanders. At various times, others also provided racer tech support, including the late Ken Jenkins, who worked at almost every major chassis company during his career and was already well-known when he came to Gambler in 1982. Spurlock was never afraid to hire the right people, especially during Gambler's hey-day from the early 1980s through the mid-1990s.

Winning races in the house car was critical to continued success, and one of the very first employees may have helped cement Gambler's reputation for

performance. Kenny Woodruff is possibly the most famous and respected mechanic in sprint car history. As chief wrench for Gambler in 1979-1980, it was a heady period that made "names" of the company, including the young driver Smith, and Woodruff, too. "Spurlock was doing whatever it took to sell the cars, and he wanted them to run up front," recalls Smith. "He told me to knock off the front bumpers. He didn't want to see any rear bumpers knocked off. As long as I was going forward and knocked off the front bumper, he'd buy as many front bumpers as we needed."

He continues, "Part of whatever it took was getting the right mechanic. That was hiring Kenny Woodruff, one of the most demanding mechanics there ever was."

An Iowa native with a Midwestern work ethic, Woodruff had gone west to California at a young age, working days in a factory while being involved at night with race cars. He quickly made a name for himself on the NARC circuit. Woodruff captured Spurlock's attention as wrench on the Jimmy Boyd ride that won the first-ever World of Outlaws race.

Woodruff's importance to establishing Gambler's reputation probably can't be overstated. But, when viewed within the context of his overall career, that was only part of his success, not the pinnacle. In fact, over many years, Woodruff has provided rides or wrenched for nearly all the top drivers. In 1989, working for former New Mexico Lieutenant Governor and Albuquerque Ford dealer Casey Luna, Woodruff guided the team and driver Bobby Davis, Jr. to the World of Outlaws title.

It was a special accomplishment in that it was a Chevy Bowtie world

Considering that they both started out in the Southwest, it's not terribly surprising that Lealand McSpadden ended up driving for car owner Casey Luna. Lealand became one of the best drivers crisscrossing the country. Casey went on to win the World of Outlaws title with Bobby Davis Jr. as driver and Kenny Woodruff as crew chief. (Win-Di Publishing Photo)

within sprint car racing. Luna was responsible for getting sufficient support from Ford to develop the 351-cubic-inch Cleveland V8 as an alternative motor, and in addition to a new name atop WoO standings, there was also a new engine.

The competition for the 1989 title chase was diluted because it was the year that several of the top drivers decamped to the brief USA circuit, but there was no such break for Woodruff in 1995. With Dave Blaney at the wheel, the team secured the championship. Curiously, the expressive Woodruff and the low-key Ohioan Blaney were a force to be reckoned with for five very rewarding seasons.

While Woodruff's later career was solidified by victories at the Kings Royal, Gold Cup and Knoxville Nationals among other significant wins, it was those early seasons at Gambler that gave him the opportunity to try new ideas and combinations, often successfully and often providing feedback that helped racers all across the country.

"There was always plenty of stuff for replacements," adds Smith. "We went through seven or eight chassis in 1980, but I was on the gas, you know, doing what he wanted."

Gambler was always changing, tweaking, trying to improve the product, but there was one particular development that made them stand out, and that was figuring out how to make the car work on dry-slick tracks. Midsummer and later around the country, racers could count on far more slicked-up tracks than heavy ones. "In the Gambler days, those cars were built to hook up when it was dry," confirms Smith. "I may have had a little overkill in the hook-up department sometimes. We would get to the heavy race tracks, and we had a lot of crashes because the cars were too tight and hooked up too much. It didn't take much to turn one over. But on the hard, slick tracks, it was a different story."

Crucial to the company's success was that what Smith learned was then shared with anyone who had a Gambler. The company was freer than anybody to that point had seemed to be. Then, when the biggest star of the series, Steve Kinser, climbed into one of the chassis, it was huge. "You could get the same car Steve Kinser was driving right then," confirms Smith. "You'd just go buy it."

But, like anything in racing, chassis are cyclical. The top dog always has others nipping at his heels, and often when a top star is lured away to a competitor, the lemmings will follow. It's especially difficult for the driving forces behind a company to retain the 24/7 intensity it takes to remain on top. After a long and glory-filled run, Gambler faded. Whether Spurlock lost interest or the contentious issues that cropped up internally hastened the demise, he now runs a motorcycle chassis company, also called Gambler. Spurlock still promotes entertainment although there are fewer A-List stars in his camp, reflecting another industry that appears to be cyclical in nature. At any rate, when Gambler folded as a sprint car company and aftermarket manufacturer, Maxim, Eagle and J&J, along with a host of smaller but effective companies such as Doug Wolfgang's

Wolfweld, have jumped into the breach.

"Spurlock wanted to win races, but then when Gambler took off, I think it became a matter of selling cars for him," says Smith. "He did what he wanted to do and then he quit going to the races, quit having his own car. The price of chassis hasn't really gone up over the years, not by very much, and there were opportunities to make some money other ways, so I think he just kinda let the sprint racing thing go."

As Kenny Rogers sang in that signature song, "You got to know when to hold 'em, know when to fold 'em."

12

Wheelmen

"I did things a lot of people wouldn't do," Lealand McSpadden reflects on his career. "If I thought I could pass everybody on the outside and nobody was up there I would try it. But, you know what? Nineteen others can't always be wrong."

McSpadden earned a well-deserved reputation as one of the most entertaining drivers in sprint car history. He won races with genuine flair—and he crashed as spectacularly as anybody ever has. "I don't want to sound like I was never scared," he says, "because I respected racing and what could happen. I thought about what I could lose a lot more than most people thought I did. But I've been flying through the air upside down and wasn't scared."

This photo leaves you wondering if you are holding the picture right side up! This is A.J. Booher flipping over an unidentified driver during a CRA event at Terre Haute in 1990. (Allen Horcher Photo)

He won a lot of respect from his fellow competitors for the way he did everything, always with consideration for others while never backing off. That comes from self-confidence, and it's a commonality among great drivers.

"You talk about confidence," says Rick Ferkel, "you see it in a guy like Donny Schatz or Steve Kinser, guys like that. Once you get to winning, it's almost like you can't stop winning. You get on a roll and you get confidence that you can handle anything, and I tell you what: It's pretty tough to beat you. But you need the whole package. It doesn't take much to upset the combination that worked for you. And once you're not winning, as even great guys like that will find out someday, it seems like it's impossible to win. A lot of people underestimate how important self-confidence is."

When a driver loses his groove it becomes something to wrestle with, as Lynn Paxton shares: "Keith Kauffman came into his own and started winning. There was nobody going to stop him—he had all kinds of natural talent. In other words, it went from me being King of the Hill at Port Royal to him taking the crown away from me. I enjoyed seeing him go from a kid who couldn't hit his ass to being competitive for so many years. But you hate to be the one who has to get out of the way."

For Paxton—and for many others—when the luster faded, so did the intense desire that had secured so many wins. He called it quits even as he was still considered one of the guys to beat.

Others are happy just to be at the track. As Richard Griffin says, "It wasn't the end of the world when the wins got harder to come by, and we were still having fun. We were disappointed but we never let it interfere with having a good time. Through my whole career we have always tried to have a good time and wherever the chips fell, they just fell. Sometimes

Richard Griffin, smiling because he's won the SCRA feature at Eagle Raceway, Lincoln, Nebraska, June 8, 2001. (Bill Taylor Photo)

Richard was one of the drivers who realized along the way that it's not a dress rehearsal, so he tried to make the most of opportunities that came his way. (Steve Lafond/Tear-Off Heaven Fotos)

I think if I had been a little more focused and done things differently, it might all have turned out a little different. But it was what it was. I'm good with that."

Walking that fine line can be especially difficult for those who are naturally talented, especially when they are young and enjoying immediate success. Such a person was Jimmy Sills. "Winning early was bad because then I thought I was *supposed* to win every week after that, and so did everybody else—my car owner, my crew and everyone. So, man, I over-drove that thing—and then I got really good at fixing it because I brought the car home with something off of it pretty much every week."

These days, Sills runs a sprint car driving school in Northern California, which allows him to keep more than just a hand in racing. If nothing else he can help youngsters understand that it's a different horse from the

(Left) Fred Rahmer qualified mid-pack on June 2, 2008, at Grandview (PA) Speedway. And he packed up and left the track after qualifying. It simply wasn't up to his high standards. (Allen Horcher Photo)

(Below) Dub and Van May, maybe the best brother-driving duo to ever come out of Florida by way of central Pennsylvania. (Gene Marderness Photos)

stock cars that so many begin with today. "Nothing relates to this type of racing except that you are going fast and there is a gas pedal and a brake," he notes. "Otherwise, it's a whole other discipline."

An experience such as Sills' school can be an enormous help in preparing for a career in sprint cars but the mental aspect of driving is just as important. Developing a philosophy isn't something a lot of drivers do, but doing so can make a more productive career.

"Dub May is a really, really interesting guy to talk to," notes Ferkel. "Dubbie has so many philosophies about stuff. He had everything always figured out. Him and his brother Van were the first to come around with coilover cars, which is part of what made them successful. But he took it beyond that to a mental deal. Like, if he wasn't running, say fifth or better, he would pull in because he figured that whatever he was making running on the track wasn't going to cover what it was costing him to be out there running."

Whether a driver thinks through all the aspects of racing in the detail that Dub did, there are a couple of areas in racing in which a driver has control: how he conducts himself *on* the track—and how he conducts himself *off* the track.

Although this car is called "Lucky Lady," many of Hooker's cars had "Rawhide" painted on the nose as a tribute to his father, who was the old television show's biggest fan. (Courtesy Hooker Hood Collection)

Few in sprint racing history have had a better handle on how to deal with other drivers, pit personnel and fans than Hooker Hood. It wasn't a calculated effort to make children adore him and ensure they would continue to be fans after they grew up, but it happened because Hooker was a sucker for the kids. As a result, he started handing out the trophies he won. "I still got about 150 of them left, but I used to give my trophies to the kids," he says. "A little boy or little girl would come up to me and I could see their eyes were big as half dollars, looking at that trophy. I'd ask if they wanted it, and if they said, 'Oh, yes, sir, I sure do,' well, I'd give it to them." He chuckles, "People come by here once in awhile and tell me that their kids still have those trophies."

Many drivers who grew up around racing came to make kind gestures toward junior fans. They realize how it impacted themselves as kids and how much they still admire those veterans who took the time to smile and talk with them. Being considerate to the adults has been no less important to many careers. However, the guy who turns out to be the biggest sweetheart in the pits after the races doesn't always bear resemblance to the guy who just ran the feature. One of those Jekyll-Hyde characters was a Midwestern driver by the name of Larry Gates.

You can take it to the bank that Larry Gates ran every bit as hard to win this race at Putnamville as any major sprint car show he ever ran. That's just his approach to racing. (Allen Horcher Photo)

Larry blows a motor–big time. (Kevin Horcher Photo)

Short, stocky, with the demeanor of a bulldog, Gates didn't even notice all the people who took the long way around him on foot in the pits. He was so intense that when Ken Schrader once told Larry about leading 99 laps only to lose on the final round, Gates' response was, "I'll tell you what—before I let somebody pass me on the last lap, I'd lean out and take a bite out of their roll cage."

No one doubted that. But, one fan recalls walking up to him (figuring, *okay, he might snap my head off, but I really want his autograph*) and being flabbergasted when Gates smiled and in a surprisingly high voice reminiscent of Tiny Tim said, "Sure, not a problem."

The vocal chords just didn't fit the earlier scowl.

Doug Wolfgang also had the reputation of being a completely different person on the race track than he was away from it. "We were all 'enemies' to him," Jimmy Sills believes. "He stayed at my house and helped me with my race cars, but when he got his 'race face' on, he wouldn't even recognize you at the race track."

One of the former sprint drivers who is still a lightning rod for controversy about his temperament is Tony Stewart. While he was always a force to be reckoned with—on and off the track—not everyone realizes what a long, long memory he has, especially for people who were good to him in the early days.

Allen and Kevin Horcher have been taking photographs for many years and were waiting on a rain delay at Bloomington, Indiana, some years ago, before Tony's stardom. Jeff Gordon was there—already a NASCAR star—and fans were literally stalking the parking lot looking for him. But Allen had spotted Tony in his car also waiting out the weather.

It was a rusty Mazda. No posse with him. Fans were cruising by the car without recognition, because his presence was not yet registering on many radars.

"I took a photo over to his car and tapped on the window," remembers Allen. "Asked him to sign it, and because it was still sprinkling rain I sort of held it inside the car. He asked if we were in the nice conversion van a little ways over, and I told him that it was our friend's. Well, he suggested we go over there, and he would sign the photo. I told him I had brought it to him so he wouldn't have to get out of his car. And he kind of looked up at the roof and said, 'Does your van leak?' Well, he came over and stayed talking until it quit raining. And from that day forward he has always spoken to us, been accessible and a truly good guy. I'm not sure how much of it goes back to that day, but I believe Tony would be exactly the same person today even if he was still driving the rusty Mazda, because he hasn't really changed at all."

Dirt is a bitch. No two track surfaces are the same and no one track surface is the same all night. That's why sprint car drivers are so coveted

Even as a young guy in 1982, Danny Lasoski was always on the gas. He figured out early in his career how to make a car work whether the track was heavy or dusty. (Allen Horcher Photo)

A smooth track invites pure speed, a great car and the perfect set-up. Those factors worked for Curt Michael at the Syracuse Mile in the fall of 2001. (Art Ruppert Photo)

The World of Outlaws ran on the Springfield Mile just once, but once was enough. The big ole track just ate up all the tires on every car that didn't blow an engine. (Joyce Standridge Photo)

And then there are the tracks that nearly shake the fillings out of teeth. Note the screen wire over the nose opening to the radiator and the cockpit that Lenard McCarl required when racing at North Star Speedway (MN) in 1972. And yet, Lenard won races and championships on rough old tracks and looked forward to racing on the most challenging surfaces. (Courtesy Lenard McCarl Collection)

by NASCAR owners. When track conditions change good drivers adjust. Smarter drivers also recognize that certain conditions are to their liking and use that to their advantage.

Almost any adequate driver can run well on a heavy, smooth track with a nice cushion. But getting side bite in the turns of a slick track requires a complete adjustment in how and when you enter, drive through and exit. If you have a lot of horsepower, it can be a trick to avoid breaking the tires loose on the straightaways. That's a condition definitely requiring more finesse, and it's not a commodity found in every driver.

Then there are the track surfaces from hell.

"We used to race at North Star Speedway in Minnesota, which is now closed, and it was really bad," says Lenard McCarl. "But I think I ran first or second about half the time I ran there. It was a terrible old track—rocks, dirt, holes and crap. But you just had to suck it up and take it into the turns hard."

"I liked a hole-y track," insists McSpadden. "Some people learn to use the holes to their advantage and you kinda have to manhandle it more. I won a lot of races on dry, slick tracks because I could be adaptable, but I feel like I really had an advantage when it was high-speed and rough. You have to give a little extra effort, and not everybody is willing to do that."

Motivation is every bit as important as self-confidence. Some drivers have responded to seeing a track just exactly the way they want it, whether it's smooth, dry or rough. Others have additional reasons for digging down deep inside themselves and finding that little extra something it takes to beat other equally motivated people.

"If I walked through the gate and all I had was $25 in my pocket," says Bobby Allen, "I knew I was going to beat anybody they could throw up against me."

When Tony Stewart and Steve Butler got together during a 1992 USAC show at Salem, Tony went sailing over the fence. Before the rescue people could even retrieve the car, Tony climbed back over the fence–and began going through the pit area in search of a replacement ride for the rest of the evening. (Allen Horcher Photos)

Money—or lack of it—will do that. So will the eternal chase for points. A fan recalls seeing Steve Butler spin out during a USAC heat race at Salem, Indiana, and Tony Stewart collide with him. Butler flipped on the track, and that served to be a ramp for Stewart—who went sailing over the wall.

At this race there hadn't been enough cars for a full feature field, so all anyone had to do was finish the race to be assured of a starting spot. But no one can ever recall seeing Tony "dog" a race.

So, he found himself bounding over the fence.

The car was destroyed, and the driver was a little battered, too. Fans who've watched racing at the high banks of Salem or Winchester over the many, many years of those tracks' histories have an abundant number of horrendous tales to tell about wicked—even fatal—wrecks. So, the "victory" that afternoon had to be that Tony felt good enough to climb back over the wall on his own.

However, instead of packing up and going home, as most sane people who've just ridden a sprint car out of the park would do, Smoke began walking through the pits, going from car to car asking whether he could drive them. He was in a serious points battle, and if you wonder whether it was worth it, think about where he is today.

"He can jump in anything and drive it. He's just a hard racer and he wants to win," says Bobby Allen about Stewart. "In Australia, I got to know him, and he crashed a car I was supposed to race—tore off the fuel tank. But it was because he tries so hard, and I love all the drivers who drive hard because their hearts are in it."

"Everybody learns from mistakes. That's just part of life," notes Paxton. "You wreck, you figure out what you did wrong, and you climb back in a race car. If you didn't, well, pretty shortly there wouldn't be any drivers left, would there?"

It's also sometimes necessary to figure out what to do by flat-out asking for help. Even veteran racers are sometimes baffled by a track, and it's always smart to pick the brain of the guy who has it figured out.

In the case of mash-the-gas Richard "Mitch" Smith and his friend Lynn Paxton, what one did wouldn't usually work for the other because of very different driving styles. However, on an impossibly hot, dusty Labor Day at Port Royal Speedway in eastern Pennsylvania, Smith was going nuts trying to figure out how to deal with the cushion-less powder on the track. After talking with Paxton for a few minutes, he announced that he was going to mount a set of double-steps (knobby Firestone tires) and raise the gear ratio.

"Oh, my God," thought Paxton, "this is going to be a disaster."

It's not hard to figure out what drew this crowd at the 1976 Labor Day Port Royal race: the track announcer is speaking with Indy 500 winner Rodger Ward and Posse ace Lynn Paxton. (Courtesy Lynn Paxton Collection)

Jerry Blundy—look at those rear tires! Knobbies were the trick deal for a while—but then so was the lack of a roll cage! (Courtesy Jeff Moe Collection)

The green flag fell, Smith shot rooster tails dozens of feet in the air and proceeded to blast from the back of the pack to the front. Nobody else could get close to him. Then after the win, he thanked Paxton on the P.A. for the hot set-up, but the truth was, says Paxton, "Every time afterwards that he went to a race track that got that way—powder with no cushion—Mitch would try that set-up, and it would never work. It only ever worked that one day."

Even the best, most adaptable drivers recognize that they have an identifiable driving style. McSpadden's style, he admits, is, "pretty wild. I don't think of it that way, but I listen to people and watch films. It's kind of funny but when I raced, I didn't really race people. I was racing the track and getting the most out of what I had that day. As a result, I've crashed leading by a half a lap. I would never intentionally take anybody out or put anybody in harm's way, but I used to do things you really shouldn't do. I would try things, and crash trying them. I tell people today that I went over the limit so many times that I know where that fine line is."

Most drivers will also tell you that they have a preference for a specific line on the track. Bobby Allen was noted for running the low line, possibly better than almost anyone else. Many drivers will tell you that's actually harder to do because it requires a good set-up. You can't just lean on the cushion or use it to help turn the car. "It made sense to me that the bottom was better because it's farther around the top," adds Allen. "But if everybody was on the bottom, I'd go up top to run. Much of the time, though, I noticed that the top tends to give up and you could win from the middle or bottom. The guys who run best consistently, like Kinser, know how to run both."

"I was usually the guy who went to the cushion first, and if it didn't work, then I was, 'Oh, shoot, guess I'm gonna have to go the bottom,'" recalls Sills. "It takes a lot of patience on the bottom, and I wasn't a driver with a lot of patience. I was always better if there was something to lean on."

Sills' fans can confirm that watching him work the high line was worth the price of admission, as was Paxton, another of the masterful rim-riders. But Paxton adds another thought that is often lost on fans, especially those who don't get to interact with drivers later: "You could win four races in a row and then you come back the next night and run fourth. Still respectable, but the worst thing you've got to face are the fans coming down, asking, 'What happened?' How do you tell them you raced a hell of a lot harder running fourth than you did to win the week before? You have to be a racer to understand that."

Successful drivers know the importance of watching and learning from other hot shoes. "When people come to my school," says Sills, "I tell them that I can teach them how to get around that specific track. But when they go to their track, there are gonna be different shut-off points, you're gonna turn in a different place, and the best teacher at that point is the guy who is going fast around there. You want to pay attention to how he's driving and watch from the outside of the track—see what line he's using and where he's lifting. When is he back in the throttle? How hard does he come back in the throttle? And then when you follow him, you see what he's doing and that helps you go faster, too."

On the World of Outlaws series, observing can be especially instructional. "When you do this long enough you figure out that the guys pretty much bring their 'A game' every night," confirms Daryn Pittman. "We put more pressure on ourselves to do good in front of a bigger stage, but I know for a fact that I don't try any harder to win at Knoxville than anywhere else. And I can promise you that Donny Schatz and Steve Kinser try just as hard to win at the smallest track we run as they do the Knoxville Nationals."

Of course, sprint car racing is much more than just a solo act. In addition to figuring out where a driver wants to run on the track, he or she has to deal with the rest of the field, too. "Racing with the World of Outlaws—I enjoyed all those years," says Johnny Herrera. "Racing with the same group of guys every week, you knew they would race you hard, but they were gonna give you room, and you were gonna give them room. They were just not going to run through you or over you."

Johnny Herrera racing at Knoxville. (Gene Marderness Photo)

"On the Outlaw tour, 95 percent of them are good racers, and we just don't crash that often. When we do, nine times out of ten it is just strictly from racing hard," notes Pittman. "We can go through less equipment than the local guys who run maybe only 15 to 20 nights, just because they get caught up in wrecks. When we do crash—it's big. But that's just because we're racing really hard."

Sometimes the guy you have to race the hardest and know you have to beat is the guy in the next pit. If he's your teammate, there are a whole new set of issues to balance. "Smokey Snellbaker was my partner an awful lot," recalls Paxton. "There were times he didn't have a ride and he'd run my second car. When we raced we could run side by side and never have a problem. Charlie Lloyd used to say, 'When you and Smokey got together it was going to be fierce but fair. You will lay it on the line without taking the other person out.'"

It was also a mutual admiration society for Paxton and Bobby Allen—sometimes to their detriment. "I can remember a couple of times we both were going for the same hole and we backed off—both of us—and let the

Aaron Berryhill has taken a few rides during his career but this one at Tri-City (IL) Speedway in 1993 during a World of Outlaws show was memorable because, while about everything else on the car was hurt, the wing was intact after he landed outside the track. (Allen Horcher Photos)

hole go by because neither of us would take a chance of hitting the other."

Not everybody races that way. Paxton labels Mitch Smith as one of those drivers who gave 120 percent every race—on *offense.* "You have to be defensive sometimes when you're racing," he explains. "I can live with an offensive racer making some contact here and there, if it's not intentional and he doesn't intend to make contact but he's got so much ability and so much belief in himself that he thinks he can put a three-foot wide car through a two-foot hole. Mitch was that kind of guy. In fact, once he bet a guy that he could take the lead—from 18th starting spot—on the first lap, and he really believed he could do that.

"He didn't make it.

"He put her clean out over the third turn, but that was his mentality. I've seen him do some fabulous things with a race car—and I've seen him do some dumb things—but he had such reflexes that he got himself out of trouble so many times. And you didn't do that with just luck."

Tony Robertson was okay, but obviously the car wasn't. (Marvin Scattergood Photo, Collection owned by Terry Young)

It can be difficult to associate with a hard-charger, though, after you've been on the receiving end. As Sills puts it, "You get into a deal where a guy does a slide job and you don't think he left you enough room. And you're pissed for a while, so it makes it really hard to get close to anybody. A lot of guys are good friends, but there's always that intensity that can get in the way."

"You race me clean, I'll race you clean. You don't race me clean," says Bubby Jones, "you're in big trouble. I didn't like to run into people but there's just some guys that sometimes you had to rough them up a little bit to get their respect."

McSpadden adds, "Jimmy Oskie and I became better friends after we quit racing just because the competition aspect was gone, and now it's just light-hearted fun."

Drawing the line between friend and competitor has always been an issue among racers, even back to the earliest days. On California's fabled tracks during the 1920s and 1930s, Ernie Triplett and Al Gordon were intense rivals. Reports from the era say that fans never sat down when the two dueled on the track, sometimes through an entire race. They seemed like the world's greatest combatants between the green and checkered flags, and yet off the track, they were great pals.

In possibly the most logical expression of how it was possible, Triplett was quoted as saying, "You can't run that way night after night, against a guy you hate. You have to trust him."

13

Diversity

Odds are pretty good that if you saw Johnny Herrera on the race track during a World of Outlaws show the thought going through your head was likely to be, "What a terrific driver." It's hard to believe that anyone was sitting in the grandstand, thinking, "Well, there's one for diversity."

The same could have been said about his dad Joe. Or another father-son duo, Shawkeet and Dion Hindi, also from Albuquerque. Shawkeet, was the 1977 New Mexico Motor Racing Association sprint car champion. Dion has been a frequent competitor on the WoO circuit in recent years, and rates an asterisk in the record books for having served as car chief on Donny Schatz's car at the tail end of 2005. That had been one of the rare

(Far left) Johnny Herrera takes a short break before climbing into his car. He's to be envied for having had a lengthy career driving race cars very well. (Mike Campbell Photo)

Dion Hindi at the 2007 Knoxville Nationals. (Mike Campbell Photo)

years in which Schatz endured a lot of frustration, but after Hindi came on board the team won six A mains. Dion is also an accomplished announcer who's been featured in a number of online racing broadcasts.

In the Southwest, diversity is part of everyday life. In big-time sprint car racing, quality finishes make people forget about focusing on the heritage under a helmet, possibly because there are no programs to propel careers on the scale of NASCAR's agenda. In fact, it's probably to sprint car racing's gain that a USCS driver with Native American genealogy, Danny "Hammer" Martin Jr., narrowly missed being selected for the NASCAR 2008 Drive for Diversity program.

Rajo Jack, born Dewey Gaston, became a premier driver on the West Coast in the 1930s. (Courtesy National Sprint Car Hall of Fame Collection)

It's usually improvident to make blanket statements, but variations within the Caucasoid or Asian races haven't seemed as big an issue for male drivers as it has been for two minority groups: women and African-Americans.

The status of black drivers hasn't moved forward a great deal in nearly a century. In fact, it has regressed since a brief, bright period in the 1920s and 1930s. That was a time of some fascinating racing tales, none more inspiring than that of Rajo Jack.

He was born Dewey Gatson just after the turn of the 20th century in Tyler, Texas, the oldest of six children. Although his father worked the railroads in the area, money was tight and teenaged Dewey was not discouraged from taking a position as a mechanic with a traveling medicine show. It brings to mind Richard Pryor's 1976 movie *Bingo Long's Traveling All-Stars & Motor Kings*.

The young Texan's racing career began in the Northwest during the 1920s, under the name of Jack DeSoto, though it's not clear why he felt the need to move or change his name. However, recall all the assumed names among the drivers through racing's history who, for one reason or another, didn't want people to know who was behind the steering wheel.

It was tough going for a while, and not just because he was a rookie. One of Jack's early match races was cancelled because the seat fell out of his car as he approached the green flag! But by the 1930s, he was fast. He had resettled in the Los Angeles area and by virtue of being the most successful salesman of the Rajo cylinder head that fit on the Ford Model T, he had been rechristened Rajo Jack.

One of the many tales about him is that he once loaded the pieces and parts of his race car onto the back of a flatbed truck and headed to a race in northern California. While his wife drove the truck over the bumps and curves of the two-lane highways of the day, Rajo Jack assembled the car and then finished an astounding second in the race.

Even with a racing record that any driver could envy, there was never any question that this was, some 60 years after the Civil War, still a time of segregation, even along the diverse West Coast. Rajo Jack often told promoters that he was Native American or Portuguese, and perhaps his reputation overcame at least some of the skepticism.

His entire career was spent as an outlaw driver, telling other racers that he would be unable to get an AAA license because he was blind in one eye and couldn't pass the physical. But observers said the lack of vision was actually with the sanctioning organization, which knew he was neither Native American nor Portuguese.

Rajo Jack always took his wife with him to the races because he knew that he couldn't kiss a Caucasian trophy girl if he won the race. He had to be sure that it was his wife who took the trophy from the girl and then handed it to him.

Nonetheless, his success earned him respect, demonstrated at least once in a remarkable show of solidarity from his contemporaries. On a particular road trip when Rajo Jack was refused food service, the white members of the group said they wouldn't patronize the establishment either. The owner caved and served Rajo Jack. Business trumped bigotry.

Rajo Jack died in 1956, almost penniless, divorced, and a nearly forgotten race driver. His passing was just a few months after Rosa Parks refused to give up her seat on a bus to a white man, the brief but signal event credited with starting the modern civil rights movement.

Another African-American driver of considerable merit was Joie Ray, who *did* get a license from AAA years after Rajo Jack's career was over. In fact, Ray was licensed on April 8, 1947, one week to the day before Jackie Robinson broke the color barrier in baseball to considerably greater notice

Joie Ray got his AAA license to race in 1947 exactly one week before Jackie Robinson broke the racial barrier in major league baseball. Here he is pictured in 1951 in the Pennington sprint car at Dayton, Ohio. (Billy Ray Collection, courtesy Dave Argabright)

and acclaim. A fine book has been written about Ray's life and career racing that featured some success in the Midwest, especially at short tracks in Ohio. He has since passed away, but Ray's accomplishments were significant enough that he was selected to be the Indy 500 pace car driver in 2003.

Among the black drivers in early sprint car history, however, there is another one whose career was so remarkable that it spawned an entire racing series.

Later, he would be known as "The Negro Speed King," but early on people called him "Wee" Charlie Wiggins. His diminutive size may have forced him to use a booster seat in the race car, but there was nothing small about his heart, intelligence, attitude or courage. Though not much bigger than a banty rooster and just as feisty, Charlie used his brains and talent far more than his fists.

For no reason other than his color, Charlie had the sign torn off his garage, rocks thrown through the garage window, and he was even attacked by Klansmen hiding in the bushes, waiting to gang up on him. "Ever try to get the blood out of your husband's shirt?" asked Roberta Wiggins during a PBS television special about Charlie and others who raced with him. "That was the worst thing of all."

Wiggins' fascinating saga began in his native Evansville, Indiana, where he worked as a child shining shoes outside an auto repair shop.

Charlie Wiggins, one of the great driving stars of the 1920s and 1930s. (Courtesy Mrs. Mildred Overton/Todd Gould Collection)

At a remarkably young age, Charlie could identify cars coming down the street by their sound. In short order, he could diagnose problems just by listening to the car, so it was no wonder that the repair shop owner invited Charlie inside to become an apprentice.

Before long, he moved to the segregated south side of Indianapolis and opened a shop of his own, but Charlie was so good that soon he was providing automotive repairs for people of all colors. In fact, as a kind of Pied Piper, he soon found that he had young men of all hues hanging around the garage, learning from a master and helping on the race car.

In July 1933, Charlie was shocked to open the local newspaper and find that one of those youngsters, John Dillinger, had been declared Public Enemy #1. Dillinger would be gunned down in the infamous Lady in Red FBI sting later, apparently without ever seeing Charlie again.

The Wiggins Special was put together with other people's rejects from the junkyard, not unlike most race cars of the day. Then in 1924, several things occurred that would forever change Charlie's life—and, to an extent, racing in general.

Charlie submitted an entry for the Indianapolis 500. The AAA rejected his entry, and Charlie was relegated to watching the race from the coloreds-only grandstand. Without excusing AAA, perhaps it helps to understand their actions in light of what was transpiring in Indiana at the time. While the South has often been the focus of this type of conflict, racism was sometimes at its ugliest in states where slavery had never existed to any extent. In 1924, the Ku Klux Klan stole the Republican party in Indiana, led by a charismatic charlatan by the name of D. C. Stephenson, who ran on a platform "in the name of Christian values and American patriotism."

The Klan swept all the statewide offices that election year and became the most powerful political force in the state. The attendant malice peaked several years later with the lynching of a black man on the Grant County courthouse lawn. Few black people were unaffected during this period. It was then that Charlie's garage—and person—were assaulted, with no follow-up punishment for those who carried out the attacks.

But some positive things were happening, even if they were framed within the Jim Crow laws of the day (separate, but equal, was the stated intention if not the outcome). Charlie had caught the eye of Indianapolis entrepreneur William "Prez" Rucker. With sponsorship backing, Rucker formed the Colored Racing Association, featuring a series of races in several Midwestern states and called The Gold and Glory Sweepstakes. The centerpiece race was the Indianapolis 100, held at the one-mile Indiana State Fairgrounds.

Not only did Charlie Wiggins win the Indianapolis 100 with his home-built Wiggins Special, but he went on to win the Gold and Glory Sweepstakes. During the brief period of the Gold and Glory, Charlie was the dominant driver. Here, he poses with his beautiful wife, Roberta. (Courtesy Mrs. Mildred Overton/Todd Gould Collection)

Critical to the new association's future, Rucker successfully enticed the entertaining African-American journalist Frank Young to journey down from Chicago and cover the race for the *Chicago Defender* newspaper. Before he made the trip, Young wrote: "Soon, chocolate jockeys will mount their gas-snorting, rubber-shod Speedway monsters, as they race at death defying speeds."

When Young arrived in Indianapolis, he sent back the following report: "Primed and groomed to the last notch, stroked and rubbed endearingly, no less than is any thoroughbred on the eve of a supreme test, 26 babies of the greatest engineering brains in America repose ready to be wheeled out on the Fairgrounds speedway..."

Hyperbole aside, Young was basically correct. The result was such a massive success within the African-American community that the young sanctioning body was assured of some future. It did not hurt that the very popular Charlie Wiggins won that inaugural event. Young observed, "Wee Charlie Wiggins, that plucky young mechanic from Indiana, had to build a special seat in his chassis to boost his tiny body so that he could reach the gears of his homemade creation. But at the end of this grand Gold and Glory event, it was not the mechanics that mattered, but the mechanic himself. As Wiggins crossed the finish line well ahead of the pack, a wild burst of applause greeted him from his hometowners, some of whom lost their heads and ran across the track, despite the yells from cooler heads, warning them that other drivers were still pushing their metal steeds at top speed for second place honors. In the end, no one was hurt, and Wiggins welcomed the stirring ovation."

Wiggins went on to victory in three more of these races and finished in the top five a total of ten times. His success did not go unnoticed across town. Journeyman racer Bill Cummings hired Wiggins to be a part of his crew at the big track in 1934. To get around the arcane rules at the Indianapolis Motor Speedway at the time, Charlie pushed a broom during the daylight hours because Negroes were limited to janitor roles back then. But after the officials went home at night, the team snuck Wiggins back in to the garage to fulfill his real role as mechanic.

And then Cummings—who had never had much success at the track and never would again—won the Indianapolis 500. You won't find Charlie Wiggins in the Victory Lane photos or listed as a team member in any of the newspaper write-ups of the time. But Cummings never did forget the contribution and throughout his remaining years acknowledged Wiggins' significant contribution.

When Harry MacQuinn asked to use Wiggins' car in a race at Louisville, Charlie agreed with the stipulation that he could hot lap and set up the car for MacQuinn. But when the grandstand crowd found out that a man of color was driving on the track—never mind that it wasn't even the official race—they stormed the infield. There was very nearly a repeat of the Grant County lynching that afternoon—stopped only when the police arrested Wiggins and took him to jail for his own protection. He was booked for "speeding."

Even during such times, great things were happening to the two dozen or so Colored Racing Association participants and their substantial number of fans. Recognizing the importance of presenting racing as entertainment, which clearly made Wiggins and Rucker ahead of their time, they offered a number of highly promotable ideas. One was a match race between Bill Jeffries and The Mystery Woman Driver.

Jeffries was a flamboyant African-American regular on the circuit. A Chicago bail-bondsman and real estate speculator, "Wild Bill" often showed up at the track wearing expensive suits and flashing diamond jewelry. Bling in the Jazz Age, no less. Jeffries was game for that Match Race in front of 15,000 fans in Cleveland— except that it never happened.

It turned out that The Mystery Woman Driver was Roberta Wiggins. And Roberta fainted dead away before the race could start—not because she was afraid, but because, it turned out, she was pregnant. That should be a happy turn to the tale, but the Wiggins couple had lost three infant sons to tuberculosis at earlier times, and this pregnancy ended prematurely. Doctors determined that Roberta would never again be able to carry a baby, a fact that was less important to Charlie than keeping his beloved wife. "Charlie said he was more afraid of losing me than anything he'd ever faced," Roberta said later.

Roberta and Charlie Wiggins share a laugh, something they certainly earned through a lifetime together that featured nearly as many tears as shouts of joy. (Courtesy Mrs. Mildred Overton/ Todd Gould Collection)

But the bad times didn't end there.

"Somebody's gonna get hurt today," Roberta told Charlie one racing afternoon in 1936.

"I don't feel good. I feel like something is going to happen," he responded. But later, before getting into his car, Charlie told her, "You can't ever be afraid. You have to face it."

Just as Charlie had faced the Klan when they marched down the street in front of his garage. Or when the racing "fans" wanted to lynch him. Or when he just butted heads with other drivers after "one-of-them-deals" on the race track. Charlie wasn't one to cower in the face of something as wispy as a strange feeling, and so, he climbed aboard the race car and started the race.

"My car was the sixth car into the wreck," said Al Warren during the Gold and Glory PBS special. "I don't know how I got out of [the car] so quick, but I got out, jumped over the fence and that's when I heard

Charlie yelling, 'Take it off my leg! Take it off my leg!' So I tried to lift the car, and about that time I looked back and heard the motors coming, so I jumped back. And sure enough, [one of them] hit Charlie's car and knocked it [sideways]…with him hanging there."

Thirteen cars were involved in what was called a fiery inferno in a newspaper account. Although Charlie was not burned, he was the only one in critical condition. Later, at the hospital, Roberta was pointed to a hard wooden chair in a lonely hallway and told to wait.

Wait, she did. Nearly 12 hours after the wreck, doctors finally came out to her and said that they had saved Charlie's life, but had been forced to amputate his leg. "They finally allowed me to see him," she said many years later. "I held Charlie tight. He seldom cried, but that day, we both sat holding each other, and we cried and cried. Racing meant so much to Charlie. And now we knew that his racing career was over."

Later, there would be a blood drive for Charlie among racing people of all races and genders. A gala would raise money to pay the exorbitant bills to follow. Charlie even made his own wooden leg on a lathe down at his garage and subsequently became a mechanic with a barnstorming show.

But nothing could change the fact that Charlie Wiggins, possibly the greatest African-American driver ever, would not wheel a race car again. With his career's demise, so went the Colored Racing Association and the Gold and Glory Sweepstakes. After 12 genuinely golden and glorious years, the circuit folded as precipitously as it had started.

Dr. Richard Pierce, historian at the University of Notre Dame, observed during the PBS special, "There are some people, and I think Wiggins is one, who can build a car and love it for that creation, but still push it because in his own life he realized that pushing yourself to your limit doesn't endanger you. It's what made you alive."

On August 2, 1924, Frank Young wrote in the *Chicago Defender* what should be the definitive words about the Colored Racing Association and the Gold and Glory Sweepstakes: "Of what will younger generations speak when they talk of the accomplishments of these great colored racers? Will it be that with heart and heavy-foot, they might become the fastest in the land? Or will it be that they did something far greater? For these men of grease and grit are a celebration of all that is grand for our Race. Let us hope that our children speak of the latter, for it is in this moment that we have achieved true greatness."

14

Women Drivers

Roberta Wiggins never did race a sprint car. But nearly a half-century later Cheryl Glass did, to considerable acclaim and anticipation. Fast forward another quarter-century, and all the promise of an African-American woman driver is no more than a fading memory, accompanied by myriad unanswered questions.

A remarkable woman on the cusp of a promising, but ultimately unfulfilled, racing career. (Tom Parker Photo)

For many who saw Cheryl race, primarily on the West Coast, hers is the story of unrealized potential. And for those who wondered about her disappearance from racing, Cheryl Glass' entire life is a tale more complex than anyone could have anticipated in watching something as focused as a sprint car on the track.

She was born on Christmas Eve, 1961, in a well-to-do area of northern California. Before Cheryl turned two, the family relocated to Seattle, where her father was a vice-president with Pacific Northwest Bell and her mother an engineer at Boeing. Even as a child Cheryl showed incredible precociousness, running a ceramics company while still in elementary school. She graduated from high school at 16 and studied electrical engineering in college. Then she stunned many people when she dropped out prior to graduating in order to pursue a full-time career in sprint car racing.

Her dad had started her at a very young age, winning in quarter-midgets and progressing into midgets, which she successfully drove until she was 18. When she started sprint cars, she told *The Seattle Times*, "I knew it wouldn't be easy. But I want it understood that I wasn't doing this as a publicity stunt. I'm serious."

Those who recall Cheryl from her sprint car racing days don't dispute that. They say she came to the track wearing her game face and that she raced with determination and skill. She wasn't one to back down to the boys but still presented herself as willing to meet people halfway.

"When I heard she was coming to the Western World Championship race in 1981, I did some press releases about Cheryl, and she did not disappoint," recalls Manzanita Speedway's long-time announcer Windy McDonald. "Everyone wanted to talk to her. She was both the first woman and the first black person to run the Western. It became, 'Never mind about Steve Kinser,' that night. She really knew what to say, and when she went out on the track there was no question she could drive. Then she got a little hot going into turn one and she flipped out onto 35th Avenue."

Cheryl with her dad, a business executive who shared his love of racing with her and was the driving force behind her racing career. (Tom Parker Photo)

According to a later press account, Glass "slammed into a post, [and] barrel-rolled along the wall 13 times. Broken blood vessels in her eyes blinded her for several hours. Several knee operations left her wearing braces on her lower legs and recovering for three months."

Probably because she had expressed a desire to go on to Indy (just like thousands of men throughout racing history) or possibly even on eventually to Formula 1, Cheryl didn't seem to make deeply personal and warm friendships at the track. She doesn't appear to have enjoyed the sense of community that makes the time, effort, money spent and unending travel worth the sacrifice for racers who make sprint cars a career.

As what might be called a "renaissance woman," with many diverse interests and abilities, her varied talents may have been—at least in terms of focusing on racing—a liability. When Cheryl married one of her race car mechanics in 1983, her extravagant, self-designed wedding dress literally attracted national attention. Even before the divorce a short time later, she made new headlines in the clothing industry, opening a clothing design studio. Cheryl was still very much in the Seattle limelight and apparently had not completely given up on her racing aspirations when that public eye had turned toward her artistic work. In a 1987 *Seattle Post Intelligencer* newspaper article, both Cheryl and her father Marvin expressed interest in making it to Indianapolis, as well as optimism that $500,000 in sponsorship money was just around the corner.

The newspaper spoke to a couple of racing participants to gauge Cheryl's potential to make it to Indy. Jerry Cope, a Tampa, Florida, engine builder who had seen Glass race said, "I don't think (Glass) is quite on that level yet. She's a very capable driver on the short track. She just needs to gain some super speedway experience. There's a great deal of difference there."

Cheryl Glass drove this sprint car for Jack Conner back in the 1980s. It has been restored and was on display at the National Sprint Car Hall of Fame and Museum in Knoxville, Iowa, during 2008. (Courtesy National Sprint Car Hall of Fame.)

Silver Crown cars often have a long life span and this one has been restored to its earliest look, but at one time it was owned by Charlie Patterson and driven by Cheryl Glass. She made the Hulman Hundred field in 1982 in it. (Courtesy National Sprint Car Hall of Fame)

Dave Craver, former president of the now-defunct Washington Racing Association, said, "I've seen her race on dirt and I've seen her race on asphalt. She was smooth and consistent and she knew what she was doing. I'd say she probably has the potential."

Cheryl got at least one Indy tryout, as well as encouragement from Lyn St. James, the multi-time Indy 500 competitor who has been instrumental in helping several young women advance their careers.

Cheryl seemed poised for a piece of fantastic racing history. And then not only did the half-million dollar sponsorship not materialize, she essentially disappeared from sight.

One bizarre night in 1991, Cheryl's upscale home was burglarized and a swastika smeared across one of the walls in lipstick. The media covered the break-in intensively. Six months later, Cheryl filed further charges alleging rape by two of the three men she said broke into her house, but the prosecutor's office—citing insufficient evidence—did not pursue the case. In the aftermath, she became a community activist, arguing, among other things, that she was not getting a fair hearing. Cheryl demanded that some of the public officials involved in the controversy resign as a result. None did. And then, for several years following the break-in, Cheryl and her neighbors waged an ugly and protracted series of apparently racially based verbal battles. Eventually the mess led to the arrest of Cheryl and a man on fourth-degree assault charges for having allegedly thrown rocks that damaged a car. "Some neighbors…need to prove all of us black people have mental problems," she told *The Seattle Times*.

Cheryl poses with her sprint car at Silver Dollar Speedway in Chico, California, September 27, 1980. (Tom Parker Photo)

When next she appeared in the newspaper, it was an article stating that on July 15, 1997, she had leaped off the Aurora Bridge, location-of-choice for many suicides in the Seattle area. Cheryl didn't leave behind a note, or apparently tell anyone what had driven her to such a shocking end. The official stance is that Cheryl took her own life. In the book *The Stranger Guide to Seattle*, published in 2001, the authors note that some of Cheryl's supporters believe she was pushed off the bridge, the victim of a Mafia hit because she allegedly had evidence of money laundering in auto racing. No hard proof of this theory has been presented in the decade-plus since Cheryl's death. No witnesses have ever come forward either, but the discussion adds fuel to the controversy that seemed to surround her life in the later years.

Did the sprinters lose a trailblazer when Cheryl quit racing? Undoubtedly.

Did the world lose a special talent when Cheryl apparently quit on life? It would seem so, and few sprint car tales are sadder on so many levels.

While gender alone is no longer newsworthy and the ranks of current drivers include a growing number of young women, the slow integration of female drivers into the ever-challenging sprint car world has meant that there are a limited number of women with a solid résumé of a decade or more experience. That becomes meaningful when viewed in the context of creating stars whom developing drivers can emulate, and fans can just appreciate.

In this 1950s photo, Helen Easton is on the left and next to Evelyn Shaheen. Helen's husband was one of the best midget drivers in AAA/USAC at one time and Evelyn's husband owned Springfield Speedway. As far as we know, neither actually drove these cars. And they don't look all that happy about posing for the photo. The other three women are unidentified. (Courtesy Jeff Moe Collection)

There were a few Powder Puff races in the 1950s and 1960s. These ladies were being introduced prior to a race. (Courtesy Jeff Moe Collection)

Youngsters have long had a plethora of male role models to choose from. The list of accomplished female drivers is growing steadily. At present, however, there are only a few, such as Sarah, Erin and Becca, whose first names are identifiable from coast-to-coast.

Sprint car racing was always simply a stepping stone for Sarah Fisher, but she drove so well and accumulated enough achievements as a sprint car driver to be accorded the respect that sprint car drivers deserve. Born in Ohio in 1980, Sarah followed in the tire tracks of most contemporaries when she began driving a quarter-midget at age five.

An only child, Sarah was an excellent student in school even though her racing career bloomed so quickly that she was featured on NBC's *Today* show when she was only 15 years old. At least some of her success can be attributed to a solid racing pedigree. Her father Dave is well-known within the racing community as her manager, but that was preceded by a sprint car career of his own. Sarah attended races from infancy to watch him, until he gave up his own interests to help his daughter. Less well known is that her mother Reba

One of the best female drivers ever–but especially so in sprint cars–Sarah Fisher at Macon (IL) Speedway, June 25, 1996. (Kevin Horcher Photo)

was a go-kart racer, and Sarah's maternal grandmother was one of the first female aviators in Ohio history.

As with every step in her career, Sarah has accumulated solid credentials. Holding the track record at the wickedly fast Winchester Speedway alone would speak to her fearlessness behind the wheel. She ran solid seasons with both World of Outlaws and the All-Stars before succumbing to the lure of big-time Indy car racing.

Erin Crocker's career development sounds very much like Sarah's. Involved in quarter-midgets from age seven, Erin racked up an impressive list of accomplishments. She raced mini-sprints while still in high school and was the Eastern Limited Sprints Rookie of the Year in 1999.

Running a second car in 2002 for seven-time Empire Super Sprint

Erin Crocker, Rookie of the Year at the 2003 Knoxville Nationals. (Mike Campbell Photos)

(Left) Becca Anderson during her World of Outlaws time in 2006. (Mike Campbell Photo)

(Right) Becca at Volusia County Speedway in Florida, February 12, 2006. (Gene Marderness Photo)

champion Mike Woodring, Erin won five A Features in the 360 class and they were named the 360 Team of the Year by the National Sprint Car Hall of Fame. The following year, in only her third time in a 410 sprint car, Erin became the first-ever woman to qualify for the Knoxville Nationals, becoming the 2003 Nationals Rookie of the Year. More accolades followed. Perhaps most importantly to her career development, Erin gained considerable respect from fellow competitors and fans alike in both the All-Stars and WoO, becoming the first woman to record an A Feature victory on the latter's tour in 2004. Not surprisingly, Erin has moved on to the challenging world of NASCAR racing.

Mike Woodring has also helped propel another female driver's career as car owner for Delaware's Becca Anderson in 2006 on the World of Outlaws. The similarities don't end there, as she has been involved with racing all her life. Becca got behind the wheel at age 11 and progressed through Micros to 358s and 360s. Eight feature victories on the tough URC circuit, including the prestigious URC/ESS Challenge at Rolling Wheels in New York, got her the kind of attention that leads to even better things. She also holds the sprint car track record at the mind-numbingly fast Syracuse mile. Although Becca has tested an Indy Pro Series car and participated in development programs, currently she is racing—and seems to be content doing so—on the URC tour, where she won again in 2008.

Mary Susan Stellfox, who became known as Mares (pronounced something like *Mare*-ess) may not be as well-known across the country, but she has something the rest of the ladies aspire to: a lengthy career. In sprint cars off and on for more than 20 years, Mares has developed a loyal following among URC fans in part for her stellar ability behind the wheel, but maybe as much for being a warm and approachable person when the engines shut off. More attractive than many trophy girls, the diminutive "Lady Outlaw" nonetheless has proven that once the helmet is on it's all about the racing—no quarter asked, no quarter given. Mares' story deserves telling if only to prove that courage isn't necessarily something that kicks in at 130 mph when a competitor sticks a wheel in.

She grew up in Pennsylvania, the fourth of five daughters, with a mother working three jobs. An absent father, she says, apparently wanted other women more than a home life and certainly didn't provide any support, financial or otherwise

Encouraged by her grandfather, she took an early interest in drag racing, which inadvertently led to Mares falling in love with and marrying a fellow drag-racing fan, Mark Stellfox. Not long after tying the knot, she found her true calling—at a mall, of all places. New Jersey's Bridgeport Speedway put on a car show at the mall in 1983 and Mares and Mark encountered old friends of his who owned a sprint car. That led to the couple becoming financially involved with the team.

Up to that point, Mares was not a sprint car nut. While most people respond to short-track racing instinctively, either loving or loathing it and not straying much from the initial feeling, Mares was that rare exception. "This sprint car dirt thing was not my bag," she laughs years later. "It was dirty and dusty. I used to sit at the track with my hands over my face, thinking, 'I can't believe I'm doing this.' But when you're in love with somebody and you are the dutiful wife, you do what your husband wants, to keep him happy."

Along the way, the girl who originally had aspired to become an NHRA top-fuel driver evolved into a young woman wanting to drive a sprint car. "Of course, at that time, it was like the biggest joke," she notes. "There weren't any girls. But I wasn't seeing much of Mark's paycheck, and I was thinking, 'You know, if he's gonna be spending all this money, I want to drive.'"

The career began with a micro sprint, and Mares first reaction to the car Mark brought home was, "You have got to be kidding! I want to drive a sprint car, and you buy me *this?*"

As things turned out, it was the right approach. "Especially being a girl, and being the first one racing in my area, if I had gone out and really messed up with a full-sized sprint car, then that would have given every woman who came later a bad name. Believe it or not, even with the micros, I had an awful time with the guys. I remember that when I first started, if there was an accident anywhere on the track, fingers were pointed at me even if I wasn't anywhere near. I was kind of surprised, but in the same breath, I realized those guys were as serious as the sprint car racers."

For example, in 1984 during her first year racing at Delaware's Airport Speedway, a frustrated racer crashed in turn four. He came raging into her pits afterward, even though she had been in turn one at the time of the wreck. He opined that she needed to be at home in the kitchen with her pots and pans, barefoot and pregnant. It was not the last time Mares encountered that diatribe.

She progressed rapidly and by 1987 was the local micro champion, although Mares and her sister had to make the argument with the officials, or she would never have been acknowledged because the officials had "forgotten" to add in one night's points.

The previous year at the banquet, Mares told Mark, "We are gonna get the championship next year because I really want that trophy."

When she garnered the championship, a funny thing happened on the way to the trophy shop. Apparently somebody forgot that the champion traditionally got a six-foot tall award. In 1987, the champion's trophy was smaller than the one she'd gotten the year before for finishing fourth.

Yet, for whatever small-mindedness she encountered—for her gender or any other reason—Mares continued moving forward as best as she could. She's been no Joan of Arc or other noble martyr along the way. There have been moments when she was so upset that she cried and told her family she wanted to quit. They, and especially her mother, gave her the kind of counseling every driver—regardless of gender, race, age, or finances—needs to hear to keep focused. She has made mistakes, admittedly sometimes said or done the wrong thing, and yet has continued on with a determination that young girls (and boys, too) ought to use as a guide. If you stay at this business long enough, there will be occasions that will threaten to break your spirit. Whether you are Doug Wolfgang recuperating from third-degree burns or Terry Average who had a bad night and flipped out of the track, you have to find a toughness inside of you that trumps the bad deals. If you don't, you'll become a *former* sprint car driver.

Mares' resiliency was clear after she became the first woman to qualify for one of midget racing's premier events, the Hut Hundred at Terre Haute, Indiana. Another competitor approached her following the driver's meeting and, out of the blue, asked, "Are you crazy?"

The driver went on to say, "Ya know, there's only two cars here without power steering and you're one of them. I wouldn't race this deal with no power steering."

She did anyway. Adrenalin kept her going and it was only during the yellows that she noticed her arms were a little tired. "But towards the end, I thought I was gonna die," she admits. "Still, I thought, 'No way am I gonna pull in—I am going to finish this race!'"

And she did. But she paid a price. That night, when Mark and their pit man left the motel to get something to eat, Mares found that she couldn't get her arms raised high enough to wash her hair in the shower. When the guys returned with a sandwich, she had to literally prop her elbows on the table to hold it.

"I think sometimes men thought they could intimidate me, and I did get intimidated a lot," she says. "I wish I could have been a different type

Mares Stellfox, racing in early 2008. (Jim Young Photo)

of personality, but growing up without a dad around, I wasn't used to being around men. But that time, at the Hut Hundred, I wasn't going to let what the other driver said keep me from finishing that race!"

Mares needed that determined spirit more than ever when she got into the full-sized sprints. "First I had trouble with the guys because they didn't want me racing with them. Then when they started to accept me, I had problems with the wives and girl friends," she recalls. "They don't want you there because they think your presence can't simply be because you like the sport. It has to be because you are after a man—maybe their man."

Whether mechanic, car owner, official or driver, almost every woman who works in some capacity at the race track, echoes that sentiment. While Janet Guthrie is often credited with tearing down the barriers for women at Indy, in fact the first licensed female in the garage area was Wanda Knepper in 1972, a legitimate mechanic on her husband's car. "Trouble and back-stabbing always came from women—the ones who were insecure or didn't want to hear their men asking why they didn't help on the car 'like Wanda does,'" she recalls.

"When I was allowed in it was with specific rules. I couldn't use the men's rest room, which was no problem because they were so bad that even the men didn't want to use them. I couldn't go over the wall on pit lane because I was told it was too dangerous—but believe me, if I had been needed over the wall, they wouldn't have stopped me any more than they were able to keep me out of the garage. And the final thing was that I had to leave the garage area promptly at 6 p.m. every day. No reason given. And they sent security to escort me out of the fenced area every single night, at the same time that some of the men were sneaking the pit lizards through the back gate."

"Pit lizards" is a derogatory term used by men as much or more than women to describe those females who really were (and are) looking for notches on the bedpost.

Mares with son Matt, the great joy of her life. (Courtesy Jeff Klein Collection)

What Wanda, Mares and a lot of other women share is a gentle firmness of spirit. They don't buy the argument that their gender should keep them from participating in a sport they genuinely love. These are not radical feminists, demanding entrance for the sole reason of gender or insisting that men should be thrown out to make room for them. Wanda wanted to be with her husband, and she knew as much, perhaps more, about a race car than many of the men there. Through race wins and championships, Mares has proven that she belongs on the track. Like many trailblazers, she has encountered significant male resistance, but some came from a source she didn't expect: her husband.

A newly divorced Mares realized that she badly needed more of what racing had given her—self-confidence—in addition to the extraordinary joy she found in raising her son Matt. At that time she was fortunate enough to connect with car owner Joe Grandinetti, and he bought the old equipment she and Mark had. In spite of the equipment's age, it was a known entity—or so she thought.

The first five nights back on the track, the car was such a beast that Mares was nearly in tears after each race. "It was awful," she remembers. "I told Joe, 'I just can't do it.' In my mind, I was thinking that I'm older, I'm out of shape, I don't have time to work out. I'm letting them down."

But then the crew chief for Joe's other car reached over and turned the steering wheel while the engine was still running—or tried to. He got a very funny look on his face. A significant repair later, Mares went out and won the heat race in a beautifully handling car. It turned out that the power steering unit was malfunctioning because it was significantly low on fluid and had plenty of air pockets. In that manner, it was worse than not even having power steering.

Today, Mares continues to be a successful racer. She is very popular among the URC fans, and that is the result of something from her childhood.

Mares' sponsor Lou Parisi (center) makes a generous donation to the Kasey Kahne Foundation. (Frank Simek Photo, Courtesy Jeff Klein Collection)

"I used to go to the drag races and I idolized Shirley Muldowney," Mares remembers. "I was really taken aback that she was not that personable. I can't tell you how many times, as a kid, I stood outside her pit with my pen and paper. I wanted her autograph so badly, and I never, ever got it. So, when I started to race I made it my goal that I was going to do whatever I could to make the kids feel included. I used to take bags of candy. I was the last person to leave the pits because I would always stay to sign the last autograph and to talk to every kid who wanted to talk to me. It was important to make them feel special. Boys or girls, if they wanted to sit in the car and have their parents take a picture—that's what we would do.

"Sure, I'd like to be the best race car driver in the world and win every race, but that's not what a winner is. A winner is the whole picture. I'm not perfect, but I want kids to feel like they're an important part of what we do, and I want them to see drivers as role models."

In an age when multi-millionaire ball players insist they don't want the responsibility of being heroes or role models for kids, maybe it's time for the wee lady in a driver's suit to take them to the wood shed and administer a few lessons in how to conduct themselves. It seems like the world could use more people who could remind us that "winners" really do more than pull into Victory Lane.

Mares and the whole team celebrate a feature win. Considering that this came on the ever-tough URC circuit, it's an accomplishment well worth cheering. (Courtesy Jeff Klein Collection)

15

Families

Not every sprint car driver succeeds in racing with the help and blessings of his or her family. Even before that wreck that discouraged Hooker Hood's father from returning to the track, an even earlier accident ended his mother's brief involvement. "She never did go to the races," Hooker recalls, "except one time she saw me race motorcycles on the half-mile track out here at the fairgrounds near Memphis. I tried to follow Leo Anthony down the backstretch and I didn't turn left enough. I went all the way through the fence out in the middle of a field. When they put me in the ambulance to take me to the hospital, I waved out the window at my mother. She had never been to a race before. She never went to another one again."

One of the most enduring clichés about racing is that it binds families together. There is a great deal to be said for shared experiences, and certainly no outsider can begin to see and understand as much as a brother, father, wife or any family member who's been intimately involved with racing. For the most part it's valued, but pop psychologists would have a bit of a field day analyzing all that goes on trackside. A racer is usually thrilled to see a loved one win the race he or she couldn't, but on the other hand, the competition dynamic with relatives can be intense. Because sprint racing demands such passion, it's natural that the person you most enjoy seeing succeed is also the person you most want to beat. Everybody wants to be lead dog in the pack—maybe even more so when it's the same litter.

There are observers who think Jeff Swindell was more naturally talented than brother Sammy but lacked the latter's determination. Sammy's results over the years seems to confirm that the bulldog approach was satisfactory. Others feel that Bob Kinser was every bit as good a driver as son Steve, but since his racing pre-dated the World of Outlaws, he never had a similar showcase for his talent. Great bench racing arguments have centered on who was the best of the four Weld brothers, the Unsers, the Tobias family, the Saldanas, and on and on.

Californian Tim Green was also a familiar face in Midwestern racing, particularly in the 1980s. He married Jimmy Sills' sister Marcy. (Gene Marderness Photo)

Overall, family involvement, whether on-track or supporting behind the scenes, does seem to be a benefit. "At least with racing, if your dad's there and your family is with you, it keeps you within yourself. You don't have time or money to mess with drugs or get in trouble. When you drive that race car you learn to be a leader," observes Bobby Allen. "But then when my dad died, I was kind of lost for a while. I missed that anchor."

Sometimes, it all becomes too much, confirmed for those who witnessed on live television the meltdown of a racing family at Knoxville a few years ago, as the camera and microphone picked up a driver yelling at his father, "Go ahead and hit me like you used to when I was a kid."

Racing against even extended family can be fraught with pitfalls, as Jimmy Sills found out when racer and fellow Californian Tim Green married Jimmy's sister. "We were great friends for a long time—we helped each other out, too. He would be in the Midwest racing one summer and I'd be home, and then we'd swap. And all the time we're calling back and forth every week with information," Jimmy recalls. "But it got more difficult after he married Marcy. She would walk back from the line-up board at the track and say, 'I can't believe you both are in the same damned heat race again!'"

Even allowing for the new relationship, Jimmy and Tim reached a point at which their friendship and Marcy's peace of mind were nearly

Daryn Pittman has just won the Kings Royal, which prompted his wife Mandy to launch herself into car owner Reeve Kruk's arms. But why is Reeve the one wearing the tiara? (Mike Campbell Photo)

shattered. The press must take at least part of the blame, as a racing magazine repeated some of Jimmy's thoughts about Tim's performance in a particular race. Tim did not agree with the details as printed. However, the claim that Tim had gotten into Sills and flipped him as they raced for a transfer spot resulted in Green reputedly telling mechanic Brian Sperry, "Well, he got that right. Yeah, I tipped the son-of-a-bitch over."

Christmas and Thanksgiving were pretty quiet for a while. Sills' mother kept saying, "Guys, can't you just put it all behind you and get along?"

While they once again resumed their friendship, the disagreement lasted substantially longer than the racing incident. It's always a little tricky where in-laws are concerned. Daryn Pittman discovered that when he married Riverside Speedway star Mike Ward's daughter Mandy. "I think we avoid talking about racing with each other, but not for any bad reason," Daryn says. "About the time that Mandy and I started dating, Mike and I had raced against each other maybe only a half dozen or so times. That probably helped our relationship, since a few of them have been nail-biters that had a few people wondering who was cheering for whom. Not so long ago, we went to West Memphis for an Outlaw show and it was really neat. Mike and I started on the front row of a heat race together. What are the chances of that?"

Son-in-law against father-in-law is one matter—son against father is another. It might seem like dads would be proud and delighted when the child goes into the family business. Often they are indeed proud of any and all accomplishments. But as for delighted? Not so much.

"I didn't want Terry to drive race cars," says Lenard McCarl. "When I was driving, everybody got hurt. There were times we didn't worry about point races or any of that stuff because the concern was just how long we were going to be out of racing, healing up. We considered ourselves lucky if we couldn't drive for only two weeks. And I didn't want that for my kids."

When the children follow in a driver's tire tracks, it's a challenge for both generations. In the case of the Wolfgang family there is the undeniable expectations created by father Doug's incomparably successful career. Knowing that everything he does will inevitably be compared to his father, nonetheless Robby has chosen to go into the family business. Considering that he also has first-hand knowledge of how mean racing accidents can be only adds to the wonder that Robby has gone forward with a career as sprint car driver.

"The timing of Robby's birth was amazing," explains Doug. "I had been burned in my accident five weeks before at Lakeside Speedway in Kansas City. I was finally beginning to regain consciousness, and the middle of the next night the nurse came in with a phone. With the daily cycle of burn scrubbing and pain medication for third-degree burns, that was a hard moment and I didn't want to talk with anyone, but the nurse insisted I answer. It was my wife Jeri, in another wing of the hospital. She said we'd just had a baby boy! May 12, 1992. It was an incredibly mixed moment in our lives."

After Doug's miraculous recovery from the burns, his career was finally ended in another

Mike Ward in 1985 at The Ditch. His daughter Amanda married Daryn Pittman. (Allen Horcher Photo)

Lenard McCarl (left) wasn't sure it was a good idea for his descendants to follow in his tire tracks, considering how many drivers were hurt or killed during his hey-day. Happily not only has Terry become a bona fide star but grandson Austin (right) has taken up the family business, too. (Judy McCarl Photo)

Proving it's in the genes, Robby Wolfgang won his first A Main in 2008 while only 16 years old and after only a few weeks of driving a 360 sprinter. Proud papa Doug was the first to congratulate him. (Doug Johnson Photo)

Sammy Swindell shares Victory Lane with his son Kevin on April 8, 2006. Although Sammy obviously still knows how to get the job done, the emphasis in the Swindell family these days is more on building Kevin's career. (Mike Campbell Photo)

bad wreck later, but he has opened his own chassis business and remains a respected figure in sprint car racing. Between the genes and the exposure to racing, Robby probably had no more chance of walking away from the sport than Terry McCarl had.

On July 27, 2008, just a few minutes after Doug was inducted in the 3/8-mile Huset's Speedway Hall of Fame at Brandon, South Dakota, Robby won his first-ever A Main before a packed house—and a very proud dad. The 16-year-old had been running 360 sprints for only a couple of weeks. "You know, I was watching and thinking how most racers never even win a feature," muses Doug. "Well, doesn't Robby go out, take the lead and win it. When he came across for the checkers, I could hear that crowd cheering right over the sound of the motors. The last time I heard that was at Knoxville when I was battling with Sammy Swindell for the lead in the Nationals. Man, did it ever give me the shivers."

Just having kids, whether they decide to race or not, can change a driver's perspective. "When I was young and full of vinegar, I didn't know if I was going to live to be 30 years old," remarks Lynn Paxton. "I wasn't worried about it. But after you get past 30 and have a family, the outlook is different. Completely different. I think you still have your moments, but it mellows you a bit. And I think it makes some of these guys better racers. Mitch Smith is an example. Early in his career he could be running a half lap behind and ricocheting off the walls because he was going to do whatever it took to catch the leader. But later in his career, with a family to consider, he realized he wasn't going to win every race, so he was more content to do the best he could and not take stupid chances. The racing was still important, but it wasn't the most important thing, and using his head more than his foot actually got him better results because he wasn't crashing so much."

There are, and always have been, three kinds of spouses: the ones who love racing almost as much as the driver, the ones who love the driver in spite of racing—and the ones who get fed up and head off into a different life.

Type One: As the daughter of a long-time driver, Pittman's wife Mandy knew a great deal of what to expect. And believe with your dying breath that any woman who had experience of the racing life before marrying a driver will hear from him,

"You knew what you were getting into," so many times through the years that eventually she will be ready to pull his vocal chords out through his ass.

"We'll argue over whether I need to sit out after a wreck, but she knows that she's in a losing battle about whether to stop racing," Pittman states firmly. "It's probably not even worth bringing up. She might win a lot of arguments, but that one isn't going to happen."

Curt Michael married a Ms. Motorsports and as a child, his Jenn had gone to the Silver Springs track in Mechanicsburg, Pennsylvania, with her dad. "She even had a birthday cake with a Smokey Snellbaker design on it," he says.

Curt Michael and Jennifer Weaver didn't begin their romance at the track, so it certainly wasn't the lure of a driver's suit that brought them together. They met when Curt was a 16-year-old kid working at a gas station in Delaware. "Then I moved back to Pennsylvania and I didn't see her for five years. But I saw her sister one night and asked about Jenn. That got us back in touch and we started dating again."

The couple has been together since 1993, but theirs was an untraditional and very touching wedding. Curt was recuperating from breaking his back in a racing accident and was still wearing a bulky, decidedly unattractive back brace. Although the ceremony could have waited a few more months until he was fully recuperated, one day Jenn told Curt that her dad's bout with cancer wasn't going to wait on the back brace.

"I said, 'Okay, let's go get our license,' and we got married in her dad's bedroom. It was just my mom and dad, her sister and mom, and her dad lying in the bed with a Curt Michael tee-shirt on," Curt recalls. "After the ceremony, he said, 'Okay, I can go now,' and he passed away the next morning."

Shane Carson's wife is another "keeper," but like many of the gypsies' spouses she has had to make adjustments. "Debi and I have been together since the '70s," says Shane. "I can tell you she lived it, from the motocross days when I came home with knocked out teeth or a broken hand, to the hi-profile promotions at the Fairgrounds Speedway in Oklahoma City, to our current arrangement that splits my time between Oklahoma, Charlotte and WoO races everywhere. She was there that cold day in January 1977 when I won my first sprint car race driving for LaVern Nance at East

Dave Hanna had apparently been able to hit the kill switch when he started to flip in 1986 because observers recall hearing only the crunch of the wing as it hit the track–and Hanna's wife screaming his name as he was going over. (Kevin Horcher Photo)

Curt and Jenn Michael moved up their wedding to June 21, 2002, held in her father's bedroom. He passed away from cancer at age 49 the following morning. Instead of a tuxedo, Curt wore a brace for his broken back. Happily, by December the couple was able to share a very happy reception with their friends and family. (Courtesy Curt Michael Collection)

Debi and Shane Carson in the late 1970s. She had already been his biggest fan and supporter for years, having been a co-conspirator when the teen-aged Shane hid his motorcycle racing from his parents. (Courtesy Mar-Car Collection)

Talk about having priorities in the correct order, Skip Jackson gave up racing in central Pennsylvania in order to return to his wife's native Knoxville, Iowa, because she and their son were homesick–and Skip felt he was missing too many special moments with them. (Max Dolder Photo)

Alabama Motor Speedway.

"Either we were in tow trucks or a Chevy Suburban, and she was always right there, going down the road. She enjoyed that life. All her friends were on the road and she looked forward to it. But when our daughter got to school age, Debi had to stay home for school days. Now I fly everywhere. My office is in Charlotte and we live in Oklahoma, so I think she misses the racing now. She went to work for a friend who owns a company in Oklahoma City and that has helped her stay busy, so maybe she doesn't miss me so much. I don't know. I do know that I miss the days on the road. We went down a lot of roads and a lot of miles, but when she was with me it sure didn't seem like travel was such a tiring deal."

It's not just wives who have made adjustments to keep a marriage and family intact. Sometimes it's the driver. Skip Jackson gave up racing central Pennsy sprints to return to Knoxville. After moving all the way from Australia, he was adaptable to differing cultures, but he was surprised to find that he also missed the small Iowa burg, and shared in his family's longing to return there. It was a seemingly minor moment that tipped the scales. During this period Skip was racing several nights a week, as happens in Pennsylvania. "I hadn't seen my son A.J. in about a week, and he woke me up at 3 a.m. and said, 'Dad, Scooby Doo's on.' He pulled me out of bed and set me on the couch while he sings to me like the television is on.

"My wife Lori and A.J. gave up so much for me to race, but even after three really good years in Pennsylvania, I knew I had to go home for them. We thought we'd go back to Pennsylvania again some day, but the reality is that you can't. But it's okay. You can't miss out on stuff like a Scooby Doo serenade."

The *Type Two* spouse may not be around to carry trophies, but she is just as deserving as any supportive wife. Every lasting marriage has to find its comfort level, and for some racing isn't the centerpiece of their enjoyment. As an example, Lenard and Judy McCarl have been married since January 1957. Judy made the Florida treks, but generally she stayed home, raised three children and pursued her own interests. Considering Lenard's long career, it obviously worked for them.

"I put my wife through living hell," admits Lealand McSpadden. "But we had a lot of give and take—a lot. We just kept working at it all the time. She really didn't like racing, and I didn't realize how little she liked it until I quit. She was so supportive and did so many things to help me, but it really wasn't her cup of tea."

Even though Janet and the kids were accommodating during Lealand's career, they did have a pact: "When I quit, I was done," he says. "We had friends who quit, then came back and got killed. She said, 'I don't care if you race until you're 70, but when you quit or take a year off, you're done.'"

And he complied.

Richard Griffin started out winning races in southern New Mexico's high desert with his parents. At those small tracks it was easy for the family to spend time together, but as he aged and began racing at far-flung corners of the country, it became very hard for his wife and daughter to go along with him. Eventually Richard's priorities focused more on his home. (Courtesy Richard Griffin Collection)

Richard Griffin's wife Charlotte had gone to the races with him from the beginning, "so she was okay with it, but she didn't go an awful lot," he recalls. "A lot of the trips were pretty fast and there was not a lot of time to socialize, so it was not really a lot of fun for somebody to just be there. Then my daughter Lindsay was born, and dragging a little kid around, staying up late at the races—it all got to be too much. Charlotte would never have said, 'You have to quit racing,' but she expressed her opinions about how much it took me away. Plus, she was with me a few times when we crashed and ended up going to the hospital. Putting women through that is hard on them and the kids, when Dad's in the ambulance and you don't know what the status is. When you really think about it, you wonder why you're doing that to your family at all."

And *Type Three*. Racing ought to have been named as co-respondent in more than a few divorces. Not necessarily just the on-track hair-raisers, but the long hours, long miles and . . . *ahem* . . . extracurricular activities that seemed to have been an ingrained part of racing. All have contributed to more than one *Party of the First Part vs. Party of the Second Part*.

"Long hours" don't come close to explaining what it's like away from the spotlight of the actual racing. Even through a layer of dust, racing can look mighty glamorous, especially when the track announcer hits a hissy-high octave in telling the fans how brilliantly a driver performed. "People don't understand," explains McSpadden. "Bubby Jones, Rick Ferkel—all of us guys running up and down the road back when—used to work a job—and race. Whatever the job, we all went home and did something to support our racing habits because there wasn't a lot of money to be made in it. In those days, $1,000-to-win was a big thing."

Then you donate the rest of your waking hours to working on the race car. Even among drivers who don't punch a time clock, race car preparation is a priority. It's not like NASCAR with back-at-the-shop team payrolls that can run into the hundreds of people. If you want to go fast in a sprint car, you had better be prepared to be part of the preparation equation. That's grease under Steve Kinser's fingernails because even Kings get as dirty as the serfs in the sprinters. "If you go to work at a Chevy dealership," adds McCarl, "you only have to work about 20 hours a day. If you work on a race car fulltime—you ain't never got enough hours."

Racers, young or old, rich or poor, will nearly always tell you that no matter how many hours they spent in the garage, they could have used more. A well-prepared race car is not always a perfectly prepared race car, and therein lies the rub. Much of the time, the car that wins is the one that is best prepared. Never mind that the driver is tired, and thereby less perfectly prepared himself.

Even the most dedicated racer—and spouse—can get weary of the road. "Road life all those years was fun, but after so many years it just gets to be a grind," says Johnny Herrera. "Being back at home, being with my family, I can have some normalcy. I enjoy helping some of the younger kids trying to start racing. I can give back. And that just can't happen when you're gone all the time."

"If I had to race today, I couldn't do half of what I did," continues McSpadden. "Because of the restrictions you have at airports these days, it's harder and harder to make connections. I couldn't make half the races or I would have to quit my job. I worked four days a week and still made three races a weekend."

Which allowed for very little else.

"I didn't know what it was like to have a family vacation," says Paxton. "You have to give up your life if you're a racer. For 23 years, I didn't know what it was to have that little part of my life."

"Didn't even know what down time was," McSpadden confirms. "Really, your families had to go through so much. I remember loading our kids in the van, and my wife and I were going down the road, not knowing where we were gonna stay, what we were gonna do, or what we were gonna eat. It all depended on how we did at the races. What a way to live."

But literally thousands of wives have dealt with playing second fiddle to the attention given a race car or the effort to make a race across country when the husband wouldn't go see a concert or play across town. Dealing with the race car as mistress is do-able for many women. Dealing with the *mistress* as mistress—less so.

"Let's face it—I have a lot of friends who are retreaded, some more than once," agrees Paxton. "Ray Kelly's been married to his wife over 50 years. Kathy and Keith Kauffman have been together for a long time, and my wife and I have been married 38 years. But when we socialize with old racers, we're definitely in the minority."

The drivers who make a commitment to their families live for these moments in racing: in Victory Lane with all those who helped make it possible, including sharing the limelight with supportive spouses. When Lynn Paxton won, he wanted his wife Barbara alongside. (Courtesy Lynn Paxton Collection)

Keith Kauffman is a rarity among drivers. Not only has he very seldom turned over, but he has kept his life—and marriage—in a straight line that's endured for many years. (Allen Horcher Photo)

If you race hard, it becomes very, very easy to convince yourself that living hard is not just acceptable—it's expected.

These days, there is far less partying, both at local tracks and among the gypsies. Part of that is that so much money and time is expended on the racing itself that not a lot is left over for silliness. On the traveling circuits, racers and their wives go back to motorhomes and socialize less than their predecessors did, agrees Pittman. But there was time when cleaving unto one's spouse was a concept sometimes left at the pit gate.

"Okay, I'm just being honest—telling it like it is," says one driver, who has married more than once. "When you're racing and traveling from place to place, not coming home for a long period of time, well, men are men. And women are women. And if you're successful at something and get the attention that goes with it—sometimes it's sort of hard to resist. In part, it was that you had to be a little obsessed. Racing was all you thought about. It was your whole life, so we got to be selfish. I never gave it a whole lot of thought. It was there. I partook of it. I'm not proud of it, but I suppose if I had it to do all over again—I'd probably make the same mistakes."

"Most of the guys who are married—their wives are going to come along with them," comments Sills. "Racers kinda got a bad reputation for not being true blue when they're out on the road. If your wife is sitting at home and she's hearing all these stories through the rumor mill, it's not a good thing. In fact, being separated from your family just isn't a good thing any way you look at it. I would come home and see my daughter, and God, there were things that she knew and had learned. She looked different, and wow, I was just missing that part of watching her grow up. That was hard. That's the down side. Racing is a great life and a great opportunity to do things and to be 'somebody,' to make your life mean something. But you can pay a big price for it, too."

Hence, a divorce rate that has probably exceeded the national average. Comfort, attention for the ego, all sorts of circumstances after the racing can conspire to hurt a driver.

Some drivers were just born alley cats and probably would have chased after women regardless. It's hardly confined to racing, of course, but still Wanda Knepper saw many things happen at every level from midgets to sprints to Indy cars, and there's no question that a lot of people, including other drivers' wives, turned a blind eye to activity that didn't even warrant the description of a "romance." It was quick and superficial in every way.

Wanda recalls a sprint-and-Indy driver who would usher his wife through the pit gate at Indianapolis and send her on to the couple's hotel room, then walk immediately to the back gate to bring in a series of girlfriends for assignations in the garage. People often wondered how he had anything left for driving, but the fact he never won at Indy, nor all that many times in sprint racing, may be attributed to expending too much energy keeping the women from encountering each other.

Wanda tells of another really famous sprint-and-Indy driver whose re-marriage made headlines in *National Speed Sport News*. "And the same week that issue came out, we were at a short track event where I saw him standing on an open trailer, smooching away," she recalls. "And it wasn't his new wife. Or the old one."

One of the better drivers ever in sprint car history admitted that he got the marriage thing all wrong from the start. "I didn't get married for the right reasons," he says. "I got married to stay out of the service, and she told me she was pregnant. When we got married, I was a little resentful, thinking now I got a wife and a kid coming. I'll never be a professional race driver because how can you be one with all these responsibilities?"

Maybe the resentment showed because the married-for-the-wrong-reasons driver got a taste of his own medicine. "My wife started running around on me, and I was crushed. But I realized that I was 200 percent racing. I told myself that I needed to be 100 percent racing and 100 percent family. I figured you had to work all day and all night or how could you beat the next guy? But now when I look back I realize what it did to our relationship.

"We've been together now for 18 years. We're still at war, but somehow we're figuring out how to continue along."

Many marriages that get to that point don't survive, however, and it's probably not surprising. A lot of long-term racers do better the second—or third—time around when they realize that the race car is not going to come visit them at the nursing home someday. Occasionally, the second effort at matrimony is actually so successful that it reminds us all that we have no business trying to sit in judgment on what others do.

Rare is the family that has enjoyed racing as much as the Hoods. Their infectious joy in sharing time together is to be envied. From left: Doug, Stormi, Carolyn, Hooker, Bill (behind Hooker), Speedy (kneeling), Misti, Rickey, Rickey Jr., Scottie and Roger. (Courtesy Hooker Hood Collection)

Here's how Hooker Hood explains how he came to remarry: "I've been here in my home since 1949 when my daddy bought the lot and gave it to me, and I built a house with five years of notes at $72 a month. My garage has always been a gathering spot for racing people. The Swindells used to stop by, the Grays, the Wards—really, everybody who's ever been seriously into racing at West Memphis at some point—and just a lot of other people who wanted to hang out and talk racing while we worked on the cars.

"One day, when Carolyn was about 18 years old, she stopped by and came into the garage. That's what started it. I was married to a lady named Doris—that's Rickey's mama—at the time. I guess she figured out that something was going on because one day she said, 'Hooker, I'm leaving.'

"She came in the house, called a cab, got her suitcase ready and about 10 or 15 minutes later she left. Never has been back.

"Anyway, Carolyn kept coming by the garage, and before I knew it I done asked her, 'When I get divorced, are you gonna marry me?' and she said, 'Sure.'

"She's a good girl. We've got two girls, one named Stormi and one named Misti. I keep telling Carolyn the next one's gonna be Partly Cloudy, but she's not going along with that!"

Carolyn is 24 years younger than Hooker, and yet they've been married for more than 36 years. Maybe their union was a bit unconventional, but, then, racing is full of people who defy categorizing.

16

Fights

It's probably not altogether surprising, in view of the tremendous passion race drivers bring to the track with them, that occasionally—just occasionally—when that ardor is frustrated and all the macho aggression has no other outlet, a disagreement ensues. Most dust-ups resemble a real fight about as closely as *West Side Story* resembles actual inner-city gang warfare. But sometimes, stuff happens.

Frequently, the event that precipitates a disagreement truly is "just one of them deals," as claimed. Not much is deliberate, and fellow racers know that. Sometimes what happens is the result of a build-up of tension over a period of time, and fame is no buffer when tempers finally boil over.

There was a night that Paul Pitzer and Jan Opperman scrapped following a hundred-lapper at Lincoln Speedway in Hanover, Pennsylvania. At the time, the real simmering feud was between Opperman and Pitzer's teammate, Kenny Weld. The two, as opposite personalities as ever took to the track, were battling for wins every night the Pennsylvania Posse ran at any of the tracks in the area, building a legendary era in sprint car racing. Also building an equally legendary grudge.

Although he was one of the original Pennsylvania Posse, Paul Pitzer ventured out to the Midwest occasionally. Here in 1979 or 1980, he meets the infamous Terre Haute ruts. (Kevin Horcher Photo)

For a while, the shaggy, hippie-fied Opp had been playing mind games with the straight-laced Weld, doing little things like driving his car up to Kenny's before the green flag, giving him a little tap that did no damage but got his attention—and then giving an impish little wave of the hand. Opp knew it annoyed the short-tempered Weld no end, and for quite some time it was an effective tool to rattle him.

In this particular race with Weld running second, Opperman came up to lap Pitzer. He may not have known Opperman was there. Maybe it was a little payback because the two had had a small run-in earlier in the night. But at the very worst, according to another driver, Pitzer did no more than slow Opperman's progress for a lap or so.

Bear in mind a time-honored tradition is that a lot of bad blood is kept alive and boiling by people other than the drivers themselves. That night, to Opperman's fans and crew, it smacked of Pitzer trying to help his teammate catch up, and thereby win, by holding up Opperman.

After the race, Pitzer came down to Opperman's pit area, which was the first mistake. And whatever was said apparently did nothing to calm the troubled waters between the two. Almost immediately, the two went at it—pushing, shoving, throwing roundhouses that failed to connect. That attracted a mob scene as such gatherings always do.

"They had just run 100 laps, and after about 20 seconds they both sounded like a car that's running at 250 degrees," says Lynn Paxton. "They were hyperventilating. Neither one of them was going to hurt the other, so the initial idea was to break it up. But I said, 'Let 'em go.' So, we let 'em go."

A little disagreement. (Allen Horcher Photo)

He laughs, "Hell, it didn't last 30 seconds. After it was over I went to Opperman and said, 'Opp, you were wrong. He didn't do anything.' And he looked at me and said, 'I know it, but it had to do with other things.' I told him I knew that. And you know what? They never had a problem after that."

Clearing the air is what the pushing and shoving, milling around is usually about. But it works only if the parties are in agreement and manage to throw a face-saving punch or two. If a party won't fight, however, it's over before it begins.

"One night Brent Kaeding and I were in a race at Placerville Speedway in California, one of my favorite tracks, and I kinda gave Brent a slide job," says Jimmy Sills. "I thought I had him cleared but he dove off the race track to keep from hitting me and he was pretty mad about it. He wanted to fight afterwards. I looked at him and he's probably three or four inches taller than I am and out-weighed me by about 30 pounds."

Sills paused for a moment, and intelligence won over macho intentions.

Jimmy Sills wouldn't fight Brent Kaeding, and Brent didn't push the matter. Maybe it had something to do with getting the last laugh, because that's Jimmy flying high over Brent in the #69, while Steve Kent (#5) just tries to get out of the way. (Courtesy Jimmy Sills Collection)

He told Kaeding, "Nah. You're just way too big for me to fight."

Sills was probably wise in his caution, although not everyone has always taken that into consideration. A blind rage is, after all, blind. Proof of that was a disagreement that escalated into words between Eastern drivers Johnny Crawford and LeRoy Felty. "Crawford's a pretty big guy and Felty was a little-bitty guy," Paxton picks up the story. "Crawford came over and was giving Felty what-for, and there was a mob scene on both sides. Well, Crawford kind of pulled his arm back—he telescoped like he was going to throw a punch. He threw a haymaker, Felty ducked down and it went over Felty's head. Then Felty jumped up in the air, one shot—*pop*—and boom, down went Crawford. The little guy knocked out the big guy, and they had to drag him off."

It's also hard to fuel a fight, regardless of a racer's size, if he knows—from experience—that it's not something at which he excels. "I learned a long time ago that there was something I wasn't doing right in a fight, so I tried to avoid that at all costs. I wasn't much of a fighter," claims Sills.

Something to think about—it's not unusual for contretemps at race tracks to occur between teams with large pit crews and plenty of family and fans for back-up. (Kevin Horcher Photo)

"But sometimes, your mouth writes a check your ass can't cash. One night we were at Knoxville and this guy comes down. He's mad as hell at me because there was this puddle coming off turn two, and I clipped the puddle. It threw mud up on him and then he couldn't see."

It seemed to Sills to be a dumb reason to be mad, especially since common sense would dictate that it wasn't a deliberate act. Sills admits that, with just a teeny bit of hot-weather sweat in his own eyes, sarcasm framed his response: "Ya know, this is *dirt* racing. Ya just reach up and grab a tear-off. Maybe you ought to get a *tennis racquet…*"

And the fight was on.

Most of the time, however, Sills and the rest of the gypsies rarely resorted to fisticuffs. They seldom needed to. "I definitely had disagreements but never anything really huge," confirms Lealand McSpadden. "When your racing is where you fly in and out so much, people are a lot

Nathan Charron has just flipped over an inside wall and into the judge's stand at Morgan County Speedway, Jacksonville, Illinois. The May 2008 incident has Nathan headed down the track to "discuss" the matter with the driver he believes was responsible, but the deputy seems to have other ideas. (Kevin Horcher Photos)

friendlier. If you're not there every week, it's like you're not as big a threat to their environment. That's why people liked Bubby Jones, Rick Ferkel, Jan Opperman so well. They didn't spend enough time in one area for the people to get to hate them. They'd go in, take the money, and go home. Go someplace else the next week and do the same thing."

Even today, with sponsorship so critical to keeping circuit racers going, the travelers *try* to avoid trouble. "Back in the '70s when there would be a fight in the pits, we're talking 50 people. It would get big back then," says Gary Wright. "If a guy wants to keep a sponsor today he better act halfway right. I found the best way is if somebody runs over you on the track, just keep your mouth shut and the next race take care of it. Nobody else has to be the wiser."

That's well and good for the gypsies, but it's harder to maintain a peaceful mantra for the weekend racer, or the drivers who routinely race certain tracks. Festering anger can erupt at any time.

Even if it doesn't lead to a fight, a wreck can result in plenty of frustration. This occurred at Bloomington in 1994 between Duffy Smith and A.J. Booher. Look closely at Smith's right hand after the wreck–it's the universal symbol for "what were ya thinkin', Buddy?" (Kevin Horcher Photos)

"Wayne Bennett flipped me out of the park on the last lap of the feature while I was leading at Manzy, I think in 1984," Richard Griffin contends. "So after the race we have a scuffle, of course, that goes nowhere and settles nothing. Later we were in our crew cab dually pick-up in the parking lot, and everybody out in the parking lot was drinking beer. And pretty soon, we see his vehicle sitting there. It's a van.

"So we just rammed it. And then we backed up and we rammed it again. Caved in the front end. And then we drove off."

That's not a new dance move. That's what happened after Donnie Gentry and Joey Montgomery got together on-track at St. Francois Raceway in Farmington, Missouri, during an August 2008 MSCS race. (Kevin Horcher Photo)

You know that after enough beer, something like that can seem like a good idea. But alcohol can also sometimes play a factor in soothing the troubled beast, too.

"I've just met so many good people in racing. And it seems like I've had fights with every one of them," says Hooker Hood after decades racing at The Ditch, a track with one of the toughest reputations that just won't quite go away. "And an hour and a half later, we was out drinking beer together. We'd just fight and get over it. We'd shake hands and get the dirt off of us—and then we'd go drink that beer."

And do it all again next week.

But Hooker didn't limit his disputes to only fellow competitors. Bear in mind that during the years that he was a top competitor, sprint car racing was not for the sissies. These were folks who believed that sometimes a fist was not only effective, it was called-for. Hooker was a good enough racer and naturally good-natured guy that he didn't fight unless the circumstances really called for it. In other words, a roundhouse wasn't the first reaction that came to mind for him—even though he had become a Golden Gloves boxer while in the military.

It's been a while since Hooker Hood was a Golden Gloves boxer, but early in his career a mouthy flagman found out first-hand what Hooker had learned in the ring! (Courtesy Hooker Hood Collection)

Apparently, Hood's pugilistic skills were unknown to a West Memphis flagman. During an event at which Hooker was on the pole, others in the field wanted a faster pace and the flagman allowed it. After the race, Hooker calmly got out of his race car, strolled casually over to the flagman's perch, waving and smiling at the cheering crowd.

He got to the flagstand and climbed the ladder. The conversation started out well enough—Hooker just wanted to remind him that the polesitter is supposed to set the pace. But apparently the flagman didn't appreciate the reminder and the discussion didn't proceed so well.

When the flagman took a swipe at Hooker with the flag, the driver climbed into the perch and proceeded to wale away at the hapless official, who just curled into the fetal position and took the beating like...an official with no Golden Gloves training. When Hooker finally ran out of steam, he climbed back down from the stand and leisurely strolled back to the pits, waving to the ecstatic crowd as he did.

It didn't occur to the flagman to call the cops and press charges for assault. Nobody did in those days. There was often a lot of milling around after most fights and threats to call the cops, but before cell phones those were generally empty threats. Occasionally, security would get in the middle of these melees and escort people out of the track, and if it was a good night the fans didn't toss half-full beer cans off the back of the grandstand at them.

But even if tire irons were waved in the air back in the days when racers still had the things, the fights were about as phony as the anger was real. It was a matter of letting off steam. Most disputes ended at the winter banquets, although a few actually did end with feuding parties sharing a jail cell for the night. That was a little tense, especially when accompanied by a hangover as they were bailed out the following morning.

There was a driver in the Midwest who was barred from his home track *for life* when he was still very young and following some particularly dramatic antics. "Life" turned out to average six weeks before he was allowed back in, and there wasn't a year in his lengthy career that he didn't get a *lifetime* ban.

A vampire couldn't have hoped to return from the dead so many times.

17

On the Road Again

It's probably not surprising to learn that a few race drivers have, at times, gotten speeding tickets.

"I hardly ever had a driver's license," admits "The Gas Man" Griffin. "Not very often did I talk my way out of tickets. But, I'm a pilot, too, so for a long time while I was racing I got to flying and that cut down on the tickets. I bought some junkers and left them at different airports so that I could just get to the airport and go to the track."

Sometimes a wreck is so hard that there's virtually nothing left on the car to salvage. Note that Ray Jo Fager's 1985 wreck at Terre Haute even crunched the header pipes coming off the engine. (Allen Horcher Photo)

This is what's left of Rocky Hodges' ride following a particularly vicious three-car wreck at Tri-City Speedway. (Allen Horcher Photo)

Considering how many miles the gypsies have run up and down the road, it's probably a miracle that any of them *ever* had a license that wasn't suspended. "We checked one year and we ran 62,000 miles to 126 races," recalls Rick Ferkel. "We had a few tickets but nothing that was earth-shattering. Mostly, we were fighting boredom, so we always had something going like betting on stuff to stay awake."

In Ferkel's time there were no big-rig haulers with all the comforts of home. Today's racers still fight boredom going down the road, although conditions have improved over those faced by the pioneers of the sport. Air-conditioning 40 or 50 years ago was 2/60—roll down both windows in the pick-up truck and go 60 miles-an-hour. There was no going back in a motorhome for refreshments or rest-room facilities. An empty coffee can with a snap-on plastic lid was sometimes the alternative to a dirty gas station where the toilet had been plugged since nineteen-ought-six. And if you got a night in a motel without cockroaches to rearrange the suitcases while you slept, it probably meant you got the winner's purse.

During their many years together on the road, the mechanic whom Arnie Knepper could count on most—at home in the garage, as well as at the track—was wife Wanda. This is 1984 with their midget, but they also raced sprints and Indy cars. Wanda was the very first woman licensed by USAC to be an Indy 500 mechanic. (Courtesy Wanda Knepper Collection)

During the years that the Knepper clan chased IMCA racing before motorhomes became common, they stayed in a plethora of really cheap motels when they weren't sleeping in the car. Wanda remembers a night in Hutchinson, Kansas, when the only room left in town meant they put six-month-old son Art in a dresser drawer because all the room had was one single bed. Arnie and Wanda got that. If the arrangements weren't enough to keep sleep elusive, the invasion of the suicidal grasshoppers was. "The next morning," she recalls, "it looked like lumpy grass grew on the sidewalks and the streets. They were absolutely green with dead grasshoppers."

It costs a small fortune to fill up the big rigs these days, but at least there's no plague of locusts—and it's not raining frogs.

Considering how much of a thrill ride just going to the grocery store in a family vehicle can be, imagine controlling the wheel of a vehicle weighing 10,000 pounds or more. "It's just a miracle to get back home some nights," says Gary Wright, in an observation that has been echoed many times over.

And sometimes, you don't.

"We had the right-of-way and a gentleman came across the road right

in front of us," explains Wright. "The wreck basically totaled the truck and trailer so we couldn't get to the races in Oklahoma City. It paid 50 points to show up, and we ended up losing the championship *by 12 points.*"

One of Wright's sponsors was a lawyer. Gary had never dreamed he was going to need the attorney's help, but suing the other driver's insurance company paid for all the wrecked equipment, as well as the difference between first and second place in points. That certainly helped get the team back on the track, but Wright's name will never be on that particular championship trophy.

There is no geographical limit to road accidents. Back in Delaware, the bumper came off a motorhome, which resulted in the trailer tongue lying in the middle of the road. Curt Michael was a rank rookie, already at the race track awaiting his very first time behind the wheel and wondering why the race car hadn't shown up. By the time it arrived, the whole incident certainly helped distract Curt from the butterflies in his stomach.

Most of the things that happen are fairly minor, injuries are rare, and the incidents actually end up being part of bench-racing lore. Nobody seems to have had more challenging trips to the track than Jimmy Sills, who somehow managed to win an awful lot of races in spite of off-track nuisances that should have straightened his very-curly hair.

One of his funniest tales occurred as he, his wife and his crew were in a motorhome on the way to a race. "My wife and I would change drivers going down the road all the time," he says. "You put the thing on cruise control and switch places. We'd made a clean switch, and I'm going back to the bathroom."

While Sills was in the bathroom, the motorhome began to sway. Not just a little, like avoiding a squirrel running across the road, but a lot—like, *zip up, Jimmy,*

The fuel tank came away from the car at DuQuoin in the early 1980s. Look closely and you'll see that Eddie Leavitt's would-be rescuer has a cigarette in his mouth. (Kevin Horcher Photo)

Sometimes it's easier to keep a car in one piece on the track than to keep the tow rig together off the track. Gary Wright knows that all too well. (Gene Marderness Photo)

and find out what's going on. "It's from one side of the freeway to the other, and she's got her arms cranking the wheel trying to correct it," he says. "I started running through the motorhome, but one of our guys fell out of a bunk, and now I'm stumbling over him. Well, I finally got to the front and helped her get control."

The Sills rig pulled over to the side of the road, and they saw that the jack-knife had rolled tires off the rear wheels of the motorhome. They went to the trailer to get the jack and found that the zig-zagging had taken its toll there, too. "It looked like somebody threw a hand grenade in the trailer," he laughs. "We had only one spare so we had to chain the other axle up so the hub didn't drag on the freeway. We couldn't run over 50 miles-per-hour because you didn't want to blow out that other tire."

Back when Sills was in the famous Weikert Farms car and was headed from Pennsylvania to an All-Stars show in Wisconsin, he was driving the

Rob Petty had spun and made contact—there's a nerf bar clearly on the track. The rescue people came on the track prematurely. Look very carefully on the left side of the first photo and you'll see a set of legs just clearing the guard rail. The yellow was out but thanks to dust on the track Chris Beaver (light-colored car) did not see it and came into the turn. He told observers later that his choice was to turn left and hit the worker or turn right and pile into Petty. Figuring Petty had a helmet and roll cage, he went into the race car. (Kevin Horcher Photos)

rig though a bridge construction zone. "I hear a big *bang* and all of a sudden it's sideways. It was a dually van and I'm trying to herd it through this little bridge. I'm yelling at my guys to wake up because they're about to get the crash of their lives."

Somehow the rig made it through the zone and was pulled over to the side. The group thought they had blown the van's transmission, but when they opened the door they realized that they had no rear wheels. None. The van really wasn't supposed to be a dually, but had been retrofitted to become one all the same. The adapter had broken, landed on the hub and torn the brake drum and shoes off. All that was left was a backing plate.

"We had to go back across the bridge to find the wheels. There was only about a foot-and-a-half of walkway and trucks are going about 70 miles-per-hour, hitting our stuff that's still in the road. One of the wheels got hit and actually came flying up through the air at me so that I had to duck."

A construction worker pointed to the wheel, which had landed in a tree. After retrieving it, Jimmy had to get the rim and rubber back across the bridge. "The steel wheel is weighted so heavy on one side that as I try to roll it in this narrow walkway, it's trying to roll out into traffic," he recalls. "So, then I turn it around and now it's trying to go off the bridge."

By this time, the Highway Patrol had put in an appearance and was able to tell Sills' group where the other tire and wheel were located. A guy had driven safely across the entire country from his college in Arizona and was about two exits away from home, when suddenly he looked up through his windshield—and saw a tire flying right at him.

"And the tire's there?" Jimmy asked.

"Oh, yeah," replied the patrolman. "It hit his grill and shoved the radiator clear back into the motor. He's not going anywhere for a while."

The team had missed out on the race at Wilmot Speedway, lost out on the appearance money, and still had to get the rig fixed. So, they drove on to the place in Michigan where the adapter was manufactured. "We need

On at least one occasion, Jimmy Sills and team did not make it to Wilmot Speedway. Instead, they retrieved the hauler's wheel and tire out of a tree alongside the highway. (Steve Hardin Photo)

Lenard McCarl at the opening of Maxim Chassis in June 1989. (Joyce Standridge Photo)

to buy one of these adapters for dual wheels," they said.

"Oh, you have to buy another deal. We don't make those anymore."

"Yeah," Jimmy replied dryly. "We know why."

It's not all frustration on the road, though. Guys and gals who spend much of their life watching the white lines figure out ways to have a little fun. And again, we turn to Sills for an exceeding immature, but hilarious, antidote to boredom.

"I drove for Lenard McCarl, and he's 100 percent racer. All he thought about was racing and building cars," says Sills. "We were at Karl Kinser's shop in southern Indiana, working on the car, and I went downtown to get a hair cut. While I was there, I decided to have a little fun with Lenard because he was too serious at the time. I walked into this sex shop and got a blow-up doll.

"Well, whoever had been in our motel room ahead of us had left a nightgown, so I dressed the doll in the gown and she was waiting when the guys got back there. I told them I had a new friend, and we named her Mildred because Lenard called every woman in the world Mildred."

Mildred went racing with the team. She sat in a lawn chair on top of the trailer so she could watch the races. Lenard told people she was a born race fan because, "you just look at her mouth and she was already yelling, 'go.'"

One of the crew was especially shy, and one day while running down the turnpike Virgil was driving the rig. When he pulled up to the toll booth, the toll-taker seemed to be staring at him with a very strange look on her face. He turned slightly to his right and saw that Lenard had propped the near-naked Mildred right beside Virgil. "Man, he just wanted to crawl under the steering wheel, he was so embarrassed," hoots Sills.

In Watertown, South Dakota, the team stopped to eat at a Chinese restaurant, and the little old lady working there spotted the Sills' motorhome outside. Since she'd never been inside one, Jimmy offered to show it to her. Although they weren't gone long, when they came back in Sills noticed a big bulge in McCarl's pocket.

"So," Jimmy said calmly, "did you clean out the till?"

McCarl dissolved in a fit of laughter. He hadn't taken any money, in fact, but had stuffed a wad of napkins in his pants to make it look like he did. The fact that their minds worked a lot alike did well by them at the race track, but that one day in South Dakota it just left behind a very puzzled restaurant staff.

Lynn Paxton and Bobby Allen were nearly as famous at one time for living life with zest as they were for the outstanding racing they provided the fans. It comes as no surprise, then, that life on the road with the duo was a real experience. People essentially lined up to go along.

"There were these young guys who would show up at Bobby's shop, he'd give them ten minutes of training and they were 'experts,'" observes Paxton. "Some of them ended up working for me, too, and one of them was a kid by the name of Bill Troyer."

Allen, Paxton and Troyer once shared the back seat of a crew cab on the way to a race. The problem was that Troyer always wore the same sneakers. They were in such a sorry state that they were covered with duct tape to hold the sides on his feet. Disgusted with the odor, Allen and Paxton grappled with Troyer, removed the stinky shoes and tossed them into turnpike traffic at about 70 miles-per-hour.

"Whaddamigonna do?" Troyer shrieked.

"Don't worry," he was told, "we'll take care of you".

True to their word, they stopped at a shoe store along the way. "Here's the deal," Paxton told Troyer as he was being sized for the shoes, "I'm left-handed and Bobby's right-handed. So, I'm gonna pay for the left shoe, and he's gonna pay for the right one."

At the checkout, Paxton got out his wallet and asked, "Sir, how much is the left sneaker?"

The cashier looked at him as if he'd lost his mind. But without batting an eyelash he said, "The left one's free. We only charge for the right ones."

Paxton thanked him, put his wallet back in his pocket and walked out as Allen was screaming bloody murder because he had to pay the total amount.

However, at least one time the tables were turned, although on this occasion it also didn't start out well for Allen. He was sick as the proverbial dog at an Ohio track. In fact, he was in the race car when the illness first kicked in, and his mistake was in letting Paxton know. Pax, of course, couldn't let it pass.

He enlisted Ferkel, who, in turn, had to enquire in the loudest voice he possibly could whether anybody else had detected that *foul smell!* Allen, waiting to qualify, just wanted to crawl under the header pipe.

"Very funny, Paxton," Allen sarcastically told his pal. By around midnight the same night, feeling fine and having cleaned up, Allen realized that his earlier problem was a virus making its way through the crowd. On the way home Paxton had to pull over to the side of the road in order to take his turn throwing up. And as he was in the grass on all fours, Allen pulled up—and put the high beams on Lynn so every other racer going down the road wouldn't miss the sight.

"Paybacks," says Paxton, "are hell."

Weather conditions often break up the hypnotic effects of driving hundreds of miles between races. What happens on the highway, however, seldom rivals the lunacy that can occur at the race track when Mother Nature is factored in, whether it's too much rain or too little.

Because so many cars had run into–and under–the guard rail at DuQuoin, in 1996 they added straw bails around the track. Bill Puterbaugh Jr. took a Silver Crown car into an explosion of straw–and when the straw settled, they found out that there was already a car driven by Tony Elliott there. (Allen Horcher Photos)

Dust was so bad at a Des Moines race many years ago that after a heat race, officials realized one of the cars hadn't pulled in off the track. He was literally missing in action. It turned out that Kenny Gottschalk had gone through the outside wooden fence and landed in a cow barn off the fourth turn. When they found him he was upside down in a stall full of straw. Observers said he was a little addled and the car was full of straw, but otherwise okay.

Skip Jackson, second from right, is part of a very cold driver's meeting at Jackson Speedway on September 27, 2003. (Doug Johnson Photo)

Because racers want to race, and common sense be damned about such matters as the weather, racing seasons often begin far too early and end well after they should. That means racing participants and fans bundled up to resemble the Michelin man without the grin. An IMCA race in Spencer, Iowa, back in the 1960s was indicative. The drivers stayed semi-warm in a changing room under the fairgrounds stage until they had to race. Race director Al Sweeney would send a runner with the line-up list, who would call out for the drivers in each race. They would hurry to the car, run the race, and skedaddle back to the dressing room. Car owners and wives would then give the drivers two cups of coffee—one to drink and one to warm hands on.

While the Midwest is ideal for racing and growing corn, that's at least in part because of rain showers. And the midsummer thunderstorms are legendary. "One night at the Knoxville Nationals we got the green flag and went through two, and you could see something happening in turn three. We got down there and it's a huge rain storm on that part of the track," adds Jimmy Sills. "Nobody really crashed, but it was too late for the flag or lights to warn us and everybody slid around in the grease."

It looks so tame when the sun is out, but it takes very little rain for that gate across Eldora's back stretch to seem to shrink. More than a few trucks and haulers have gotten an Eldora Smack trying to get through the gate. (Steve Hardin Photo)

Anything less than a downpour of rain, however, and the races go on, even when wiser heads should have prevailed. "We were at Lincoln Speedway in Abbottstown, Pennsylvania, and it was fog like you can only imagine," says Sills. "Everything was fine as long as the races were running because the wings were blowing enough air that it kept the fog elevated above the track. So you could see, the fans could see—sort of—and the officials could see—sort of. I was running second to Sammy Swindell but the car was running tight and I kind of lost it for a moment. The red flag came out because they thought I'd flipped it, but actually I'd saved it and somebody else had flipped.

"We sat there while they cleaned the track, but by then the fog had settled back down and you couldn't see even halfway

down the straights. We ran some hot laps, but smarter minds took over and they ended up canceling the rest of the race."

Eldora is the most notorious track in the country for rain interruptions of epic proportions. Because of the high banks, getting out of the infield is entertainment to rival Marx Brothers slapstick. In days of yore when everybody pitted in the infield, it could take literally hours to pull all the equipment out. "It was a bigger spectacle than the racing, trying to watch the haulers get out the back gate," remembers Lealand McSpadden.

There's another track, across the country from Eldora, which earned a reputation for rain misery, too. At Manzy, the desert dust grains turn to teeny-tiny ball bearings when mixed with a downpour, and it can challenge racers far more than what gear to put in the car.

"My crazy dad decided he was gonna pull another driver's hauler out at Manzanita, with our motorhome," says Richard Griffin. "He strapped the truck to the motorhome and backed up, which allowed for a lot of slack in the strap, and then he got about a 20-foot run. Well, when he got going and the strap got tight, it pulled the bumper off the motorhome. Then it flings the bumper back—and it went clear through the side of the trailer."

So much for trying to help. From that point on, when the rain moved in, Mr. Griffin moved out.

Richard Griffin (left) and Davey Allison at a Manzanita CRA show, February 1, 1992. They look so serious. You don't supposed Richard has asked Davey for advice in how to pull rigs out of the mud without yanking off the motorhome bumper, do you? (Bill Taylor Photo)

18

G'day, Mate

Tim Kaeding proudly displays the American colors during the running of the Coca-Cola Classic at Parramatta City Raceway in Sydney on New Year's Day, 2000. (Steve Lafond/ Tear-Off Heaven Fotos)

I t was not bad enough that the steering wheel was located on the right side of street vehicles in Australia, but when Jimmy Sills got ready to head out to far-flung race tracks during one of the earliest of his 18 trips there, he found that the tow vehicle was a Ford Falcon station wagon hitched to the trailer. Later versions of that small Focus-sized Falcon are still marketed Down Under, but it's not been available in America since 1970. Nor is there anywhere in the world where that would be the first choice for a tow vehicle.

"The rear bumper was dragging the ground as we left," Sills recalls. "We started in Adelaide and we're gonna tour all of Australia. But we barely got down the road until we had to call back and tell them to send a truck because the station wagon had overheated."

Restarting with a Ford F-100, the Sills party headed into the Outback, and found another fact of life in Aussie Land. Gas stations are few and far between. "We were so far out that you couldn't even see lights from a farm house anywhere," he says.

They weren't totally unprepared when the tow rig ran out of fuel that night. They had several fuel cans with them, so they got out and turned on a Safari light bar. Mounted on top of the truck, it can illuminate the entire surrounding area. That's when they learned yet another fact of life: The Outback only *appears* to be empty. In fact, it is full of bugs.

Millions and millions of flying bugs.

Sills remembers, "There were so many bugs we could hardly pour gas in the truck. They're biting us, they're trying to eat the gas, they're so thick you have to beat them off to get to the fuel fill."

From left: Jimmy Sills, Gary Patterson, Larry Burton, and Larry Rice, with car owner Bob Davis kneeling, at the Sidney Showgrounds in 1975. (Courtesy Jimmy Sills Collection)

Jimmy Sills racing with Dick Briton at the Sydney Showground in 1974. (Courtesy Jimmy Sills Collection)

Sills is just one of scores of sprint car drivers who have traveled to Australia during the American off-season, ideal timing because the seasons are reversed. Now that there's nowhere left to pioneer in America, the free-spirited find Australia appealing. Australia (and New Zealand, where racing also abounds) are not the new Wild West. Australia is as modern as any well-heeled North American or European region. However, Australia has rural areas where, if time hasn't stood still, it just hasn't been in as much of a hurry as the sophisticated cities. With less competition for entertainment dollars, racing has been especially solid in small towns scattered throughout the continent.

Aussies are not the only ones to cross the water and race in the U.S. This is the Kiwi Kid Stevie Walsh from New Zealand after a push-off for hot laps at Spoon River Speedway in 2006. (Keenan Wright Photo)

It doesn't matter which continent he's on, Skip Jackson knows how to get his game face on. (Mike Campbell Photo)

Aussies have long been fans of American racing as well. "When I was a little kid, my Dad was interested in American racing," Aussie native Skip Jackson tells. "We knew what the Indy 500 was and American drivers were always coming down to race. A.J. Foyt—I'm actually named for him, Skip being my nickname—raced here in 1975. Even in the 1970s, the Americans were coming."

Gary Rush was the acknowledged king of Aussie sprint car racing back then, winning 10 Australian championships during his career. After failing to get into Formula 1 racing, he instead turned his attention to the U.S. during the Aussie off-season. Because he had some success, it piqued interest in what Australia had to offer. And while they had lagged behind in technology up to that point, all that changed in a rush. Or perhaps more accurately, a Rush.

"Gary bought a Stanton car and did extremely well with that," recalls Jackson. "He brought it back to Australia and did really well for a long time with that particular car."

In the U.S. the battle between winged and wingless cars was being waged—and continues to a degree today—but Down Under there was always a roof. "They were quite primitive at first, but we've always had wings," confirms Jackson.

Parramatta, near Sydney, is the most famous of the tracks, a clay surface that has been fast and easy on tires. In fact, in the 1970s and 1980s, unless they were flattened in a wreck, tires lasted all year. Even with the low cost, however, they got maybe 20 or so cars per event back then. The attraction to sprinters has grown so much over time that now they draw 50 or 60 cars.

Gary Rush Sr. and Gary Rush Jr. are names well-known in Australian circles. Senior was among the very first Aussies to come to America to race, and he made a terrific impression that has naturally led to many driver exchanges over the years. (Steve Lafond/Tear-Off Heaven Fotos)

"I think the biggest thing was that back then if you bought a car for $20,000 U.S., you then had to convert it to Australian dollars, so now it was up to $30,000," says Jackson. "Add a 40 percent import duty on top of that and a 22 percent sales tax. Instantly the car was nearly $50,000. As a result people got quite...umm...ingenious in those days in figuring out how to get a car into the country."

Tobacco company sponsorship also pumped up the racing, sponsoring drivers, cars and tracks. One even developed a World Series that attracted tremendous attention domestically and overseas. "In Australia, there are 30 million people, while in America there's 300 million," Jackson continues. "Percentage wise, probably one percent of the population in Australia knows about and follows sprint car racing, where it's maybe only a tenth-of-a-percent in the U.S. But comparing percentage-wise, sprint car racing is bigger in Australia even though there are fewer tracks and cars. The ban on tobacco advertising had an adverse effect on sprint cars there, but the racing had gotten big enough that it's still solid."

Although the cars are identical to their American cousins, right down to 410-cubic-inch versus 360-cubic-inch engines, when Jackson and his brothers got started, cost inhibited development. They got their parts from a junkyard back then, including a four-cylinder Nissan engine for which they had to build the injectors, headers and oil pan. Nonetheless, they went out and won races with it.

But times change. Probably most significantly, Gambler Chassis had an impact on Australian racing at the same time it was changing American sprint car racing. Not only did Gambler send down cars with American drivers for the season, they signed up a distributor and ensured

When a fan came down after the race and asked Team USA–Rocky Hodges, Shane Carson, Danny Lasoski and Jeff Gordon–to pose with her pet, the guys expected a puppy. What they got was pure Australian–a baby 'roo! (Courtesy Mar-Car Collection)

As part of Team USA, Shane Carson wheels the Trostle car around the track at Perth in 1987. (Courtesy Mar-Car Collection)

that frames and parts were readily available.

Bob Trostle also had significant impact as he realized the potential market there. "Trostle supplied the cars, and I went over as part of Team USA in 1987," says Shane Carson. "Rocky Hodges was sort of the manager of a team that included Danny Lasoski and a new kid nobody really knew—Jeff Gordon. It was kind of interesting—we made him bring his own car because we weren't really sure if he could drive or not. By the end of the trip, though, we realized he could drive all right. John Bickford, Jeff's stepfather, was pretty instrumental in keeping his equipment up and coaching Jeff along. So it ended up being great to have him over there. He was a lot of fun."

Kinser, Schatz, all the big American stars raced there, although one of the biggest names to the Aussies for a long time was Gary "Preacher" Patterson.

A contemporary of Opperman's, Patterson became absolutely legendary there in the 1970s, but for maybe the wrong reason. He was notorious—*absolutely notorious*—for inciting near-riots in the grandstand by getting on the public address system and calling the Aussie drivers "amateurs," and following that up with put-downs of all things Australian-racing.

"I was just six or seven years old, but he used to race at our track quite a bit," recalls Jackson. "I'd never, ever say 'hello' to him because…*whoa*…he looked mean. I found out later from talking to different people who knew him well that he was actually the nicest fellow in the world. But as a little kid looking at him, he was just plain scary."

No Aussie driver appears to have donned a black hat and chosen to be boorish after crossing the ocean. Instead, many who've come to race in America have been warm, charming and reasonably successful, particularly Brooke

Brooke Tatnell has become one of the most enduringly popular Australians to craft a sprint car career in the U.S. (Mike Campbell Photo)

Tatnell and Max Dumesny, in addition to Rush and Jackson. Often Aussie fans come to visit, too, and see for themselves the places they've only heard about, such as Knoxville, Eldora, The Grove, Manzy and many more up and down the highway. They blend in well with Americans at the track.

Off the track—not always so well.

One American driver tells of hearing a group of Aussie fans talk about "wingies," and his curiosity prompted him to ask what they were talking about.

"It's a beer, mate," was the response. "When you're done, you throw it out the car window."

"Umm, how fast were you going?"

"Not so bad. Kind of what we do back home—about 90."

"90??? Going 90 mph down the Interstate, drinking beer? You can't do that over here—they'll throw you in jail! You'll have to call your ambassador or somethin'. They don't care about diplomatic immunity in rural Iowa!"

The Aussies just laughed. And popped open another one as they headed toward the next race track. American fans have also followed their heroes Down Under, and probably behaved no more sensibly, which is likely why there is such a warm understanding between the groups.

American drivers have often fared well in the Southern Hemisphere, but probably no one has gotten more out of the exchange than Daryn Pittman. He was originally planning to go over in a deal arranged by an acquaintance he'd met in the U.S., but the telephone remained quiet for weeks, and then months. Finally, he dug out the phone number and called.

The deal had fallen through, and the fellow apologized for not calling. Daryn figured he had to write it off, a bummer at least in part because he didn't really have anything going in the U.S. at the time either. And then the phone rang again. The gentleman felt so bad that he had gone out and leased a car for Pittman to run at four events in Australia.

"We won three of the four," Pittman says. "I was supposed to leave in a couple of days to come back home, but Reeve Kruk was in the grandstand watching."

Kruk, owner of the largest garage and carport firm in Australia as well as a sprint car team, had been preparing to sell off all his racing equipment. In fact, he'd taken out a full-page ad, but after seeing the young American, he said, "Nope. I'm gonna keep racing."

Kruk sent his crew chief, Brent "Glenno" Inglis, down to the pits to

Kerry Madsen is nearly as well known in the U.S. as Australia. In recent years he has been a Knoxville Raceways regular and occasional visitor on the WoO circuit. (Steve Lafond/Tear-Off Heaven Fotos)

Reeve Kruk, a successful businessman in Australia, became Daryn Pittman's car owner in America, too. When the team won the Kings Royal in 2008, it was the realization of a long-sought goal. (Mike Campbell Photo)

hire Pittman, and, what a great deal it turned out to be for them all. Pittman raced for Kruk in Australia for three years, and then the businessman bought equipment in the U.S. for Pittman to drive on the World of Outlaws series and in various independent events at various tracks around the country. Glenno has come over to be his U.S. crew chief, too.

"We went from coming home to nothing to having probably one of the best rides in Australia," Pittman remembers. "Even though I didn't win any races for Reeve that first time over there, we got along really well. So he asked me to come back over and run the whole World Series thing, which had been my goal to begin with. I went back the next year and it pretty much went to plan. We didn't win as many races as we should have, but we pretty well dominated the series. Won the points deal."

To date, Pittman is the only American to have won the World Series. That's made him a huge favorite with the fans there, too.

"They're a lot like the fans here," he continues. "And it's a lot like here in that the smaller towns are the places where they're having the most success. They'll run five- or six-page articles in the local newspaper. The whole town is behind the races."

There is special commotion around the most important race of the year—the Grand Annual Sprint Car Classic, held at Premier Speedway in rural Warrnambool since 1973, and the equivalent of the Knoxville Nationals.

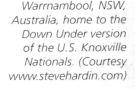

Warrnambool, NSW, Australia, home to the Down Under version of the U.S. Knoxville Nationals. (Courtesy www.stevehardin.com)

Jackson agrees with Pittman's assessment of the fans. "The people who come down to see you after the races are nice people, and they really know the racing."

"It was cool because everybody over there was really jazzed up about the racing," adds Carson. "I don't know what else they had going on in sports at the time that might have competed for attention, but the sprinters were really big there, and the fans just loved it."

"Australians are big on beer drinking! That is one place where it is socially acceptable to be an alcoholic," laughs Sills. "Those guys like to have some fun parties."

Just going to Australia is just so plain enjoyable that many go back again and again, sometimes for decades. Drivers and their families get to indulge in foreign travel but in a setting that is exceptionally comfortable. Australia also sometimes represented the opportunity for a different approach to racing. For example, Bobby Allen nearly always drove for himself in America, but raced for car owners in Australia. Conversely, Jimmy Sills nearly always drove for others in America, but took his own car Down Under, at least once.

"When you spend every dime every day to race at home, it makes you not as aggressive because you're protecting everything," notes Allen. "When I went to Australia that last time, I didn't worry about it. You want to perform good, but if you crash it, they're going to fix it."

When Sills got a chance to go, he had to take his

own race car and actually borrowed money from his mother to buy the car. "I really have respect for guys who drive their own equipment because you just can't drive them like you can for someone else. That was definitely a whole different deal and I ended up making some money off the car at the end of the tour. We actually broke a track record at Adelaide with the car, and I told the guys there I was selling it to that they should go through the motor because it had a little vibration in it when I ran the pavement track. Well, they didn't. They were just excited about racing—and they blew the engine the first night out. So, I guess I dodged a bullet as a car owner—and I found I didn't care for being one."

Even after Lealand McSpadden won the Chili Bowl in 1991, he passed on the marquee midget race the following year to go to Australia. He returned several more times during his lengthy career. "For me it was like getting to be Steve Kinser because I went there and raced full-time—didn't have to run home to work at my job," remembers McSpadden. "My wife

Danny Smith, a frequent visitor Down Under, is interviewed by Aussie announcer Wade Aunger. And then Danny went out and flipped 'er. (Steve Lafond/Tear-Off Heaven Fotos)

It's never unusual to see Donny Schatz (center) in Victory Lane, but this time it was Australia. That's Skip Jackson to the left and Phil Gressman at right. (Steve Lafond/Tear-Off Heaven Fotos)

and I got to do a lot of sightseeing. It was a vacation and getting paid to race, and the people there treated us wonderfully. It wasn't a hard decision to go back."

In the 18 times Sills went to Australia (and six times to New Zealand), he saw a lot of change, beginning with priorities. When he first started going, the emphasis by the tracks was preparation for Speedway Bikes, noisy, lightweight motorcycles that race four bikes four laps at a time. ESPN showed them late at night some years ago. They're exciting, but they like a track that's dry, one that's even dusty. As a result, when the sprinters ran concurrently they found all the tracks except Parramatta got slick very quickly. "One night we were racing and I talked the guy into digging the track up so it would hold moisture and be better for us," Sills says. "Well, they crashed the bikes that night. I wasn't too popular with them after that. But over time the sprint cars got more popular overall than the bikes, so the tracks paid more attention to us. The result was that they have developed some really good drivers compared to…well… anywhere."

But as much as Americans and Aussies are alike and have progressed in racing apace, Australia is still another country more than 7,500 miles as the crow flies from Los Angeles to Sydney. (And the crow doesn't fly, so the airlines add many more miles—and hours—to the trip.) For all of our similarities, there are significant differences, too, beyond simply driving on the wrong side of the road. There's also the food.

"That's the biggest thing over there," recalls Carson. "You had to get used to what they called 'food.' I remember Jack Hewitt and Jac Haudenschild complaining about it. So, we tried to make chicken-fried steak one night. I went to the store and tried to get cube steak, but they had never even heard of that. I got something that looked like it, and they beat on it for a while. We made up some fries to go with it, and the people we were staying with—they wouldn't eat it. They didn't touch it. Turned out that even the flour was different. I didn't know you could get different flour."

Well beyond the kitchen, obviously, kangaroos and wallabies are indigenous to Australia and won't be found in the U.S. except in zoos. But even shared species can be different—such as spiders. "We saw a funnel web spider in a museum exhibit," explains Sills. "They are so venomous that just a little while before a kid had been bitten by one and died. So, we saw at the museum what they look like."

A short time later, Sills was about to get into his truck when he

Dave Darland; Warren Eikens from Darwin, Australia, and wearing vintage racing gear; Jimmy Sills and Tony Elliott were invited to drive vintage midget cars in 1996 at the Rosebank track in Auckland, New Zealand. Of course, Jimmy couldn't leave it there—he ended up as a passenger on a motorcycle, too. (Courtesy Jimmy Sills Collection)

happened to look down. Whether it really was one or just the power of suggestion, he thought he saw a funnel web spider. "I was barefoot," he says. "It looks just like one of those spiders by my foot, so I dove into the truck! Banged my head on the door, but I didn't care. Headache? Dead? Which would you choose?"

Rattled by the encounter, Sills forgot to stop at the gas station, even though he'd already had experience of running out of fuel and survived an all-out flying insect assault. "We ran out of gas—and we didn't have any in the carrying cans either," he recalls.

A flat-bed, tractor-trailer pulled over to where Sills and team were stranded. The driver got out and asked, "Got a problem there, mate?"

"Yeah, we ran out of gas," Sill responded. "Can you give us a lift to a petrol station?"

"I'll do better than that. I got a chain, so I'll just tow you in."

Well, hell. Why not?

"Now try to keep the slack out of me chain while I'm goin' through me gears, so we don't bust the chain," the driver told them.

They took off, but Sills' truck didn't have the lights on because they didn't want to run down the battery. As it turned out, that was the least of their worries.

"No power steering," says Sills, "no power brakes, so it's kind of a handful, but I'm keeping the slack out of the chain and we go for a ways. Well, then the guy finds another gear somewhere, so my rig runs clear up to the flatbed before I can get on the brakes. But when I get on the brakes, he takes off, and I thought it was gonna tear the whole front end off the truck.

"So, now this guy's going as fast as his truck will go. Probably 80, and the roads there are so narrow that if two trucks pass each other, you're both off on the shoulder. Out in The Bush, people have screens over their windshields to keep from getting them broken with the rocks that get kicked up."

Absolutely helpless, they could do nothing but literally hold on and pray. Convinced that, short of death, it can't get worse—it did. It began to rain.

"We're doing 80 and it pours so hard that we can barely see the glow of his taillights through the spray. Then the road has some dips in it, and they were full of water from this downpour, so our truck hydroplanes across the dips. The front end would pull off to the left, but then the chain would jerk it so bad that my hands came off the steering wheel.

"We did this for probably only 10 miles—but it felt like 30."

And if that wasn't enough, as Sills was finally gassing the rig at the station, he happened to look over and saw the truck driver in the coffee shop, laughing and pointing at the crazy Americans who'd literally had their chain yanked but good.

Guess Jimmy should have tossed a wingie the trucker's way, eh, mate?

19

Abrupt Endings

Just as Bobby Allen thinks his brother was more innately talented as a driver but not as driven to succeed, there have been many, many more instances of unfulfilled expectations. More often than not there is a positive spin to the story—a driver who has been able to keep racing in perspective, avoiding the pitfalls of putting it ahead of family and friends. But occasionally, the cause is out of their control.

"Billy Shuman could have been a world champion in any type of racing he wanted," is Lealand McSpadden's opinion. "He had so much natural talent in everything he drove. He was driven early on, and then he got hurt a couple of times and he just kind of didn't pursue it as much after that. If he had, I believe he could have been better than his brother Ronnie or me—he just had that much ability."

It's a given that anybody who races for any length of time will end up waiting for x-rays to be read in the emergency room. There have been times when the possibility of something a lot more permanent—death or maiming—could be in the cards. Roll cages, arm restraints, better helmets, firesuits, disintegrating cars that dissipate the energy of a crash, and many other improvements have reduced the seriousness of most wrecks. Not eliminated the threat, but made it much easier for drivers to think about something more than just the "what if" factor. Still, throughout the history of racing too many promising careers have ended prematurely.

"When I started racing in the early 1960s there were two very consistent, strong runners, Bobby Hersh and Gene Goodling," says Lynn Paxton. "They both got severe neck injuries of the type that the seat rolled in and apparently broke the base of their skulls. It was all because of the inferior way the seat belts were put in and the way the seats were mounted. Stuff that everybody knows about now, but back then we just didn't know.

Jack Hewitt has known more single-day success at Eldora than any other driver, but occasionally he's been bitten by Lady Luck. During the 1993 4-Crown race, he tangled with Mike Mann and was badly injured. Observers say that his helmet hit Mann's roll cage during the tumble. (Allen Horcher Photo)

They weren't killed, but they were in comas for a long time."

Goodling, in fact, came back to racing as an official at Lincoln Speedway after his 1964 end-over-end accident. He is still alive, but Hersh passed away a few years ago.

"Ray Kelly was another absolutely fabulous racer, but he got hurt at Langhorne," Paxton continues. "I'll tell you what—if those three guys had been able to race into the late 1970s, there wouldn't be as many of us in the Hall of Fame because they were that good. It was definitely a case of careers cut short because of injury."

"Another one was Bobby Davis," believes Rick Ferkel. Davis had been the 1989 World of Outlaws champion, and many people believed he was poised to be a serious threat to the Big Three: Kinser, Swindell and Wolfgang. "But

(Top left) Bobby Davis (#29) tried to take away the final transfer spot in an Eldora heat race during the early 1980s, but Dewayne Barker (#33B) didn't yield. (Top right) As a result, both flipped, Davis caught on fire, and neither made the transfer. (Kevin Horcher Photos)

Rick Ferkel (#0) goes low and avoids the wreck at Eldora. (Kevin Horcher Photo)

then he had that bad wreck at Knoxville and it sort of took it out of him. He ran a bit after that but not really, really good It was a shame because he was young."

Wolfgang's career, on the other hand, had lasted years and accumulated significant accolades before his first life-threatening accident at Lakeside Speedway in 1992, when he broke his neck and suffered third-degree burns. Like Opperman before him, Wolfie overcame incredible odds to race again, but when he broke his neck a second time at Tri-City Speedway, Illinois, in 1997, it signaled the premature end to an incredible career.

Throughout sprint car history there have been too many instances of drivers losing limbs or suffering paralysis. Just one example was Terry Turbak, who was paralyzed in a wreck at Sioux Falls in 1979 and then passed away several months later. But in a bona fide case of making lemonade from lemons there is the story of Brad Doty.

The roll cage collapsed on him during a flip at Eldora in 1988, leaving him a paraplegic. Following his recuperation, Brad became a highly respected and admired sprint car television commentator. His charming personality translated well from the track to the camera, and he has won awards for his communications work. "He was a great racer, so the wreck and injury were a shame," says Johnny Herrera, who recalls Doty's skills well. "He is a wonderful person, too, and he is still trying to give back to the sport all he can."

Jimmy Caruthers survived the cage collapse at the Terre Haute Action Track on August 8, 1971–but he didn't win the battle against cancer a few years later. (Joyce Standridge Photo)

Although he had retired from racing after the 1995 season, Lealand McSpadden found himself in the biggest battle of his life when he was diagnosed with cancer in February 2003. Radical surgery on his neck, followed by additional treatment did not initially leave his medical support team especially optimistic. Doctors found that the Stage 4 cancer had metastasized and they weren't even sure of the source. Radiation was done to improve his odds by 10 percent, but as his wife Janet said at the time, "Stand 10 people in a row and only one succeeds, and Lealand will try to be that one."

One of the most tenacious racers ever, Lealand McSpadden needed every bit of his legendary toughness to fight an even greater battle off the track. Here he is in a pensive moment prior to a race at Imperial (CA) Speedway, November 3, 1995. (Bill Taylor Photo)

Dr. Chris Sloan, who saved several lives in the pits at Little Rock in 2007. (Courtesy Jeana Sloan)

Two hundred race victories over a 26-year career pales in importance when compared to seeking this kind of victory. But anyone who ever saw Lealand's truly tenacious style behind a steering wheel would not be surprised to learn that he was interviewed for this book in February 2008, five years after the original diagnosis. Has he ever extended this heat race!

Even as safety equipment and track response have steadily improved through the years, there are always new things to think about. An insidious new threat to racing, one that potentially affects nearly everyone in the pit area is carbon monoxide poisoning. This comes, not from the race cars, but rather from the oversized haulers and generators that run almost continuously during events. With the haulers parked so closely together at most events, the fumes become trapped and can become deadly.

At the Little Rock Short Track Nationals in October 2007, Illinoisan Jimmy Hurley and his family found out firsthand just how dangerous CO can be. They had already experienced a series of incredibly unlucky events. During the previous year, a race car flipped out of Jacksonville (IL) Raceway and landed on four people with their team, putting dad Jim in the hospital with serious injuries. An Interstate highway wreck completely demolished their hauler and trailer. Then a bracket broke inside the new trailer, falling and gashing mom Joyce on the head. The Little Rock weekend was supposed to be a respite after such a string of nightmares.

If they had any good luck at all, it was that the very popular physician/driver, Dr. Christopher Sloan of suburban St. Louis, was changing clothes in the next hauler after finishing his race. When he heard a frantic voice just outside, calling him, Doc didn't even take a moment to put on his shoes. "I knew from the tone of voice it was urgent," he says.

Jimmy had found his mother slumped between the driver's and passenger's seats in the hauler, unresponsive. Since Doc is a good-sized man, he lifted her over his shoulder and got her out of the cab to lay her on the ground.

His immediate assessment was alarming. Her pupils were fixed and dilated, skin a pasty white, and her lips nearly purple, Doc realized immediately that he was dealing with serious carbon monoxide poisoning. Although she had a thready pulse and weak heart beat that said she was still alive, Joyce was perilously close to death. If Jimmy hadn't gone to the cab for something else at that given moment, it's unlikely she would have survived.

His serendipitous action saved his dad and sister, both of whom also were in the hauler and minutes from death. Amy was "anesthetized," according to Doc, able to sit up but she could not respond to commands or to speak, with symptoms similar to her mother's. Dad Jim stumbled out of the cab on his own, but was incoherent. Ironically, although he appeared to be in the best condition initially, later he was assessed as having the greatest concentration of CO in his system and spent the most time hospitalized.

Jimmy Hurley
needed Doc
Sloan's help to
save his family's
lives. (Keenan
Wright Photo)

With assistance from the paramedics at the track, Doc Sloan cleared airways and got oxygen going, stabilizing the Hurleys so they could be transported to the hospital for further care. But not every situation is going to have a physician in the next pit, and some drivers have been forced into retirement because of chronic CO-related headaches. That is why carbon monoxide detectors are overdue as basic equipment in every hauler.

Although he did not pass away until 1997, it's fair to say that racing used up Jan Opperman long before he was gone. Few people recall that his brother Jay died in 1970 at Knoxville, in the first sprint car race he ran in the Midwest while trying to follow in Jan's tire tracks. Jan rarely spoke

Jan Opperman nearing the end
of a brilliant career, 1980. (Allen
Horcher Photo)

Jan Opperman, early 1970s. (Courtesy Jeff Moe Collection)

of that, but it was the first of several racing incidents that took a toll.

On the 51st lap of the Hoosier Hundred Silver Crown race in September 1976, Johnny Parsons Jr., Bubby Jones and Jan Opperman were battling for the lead when Parsons inexplicably slowed. Opperman rode over the rear tire and flipped. All three cars ended up involved, and when he

"Indiana" Andy Hillenburg wrecked at the Indianapolis Mile and the fuel tank ruptured, setting on fire the tarps hanging on the fence. Fellow driver Ron Dunston realized that Hillenburg was injured and couldn't get out of the car on his own, and Ron helped Andy out of the fire. (Kevin Horcher Photos)

apparently thought it safe to do so, Opp began to unbuckle and get out of his car. However, a backmarker came around through turn three well behind the pack and slammed into Opp's roll cage.

While Jan came back to racing after recuperating from that wreck, there was no such inspiring resurgence after a 1981 Jennerstown, Pennsylvania, crash that resulted in serious brain injury. His devoted parents, June and Pops, took care of him the rest of his life. Even with frequent financial support from the racing community, the slow demise of Jan Opperman was a heart-breaking coda to a brilliant career that had thrilled thousands of fans from coast to coast.

There have been numerous instances of disabling injury eventually taking a life, but racing-related death often happens quickly, violently and unforgettably.

Of the litany of those killed racing, it's always particularly difficult to cope when the young ones go. One such was Robbie Stanley, who was only 26 years old in 1994 when he spun out and was tee-boned by another car at Winchester Speedway. He had already accumulated an All-Stars championship and three USAC championships in a row.

But even for those who aren't well-known, it is a terrible truth that racing can be indiscriminate in taking drivers away. When 27-year-old Billy Kimmel was killed at The Grove in 2007, it was as devastating to his admirers as Stanley's violent demise had been to his. "If anybody could define the term 'underdog,' that was Bill," friend Gregg

Robbie Stanley is interviewed by Dave Despain on ESPN's Thursday Night Thunder in the early 1990s. (Allen Horcher Photo)

Obst was quoted in Carlisle, Pennsylvania's *Sentinel* newspaper afterward. When Kimmel had shown up at an earlier race without fresh tires, Obst had bought enough tee-shirts to pay for the tires. "He was standing there with tears in his eyes. He was never going to win the race, but, by God, he would capture the hearts of the people watching."

Though no more important to their families than all the others have been to theirs, there are three other drivers who stand out because their deaths were sucker-punches to all of racing.

He got his nickname by way of a mail-order divinity degree. Gary Patterson certainly didn't look like a typical preacher, nor did he take the whole deal very seriously. It was the anything-goes 1960s.

If he looked tough, that part was no lie. Not long after he got out of the military, Patterson ended up doing two years in a Georgia prison for assault. He had gotten into a fight at a bar, and while he had viewed

Gary "Preacher" Patterson, one of the most colorful characters ever in racing. (Gene Marderness Photo)

it as self-defense, the legal system saw it differently. Those stereotypes of Southern jails as exceedingly unpleasant aren't off the mark, so anything racing could throw at him in the future couldn't be any worse than the time in jail. "In Australia they called him the Hostile Hippie, and he looked the part," remembers Jimmy Sills. "He wasn't a guy I wanted to race wheel-to-wheel with, and we had a few problems. Our friendship was strained a few times, but you got over it."

Yet, in spite of the prison-yard stare that chilled nearly every competitor or racing fan within range, and his hard-nosed approach to driving, Patterson was equally well-known as a gentle and kind spirit, especially with children and animals. He could be insightful. "In 1977 I didn't win a race and was crashing a lot," Sills continues. "Gary said, 'You know, you can't take that to the next race. You're only as good as your last race—you gotta re-prove yourself all over. Pretty soon all the bad stuff ends and you'll be back to winning.' I took that advice, and he was right."

Throughout the 1970s, Patterson compiled a string of wins, particularly on the West Coast. For a guy who hated organizations and clubs, he was winning within the acronyms as much as he was creating a legend as a free spirit. Unlike a lot of people who just say they don't care

People like Gary Patterson were good to Jimmy Sills when he struggled, so Jimmy has always tried to give back to racing. Using the two-seater from his driving school, Jimmy took quadriplegic Shawn McDonald for a ride. They couldn't get a driving suit to fit, and they had to tape Shawn's helmet and hands in, but then Jimmy did the best thing he possibly could have for Shawn—he opened that baby up and took him for a real ride! (Courtesy Jimmy Sills Collection)

what others think, it seems that Patterson really didn't. His friendships ranged from fellow maverick Jan Opperman to the straight-laced former school teacher (and USAC champion) Larry Rice. Not a lot of drivers could have stretched it that far, but if Patterson was your friend, it was the same as blood.

On Memorial Day weekend of 1983, The Preacher perished in a wreck at Calistoga Speedway. The fussin', fightin', feudin' and fun were dimmed for a lot of West Coast fans. There surely were some unwritten chapters in that extraordinary life.

Dick "Toby" Tobias, a truly brilliant star taken too soon. (Above left) Toby in 1977 at East Bay. (Al Consoli Photo) (Above right) Racing in the era before roll cages. (Gene Marderness Photo)

When Dick "Toby" Tobias sheared off his roll cage and was killed during a USAC sprint race at Flemington, New Jersey, on June 23, 1978, the entire racing world was shaken to its roots. Toby had seemed unsinkable. He was a smart driver on the track and he seemed more at home in the winner's circle than picking up the pieces of a wrecked car from a wrong move. Toby won the very first race he ever ran, joking that he was so nervous he closed his eyes at the green flag and when he finally opened them he was leading.

His career was interrupted by military service, and then later he promised his bride he wouldn't race. To the future delight of thousands of fans, he didn't keep his word. While he rather routinely whupped the competition, he earned many friends among the racers, too. Lynn Paxton was just one of them, and he remembers a particular race at Susquehanna Speedway. "Toby was leading this thing, it's getting late in the race and I get into second," says Paxton. "I thought to myself, 'I've got my hands full here, 'cause Toby's a hell of a racer.'

"About halfway up the backstretch, this big paw comes out of the left side of the car and makes a motion like I'm supposed to pass him on the inside. Well, it shocked me. I went in so hard I overshot, especially since we weren't running wings. He damned near got me back, but he let me go.

Mitch Smith walked away from a Hall-of-Fame career while he might still have had a few wins left in him but in the shadow of fellow competitors returning to the sport only to lose their lives, he put his young children's interests first and quit for good. (Courtesy Lynn Paxton Collection)

"We're in Victory Lane and he said, 'Well, kid, you about give that one back.'

"I said, 'Toby, that's not you. What was your mindset? I was expecting to do battle with you.'

"And he said, 'I looked in my mirrors and I saw you and I saw Ray Kelly coming like hell. I couldn't hold you both up and Kelly's been winning all the races.'"

Toby was right that Kelly had about three times as many wins as all the others combined. Add to that the fact that Paxton owed some money to Tobias' speed shop, and well, heck, when Toby realized he didn't have the horses to win, it was probably a pretty easy decision for a thinking driver.

"Toby was the guy who never took chances," Paxton continues. "He was 'Steady Eddie' because he was the consummate professional. With his eyesight the way it was, he didn't stick it in where he didn't know he could make it. He got to where he didn't like running Port Royal because of the shadows on the track. He didn't like Flemington either, and he really was there to fill out the field for USAC. He was already qualified for the A Main, but he went out in the B to help them out, make them look better."

If there was anything good at all to come out of the death of a driver who had impacted DIRT modifieds as much or more than his beloved sprint cars, it was that Toby's death made another terrific driver pause.

"I called Mitch Smith about two in the morning and told him that Toby had been killed that night," say Paxton. "Mitch had just come out of retirement. He's in his fifties and he's got young children because he had them late in life. I said, 'Stay the hell out of a race car,' and to his credit, Mitch never ran again.

Sheldon Kinser (#3) and Rich Vogler (#2) compete at Eldora in 1984. In less than a decade, they would both be gone forever, Sheldon to cancer and Rich to a vicious crash. (Allen Horcher Photo)

And it wasn't because he was afraid—he just understood what it meant to Toby's kids to lose him, and he didn't want his three young children to go through that. There wasn't anything left to prove anyway."

When Rich Vogler died in an especially grisly accident at Salem, Indiana, on July 21, 1990, he was just days away from his 40th birthday. He was also qualified for the NASCAR race the following day at Pocono, in what might have been a new twist to a fascinating career. Vogler was awarded the win at Salem because he had been leading when the race was red-flagged for the wreck that had left his car impaled on a fence post.

It wasn't that Vogler didn't know how mean short track racing could be. His father Don had been killed in a 1981 midget crash at the Indianapolis Speedrome, but Rich could no more turn off the desire to win than he could have voluntarily stopped breathing.

Sprint car racing has always drawn hard-nosed, determined drivers, but Vogler was extraordinary. He had a real love-hate relationship with his fellow competitors. It wasn't possible to even talk to him during the race—unless *he* wanted to.

"If you walked up to him after hot laps, from then until the show was over, when you asked him a question he'd act like you didn't exist," recalls photographer Allen Horcher.

"When Vogler went to race, he didn't go to socialize," adds Kevin Horcher. "He didn't go to run second either. You might get a one-word answer from him and that was all. But if you watched him, it was obvious that he was thinking. A lot of times, he'd be standing ten feet from the car, just staring at it. He'd maybe go talk to another driver or car owner, but while he's standing there talking to them, he'd be kind of leaning on his hand on their tire—he'd be picking at it to feel the compound. He would never look down, because he didn't want them to know what he was doing, but he'd have his thumb down there just picking away to see how soft that tire was."

The intensity made him a sensation for fans to watch. "He was

Rich Vogler, March 1990. He's not picking at the tire, but then, it was his own rather than a competitor's. (Allen Horcher Photo)

The irony of this photo is that it is Wayne Hammonds (#66) and Rich Vogler (#1), racing side by side at Bolivar, Missouri, in early 1990. A few months later, they would touch tires at Salem, propelling Vogler through the air and to his death. (Allen Horcher Photo)

ESPN's Gary Lee interviews a very unhappy Jeff Gordon after Rich Vogler has taken him out of a race at IRP. (Kevin Horcher Photo)

absolutely fearless, especially at a place like Eldora, including when they ran without the wings," says Allen. "He was absolutely fearless—or just a complete idiot. I'm not sure. But he sure never drove with any caution at all."

At Terre Haute, he got in Ben Bowen's car for a USAC show, started dead last in a car he'd never even sat in before—and won. He hit a lot of other cars on the way forward, and that was pure Vogler.

He probably cemented his reputation as a "screw-you" guy one night at Indianapolis Raceway Park, during an ESPN-televised show. Doing well was critical during those races because a lot of big time car owners tuned in and it was a great way to get attention, especially if you were an aging driver with a reputation for being hard on equipment. This particular night, he got together with a young kid by the name of Jeff Gordon. And after Gordon was punted out of the race, he ended up at the edge of the track, shaking his fist at Vogler.

The crowd was booing Vogler, but that was hardly a rare occurrence. Things like that never shook his confidence. So, when the race was over and the inevitable television reporter stuck a microphone under his nose with a camera in his face, the demand was, "Tell us about the problem you had over in turn three."

"Problem?" he snapped. "I didn't have no problem."

"With you and Gordon," the TV guy insisted.

"I didn't have no problem," Vogler smiled. "I guess *he* had a problem."

It was not uncommon for other drivers to have Vogler problems. Shane Carson recalls, "The USAC champ cars came to Oklahoma City for a race, and I won it. That was a big deal to me because it was on my birthday and in front of my hometown crowd. I passed Vogler to win, and that was pretty important to me. I'd raced with him a little bit before but I knew he was all about winning. He didn't like to lose, and the USAC-ers—they really don't like outsiders.

"Right at the start of the race, Vogler nailed John Johnson, and he flipped. We rolled down the back straight and the red was out. Vogler stopped on the front straight and another local driver just rammed into him—letting him know he didn't appreciate what he'd done to Johnson. The fans were going nuts. You could hear them yelling over the engines.

"I got out of my car and went up to Vogler's. I told him not to give me the same treatment. Of course, he told me it was *not* his fault, but I'd raced him enough to know. He was the classic USAC driver of the time. Back in those days—the '70s and '80s—the USAC drivers were treated pretty badly by the owners. If you didn't win, you'd get a Coke and when you came back there might be somebody else driving your car."

Unquestionably, Vogler was under a lot pressure to perform, but probably no car owner exerted more pressure than he did on himself. "Controversial" doesn't begin to describe how he was viewed. Fewer drivers inspired more love or loathing. Hard feeling got to the point he was blamed for everything that happened, whether he did it or not. The Horchers note that more than a decade after Vogler's death, driver Chris Cumberworth had a running joke that scoffed at those who had always been so quick to point a finger at Vogler as the source of all evil.

"It's raining! Can you believe this rain?" Cumberworth's booming voice preceded him through the pit area. *It's Vogler's fault! Everything is Vogler's fault!*

"There were people who thought he was a complete asshole," says Allen Horcher. "But he wasn't a bad guy. He was just different. Really, really different and the bottom line was that he always gave you your money's worth."

On July 19, 1986–his birthday–Shane Carson won the Silver Crown race over Rich Vogler, which was always a benchmark in USAC racing. (Courtesy Mar-Car Collection)

Easily 99 percent of drivers come into racing without a calendar, and leave without one, too. Even if promises have been made to spouses, they are rarely kept because racers usually go until they can't afford a car or they can't find somebody else who will pay the bills for them. If they contemplate going out by paying the ultimate price, almost to a person they will say, "Don't feel sorry for me if I die doing what I love."

Easy for them to say. It's the families who are left to deal with the emptiness, pain, and, often, financial issues. As Wanda Knepper has noted, "The attitude of race drivers is that nobody makes them do it. They love it and are willing to take the risks involved. To them, racing is life, and *not* racing is *not* worth living. Work your way through the bad times as best you can, but remember the good times."

Most drivers, to their families' relief, end up retired. For the driver who decides to hang up his helmet by his own choice instead of simply not being able to put together a ride, there's always a reason behind it. Count on it.

Lynn Paxton retired at 39 years old, and many knowledgeable observers believe he still had a lot of feature wins that he left on the track by quitting so early. But listen to his thinking on the matter: "I had done everything there was to do in central Pennsylvania. For me to tackle any new ground I'd have had to go on the road and I had too many roots at home. I didn't like the road—being a gypsy was not my cup of tea. Ferkel and guys like him loved it, but I was a homebody and I like sleeping in my own bed. I realized I had a young family I didn't see grow up and I wanted to spend some time with them.

"I didn't decide to retire. There was never a plan, and the racing was always exciting. But there were plenty of good reasons to quit. So I stayed busy for five years afterward—and it was very difficult for those first five years—but then I got cured."

Paxton loves racing to this day to the point that he is actively involved in preserving memories through the Eastern Museum of Motorsports Racing near The Grove, and in keeping in touch with so many racers.

Having that extended "family" in racing, too, can be extremely important for the driver who faces illness at any time in his life. When McSpadden was presented with the diagnosis that every human dreads, "It was unbelievable the support I got from the racing community," he says. "I think the mental toughness from racing might have helped through all this mess, but I think I was a very fortunate person to have gotten to know all the people who came forward and helped our family get through it. I guarantee, I didn't face it alone."

20

Last Lap

"When you get up in the morning, if your elbows don't hit wood, you're in good shape." –Quincy Jones

Retirement sucks.

Even for people who willingly walk away and find other things to do with their lives, there are moments when drivers *know* they could still do it. Lynn Paxton has told us of instances where drivers followed up on that instinct to sometimes disastrous results because time really had passed them by and sprint car racing can be so unforgiving. But occasionally there are drivers who get back in a race car and find that there's still a win or two left in them. Like Luke Warmwater.

Who?

It was 1988. He had spent the racing season in Pennsylvania, far from his California home. Brad Doty's life-altering wreck at Eldora had hit home with this driver, who had also just gone through a painful divorce. "I thought, 'You know what? Maybe I just need to find something else to do." So, I quit racing and I went to work for Carrera Shocks as a sales rep," he says. "When I announced my retirement, I got $1,000 from Baylands Raceway. I got paid to go run the Gary Patterson Memorial, which was my last race, and Trophy City in San Jose made up a beautiful plaque from all my fans. And then everybody said, 'This won't last. You'll be back in three months.'"

You can't let *everybody* be right. It's a matter of honor.

However, there was also the little matter of the Great Shrinking Bank Account. He was quickly learning that it often takes a while for commissions to accumulate out in the real world of sales. So when a former car owner called about going to run midgets in Australia, the new retiree figured, "What the heck? Nobody's gonna recognize *Luke Warmwater from Hot Springs, Arkansas.*"

But when he won a race there, and stopped on the front straightaway,

You might think this is Jimmy Sills, but some people believe it's actually Luke Warmwater. (Courtesy Cookie Pool/ W.O.W. Photos, Jimmy Sills Collection)

the announcer asked what he was going to do next. He replied, "I believe I'll just leave my helmet on."

Well, everybody was wondering what the deal was with this Luke Warmwater dude, with his rookie red flag on the tail of the car. He sure hadn't driven like a rookie. The natives got restless and it became clear that curiosity was not going to allow Luke to hide under a helmet. Eventually, he had no choice, so he gave in.

"I pulled it off, and then I heard somebody yell out of the grandstands, 'Oh, bullshit, *that's Jimmy Sills!*'"

The voice didn't carry all the way to America, so it was that *Luke* won three out of the first five races when he first returned to the States. Of course, that brought attention, and attention brought recognition. Even though this was a time when a lot of drivers were getting their hair permed, there really was only one curly head of hair quite like Jimmy Sills'. Eventually, Sills really did hang up the helmet, although by opening a driving school near his home in California he found a way to keep his hand in, while simultaneously giving back to the sport.

Then and now:

The years have been kind. Steve Kinser and Rick Ferkel, Sammy Swindell, Doug Wolfgang, Shane Carson and Lynn Paxton.

Steve Kinser and Rick Ferkel share a laugh in the pits at Eldora in the summer of 2008. (Mike Campbell Photo)

Steve Kinser in the 1970s. (Gene Marderness Photo)

Rick Ferkel at Devil's Bowl in 1980. Note the bits of mud clinging to his shoulder. (Gene Marderness Photo)

*Sammy Swindell in the 1970s.
(Gene Marderness Photo)*

Sammy at Knoxville in 2007. (Mike Campbell Photo)

*Doug Wolfgang at Lake City, Florida, in
January 1978. (Gene Marderness Photo)*

*Doug at his induction into the South Dakota Sports Hall
of Fame in 2007. (Courtesy SD Sports Hall of Fame)*

*Shane Carson, around 1980.
(Gene Marderness Photo)*

*Shane in 2008, still playing around with cars.
(Shane Carson Collection)*

Rick Ferkel has been a key World of Outlaws official and has managed a USAC championship team. He is still active behind the scenes and probably will be as long he has mobility. Bubby Jones continues to build cars and help young drivers. In fact, it's not at all unusual to find that some of the great driving stars of the past have taken a step back out of the limelight but continued to contribute to racing, even when they didn't necessarily plan out that path.

"We were going to race forever," laughs Ferkel. "Not that we were spendthrifts because we were always pretty frugal. But you didn't race in the wintertime, so you had to put back money to live on then. We didn't invest money and we paid cash for everything. Probably, if we'd put more thought into things, we'd be in better shape financially today."

"Thinking" for all those years had centered on tire selection, wing adjustment, which race to attend—things that simply pushed the future to some fuzzy, unimportant thing way beyond next week's feature race. But eventually the future comes rushing into focus for them all.

Retirement also allows drivers time to reflect. Thinking back, most wouldn't change a whole lot because the memories are simply too precious. But often there are tweaks—small things they would like to alter a bit. Ask Lenard McCarl if he would do anything differently, and he says, "Yeah. I would quit running into the fence."

More seriously, he notes that, "I got hurt pretty bad and I probably should have quit driving at that time, but it turned out that I really wanted to drive those race cars, so I went to an IMCA race south of Des Moines—and I won. I swept the show, in fact—fastest qualifier, won the heat and won the feature. But when the feature was over, this guy tried to protest me over some stupid thing that didn't really matter at all. The guy who ran IMCA then said it didn't matter because, 'if Lenard started on the tail, he was still going to beat you.'

"But going home I was kind of depressed about that. I never put it into words or anything, but it was kind of like, "I won everything and I'm not happy." I knew that racing couldn't get any better than that, so I knew it was time. I just turned it off like a switch. No deep thoughts—just quit driving. I stayed involved, owning cars, turning wrenches, doing a bunch of other things, but it was just time to get out of the car myself."

Retirement is also the point at which many drivers take a look at the so-called Big Picture—a lifetime of racing as opposed to just a race or a season. "Looking back, none of the people I drove for or dealt with over the years are enemies," says Shane Carson. "Sometimes a guy will get out of a car after a crash, and they never talk to the car owner again, but I guess I had the knack to pull the good out of a situation, even if I had crashed at the end. I'm kind of proud of that."

"When we ran a lot of Outlaw races in the early '90s, it was more laid back," recalls Gary Wright. "Like, we would go to Fargo, North Dakota, and they had a big cookout at the hotel. Everybody stayed in a hotel then instead of a motorhome, and there would be a keg of beer, everybody at the pool and we'd have a good time. It doesn't happen anymore. The motorhomes and haulers have cut out some of the cost, but it's also ruined that sense of community we used to have."

"Cars would pay their own way back when, so we had more fun," confirms Lynn Paxton. "People ask me, 'Don't you wish you were running for $10,000-to-win like they are now? My point is that the $500 or $1,000 we ran for—do you realize how far that money went compared to today? Start thinking about what gas costs, and tires and engines—and we were far ahead of the curve."

Paxton also sees a difference in how on-track relationships have evolved, too, by referring to a driver who's been around for a long time, still racing and has seen it all through the years. "Fred Rahmer said the game has changed. There used to be an 'honor among thieves.' He said that when you were racing a guy who got farther into a corner you'd back off for him—remember he was there and race accordingly. Now, they're paying you to win and nothing less, so if you thread the needle—and miss—somebody's going for a ride."

"I think if you really want to succeed in racing today, then you have to take every opportunity that comes along, regardless of whether it burns a bridge," adds Richard Griffin.

Another consideration today's racers have is image. It would probably be impossible for any current racer to secure a ride and major sponsorship if he or she had some of Hooker Hood's exploits in their background.

"Oh, yeah, I hauled a little whiskey," he laughs in his wonderful way. "I'd heard about Junior Johnson and I said, 'Well, he got by with it, maybe I can.'"

Hooker forgot about the part where Junior got caught and did time. So, then Hooker followed in Junior's tire tracks more than he intended. He was returning to west Tennessee with a load of about 200 gallons from down on the Gulf Coast when he was caught in a sting, in a school zone, no less. In the one phone call allowed to arrestees, he said, "Pop, I'm up here at the jailhouse. They caught me hauling some whiskey."

His daddy told him, "You shoulda run, boy."

"We didn't have no chains in jail," Hooker continues. "You wore just blue Levis and a blue Levi shirt. Shucks, they'd send me uptown without anybody and I'd go by all my racing buddies' places. And then I told them I had a hurt back and them cats put me in the hospital. My wife came down there and stayed in the guest house."

Meanwhile, the West Memphis track owner had been busy. "Mr. Montgomery got hold of our congressman and said, 'Now, we need to get Hooker back here for the race car season.'

"For that little deal I got sentenced to three years and a certain amount of days, but I was home in 15 days. When I heard I was coming home, my back got well real quick. Then I finished up the season at West Memphis, and I won the points."

❖   ❖   ❖   ❖   ❖

Sprint car drivers retain respect more than almost any other athletes enjoy, but that seems especially true among contemporaries in other types of racing. As Curt Michael notes, "We went down to tour the NASCAR shops with some guys I know who went there to work. When you get introduced and you tell them you drive a sprint car, they go, 'Oh—*real racing.*' And when you look at how many of their stars have sprint car experience, you begin to realize that if you can drive a sprint car, you can pretty much drive anything."

The Gas Man contemplating the feature about to start, February 4, 2000. Richard Griffin is among the majority of racers who figured out how to have a lot of fun along the way, but when it was time to go to work, he knew how to gather his thoughts and bring his "A" game to every race. (Bill Taylor Photo)

When Richard Petty and Hooker Hood got together, there was some serious bench racing, especially since Hooker is a NASCAR veteran as well. Do you suppose he's told the King that Junior Johnson wasn't the only race driver to haul hooch and then spend time in jail for it? (Courtesy Hooker Hood Collection)

But if a sprint car driver never steps foot in a NASCAR ride—or any other kind of race car—there are a couple of very special aspects about what they do. One is that the sprint fan base is so knowledgeable and supportive. "I get stuff from all over the country from people I've never even heard of, who say, 'I watched you race here and there and whenever you're nearby I come watch you,'" says Gary Wright. "It's amazing to me how many people follow you and the fans you get from all over the country that you don't ever even meet."

While a stock car driver might like to measure his ability against that of Jeff Gordon or Tony Stewart, if he didn't catch a race with a NASCAR driver during the increasingly brief period between short-track racing and the big time, he will never get the chance to find out. Most of those drivers have contracts that limit how much mixing it up with the Saturday Night drivers they can do. With sprint car racing, however, you can race with the best just about any time they come around, if you're so inclined. In fact, the traveling circuits would like it very much if you did, as they often depend on some local racers to fill the field and add a ripple of excitement in the grandstand for fans who also want to know how their guys stack up to the pros.

"Like Steve Kinser—it seems like he's won millions of races," says Bobby Allen. "Well, one race I beat him. He probably doesn't remember it, but I remember that race like it was yesterday. That's something nobody can take away from me."

Wanting to go head-to-head with the best is just one of many characteristics that make sprint car drivers a special nut to crack. Rare is the sprint driver who is content simply to be a part of the pack. While there is nothing wrong with being a little laid-back, it seems that sprint car drivers retain a hunger for accomplishment that never goes away. How else do you explain Steve Kinser? Or any of the rest, for that matter.

"It's a fine line between being good and being a Tony Stewart or Jeff Gordon," adds Bubby Jones. "There's not a lot of guys who are real exceptional, but regardless, you gotta have a lot of gunfighter in you to drive them sprint cars."

"I can honestly say that I don't think there's anybody who drove a race car and had more fun than I did," adds McSpadden. "For me, it didn't matter if it was a heat race or a feature. To me it was competition and I didn't care if it paid $10 or $10,000. It wasn't the money or the points. I believe that to guys who pull those helmets on it's the *racing* that means everything."

Bobby Allen's nickname was Scruffy, because his race cars often ran much better than they looked. When time was at a premium, Allen worked on the motor and the chassis, and then made do with whatever body parts were around the shop. Later in his career, the cars got better looking–even when covered in mud. (Joyce Standridge Photo)

"I'd do it for no money," says Allen, confirming the worst-kept secret in racing because so many drivers share that sentiment. "What I miss most are the people. I miss going out there and beating the big guys and hanging out with the fans. I miss it all, really, and I loved it."

"I don't think there's anything that puts out that kind of power and has that much acceleration—and you still have to turn the corner," Ferkel says. "Every fan should drive a sprint car at least one time. And here's the experience they'll have—the first night I drove, when they were pushing me to start, I was scared to death. I thought we were going way too fast—just having them push me. And then I made the corner, the car started, and there was just no going back to a life without sprint cars. *Ever.*"

"Once you go to a good sprint car race, nothing else comes close to it," concludes Sills. "The acceleration and speed a sprint car has is unique. The sound. The close racing. And if you like a good crash, you don't have to wait long for that.

"Sprint car racing has it all."

❖ ❖ ❖ ❖ ❖

Since I began this book with personal observations about racing, it seems comfortable to conclude with a few bench-racing *win it or wear it* tales from my family.

Back in the *Introduction*, I told of Robbie surmounting the third-turn fence at Springfield Speedway. But he wasn't the only one to go sailing. My husband Rick set a few altitude records himself. After a particularly violent crash at Robinson, Illinois, one night, I drove him home afterwards even though he walked away relatively unscathed. Apparently, I didn't come through the experience as well as he did because he tells me that I ran every red light on the way. With the wild look in my eye, he thought maybe it was safer to just ride along rather than suggest he move over to the steering wheel.

This is what was left of Rick's ride after a wreck at Robinson, Illinois, in 1976. That's car owner Frank Siciliano in mourning behind the car. (Courtesy Rick Standridge Collection)

Rick is the oldest, but close behind is brother Randy. What I remember is an experience in the mid-1980s at Springfield, after which the race car was fine but for a couple of weeks, Randy looked like he was ready for Halloween. A rock had been kicked up off the track by a competitor's wheel and actually managed to penetrate his helmet shield. With God watching out for him, the rock hit the bridge of his nose and broke it. But a centimeter one way or the other and he would have lost an eye.

Fuel tank flying off Randy Standridge's car during a flip series at Springfield Speedway. (Photo by Marvin Scattergood, Collection owned by Terry Young)

A friend remembers going with Randy to the hospital after a post-race slide job by another guy (and don't get me started on the feud that came out of that deal). Randy had seemed okay, but in fact, told his team that he was supposed to be in the race that was on the track—and it wasn't even a sprint car race. Randy's car owner said, "Boy, you need an ambulance," and they all trooped off to the hospital to watch cartoons in the waiting room until six in the morning. At least Randy got to sleep in the exam room.

It was Randy's wife who got the goods scared out of her one night at Tri-City Speedway when younger brother Ronnie flipped. "They had to walk me back around the track to find my

Ron Standridge exiting the track at Putnamville during a 1985 USAC sprint race. He took an ambulance ride on this one, but was released shortly thereafter. (Kevin Horcher Photos)

sandals later on because I had run right out of them," Rita remembers.

That turned out to be another late night of television in a waiting room—Jerry Lewis, this time—but the goofiest part had happened on the way to the hospital. Ronnie's best friend Bruce had to literally hold the ambulance's back doors closed because they wouldn't latch, and then Dad held on to the gurney so it wouldn't slide back to knock Bruce through the doors and onto the road.

At St. Charles, Missouri, Ronnie cleared an eight-foot fence, hit a light pole, causing the light bulbs to explode. Fourth of July without a calendar. But the most memorable wear-it experience was probably when he flipped big time at Eldora. His wife Nancy had been filming the race, but nobody got to see the wreck because the second she sensed something was wrong, she took off running. And all you could see on the tape was the ground flying by as she ran.

That's some of the *Wear It* part of our lives. I won't go into the *Win It* part, although there's plenty. All four brothers, having learned well at their dad's knee, won a lot of races, set a lot of records, and took home championships. It's a source of pride that they have done it mostly with so-so equipment. "At one point, we blew the motor seven weeks in a row," remembers a crew member. "We'd put it back together and run the next week. Today, you blow the motor, you can't go to Dad's garage rafters and find some replacement parts to be back on the track tomorrow."

Randy and Ronnie are (supposedly) retired, although I'm never shocked to hear they've climbed back behind the wheel yet again. Robbie, who broke his collar bone and some ribs in a sprint car wreck that occurred while this book was in process, probably has a few more years left in him even though he's past 40 now. Rick is racing late models. Of the next

(Joyce Standridge Photo)

generations (14 children, six grandchildren), only Ronnie's son Jeremy is racing sprint cars. (Our son Richie is the only other racer, driving modifieds.)

But for all that we've had to give up, what no one can take away from any of us are the wonderful, wonderful memories we have. We are all convinced that we stayed close because the race track brought us together, and that thought is echoed by racing fans and families all across the country. Now that the home track is closed and there's less racing going on, we find we get together far less often, too. And that, for racing people all across the country with their own experiences, is the greatest sadness as tracks close.

It is also why it is so very, very important to record and preserve the memories of those who have raced with such passion and joy because there is unlimited beauty in a life lived to the fullest. As Jimmy Sills summed it up with brilliant simplicity, "Sprint car racing has it all."

And we need to savor that fact.

INDEX